Helping Your Gifted Child

Helping
Your Gifted Child

By RUTH STRANG, Ph.D.

Professor of Education, Teachers College
Columbia University

With an introduction by
DR. CYRIL WILLIAM WOOLCOCK
Principal, Hunter College High School

E. P. DUTTON & CO., INC., NEW YORK

COPYRIGHTS FROM WHICH PERMISSION TO QUOTE HAS BEEN GRANTED

Barclay, Dorothy. "A Set of Basic Family Values." *The Times Magazine*, July 13, 1958, reprinted by permission of *The New York Times*.

Bissex, Henry. *If You Want Your Child to Read*, printed for Essie Olive Abeel Private School, Inc., 293 Lookout Ave., Hackensack, New Jersey.

Dostoyevsky, Fyodor. *The Brothers Karamazov*, The John C. Winston Co., 482.

MacFarlane, Jean W. "Intellectual Functioning in High School Girls and College Women," *Journal of the N.A.W.D.C.*, XXI (October, 1957), 5.

McCarthy, Dorothea A. *Measurement of Cognitive Abilities at the Preschool and Early Childhood Level*, Princeton, N.J.: Educational Testing Service, 1958 (unpaged).

Mearns, Hughes. *Creative Power: The Education of Youth in the Creative Arts* (second revised edition), pp. 116, 118, reprinted by permission of Dover Publications, Inc., N.Y. 14, N.Y. ($1.50).

Miles, Catherine Cox. "Gifted Children," *Manual of Child Psychology* (second edition), 1954, Leonard Carmichael editor, 1002, 1008, reprinted by permission of John Wiley & Sons, Inc.

Murphy, Lois B. "Emotional First Aid for the Young Child," *Childhood Education*, XXXII, No. 5 (January, 1956), pp. 206–207, reprinted by permission of the Association for Childhood Education International, 1200 Fifteenth Street, N.W., Washington 5, D.C.

Myers, Garry Cleveland. "Parents and the Gifted Child," *Education*, LXXIX (September, 1958), pp. 17–18, used by special permission of the publishers, The Bobbs-Merrill Company, Inc.

Ojemann, Ralph H. "Basic Approaches to Mental Health: The Human Relations Program of the State University of Iowa," *Personnel and Guidance Journal*, XXXVII (November, 1958), 198-206.

Strang, Ruth. *The Adolescent Views Himself*, 95,170, New York, McGraw-Hill Publishing Co., 1957.

Strang, Ruth. *An Introduction to Child Study* (fourth edition), 1959, reprinted by permission of the Macmillan Company.

Strang, Ruth. "Manifestations of Maturity in Adolescents." *Mental Hygiene*, XXXIII (October, 1949), 567-569.

Schweitzer, Albert. "Schweitzer's Words: Light in the Jungle," *The Times Magazine*, January 9, 1955, 73, reprinted by permission of *The New York Times*.

Terman, Lewis M. "The Discovery and Encouragement of Exceptional Talent," *American Psychologist*, IX (June, 1954), 224, 228.

Terman, Lewis M., and Melita H. Oden. *The Gifted Child Grows Up*, Vol. IV, Genetic Studies of Genius, Stanford, California, Stanford University Press, 1947.

LIBRARY OF CONGRESS CATALOG CARD NUMBER: 60–5974

Introduction

Helping Your Gifted Child by Dr. Ruth Strang is one of the best books that I have read on this subject. I honestly believe that it will become *must* reading for anyone interested in the gifted child.

Primarily, the book is for parents of gifted children and contains basic, essential, and helpful information about the proper rearing of these promising individuals. However, teachers, school administrators, psychologists, pediatricians, social workers, and others interested in and working with gifted children will find this book most helpful.

Dr. Strang, long associated with the education of gifted children and a recognized authority in this field, sets forth in delightful and careful fashion in this book what we know for sure about gifted children and the reliable possibilities of developmental growth for them. She does this by means of citing interesting and cogent examples of the best ways to help gifted children at the various age levels, and by review of pertinent, concise, and related case study materials. Her presentations are brilliantly arranged and her analyses commanding of full respect.

Readers will find this book easy to read and pregnant with humorous anecdotal incidents related to the points under consideration, culled from Dr. Strang's rich and full experience with gifted children.

I heartily recommend this book to parents of gifted children and to all others who are interested in or who deal with these unusual individuals, and who wish to help the gifted realize their full potentials for their personal satisfaction and social usefulness.

DR. CYRIL WILLIAM WOOLCOCK

Principal, Hunter College High School, New York City; President, Metropolitan Association for the Study of the Gifted, New York City; Member: American Association for Gifted Children, Advisory Board, National Council for the Gifted; Consultant for the Gifted, State Education Department, Albany, New York.

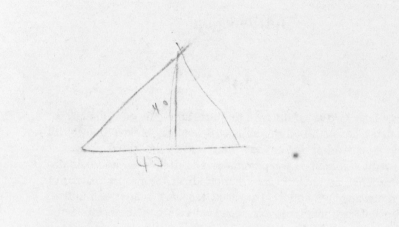

Contents

Helping Your Gifted Child

Preface for Parents

I⊤ is difficult to write about gifted children because they vary so widely. Many are attractive and physically well developed; some are not. A few very gifted children are physically handicapped; Helen Keller is an outstanding example of the person who is brilliant though physically handicapped. Some children are especially gifted in mathematics, others in music; still others are socially gifted. They come from all sorts of home backgrounds. Some need control; others need freedom. Some are overstimulated; others need to be challenged. Some are self-centered and egotistical; others have feelings of inferiority. Some need more challenging standards and goals; others have too high a level of aspiration. Some receive an embarrassing amount of praise and recognition; others need more outspoken appreciation. Whatever a child's special abilities, we must remember, as one mother said, that "he is first of all a child"—and that children are different.

There is no substitute for your own firsthand understanding of your child. Only you can note, day in and day out, what he can and cannot do, under what conditions he learns best, what gives him the greatest satisfaction. You have to believe, as Dorothy Barclay has said, in the evidence of your own eyes and ears.

There is seldom any such thing as the one best way of handling a human situation. With respect to gifted children, everything depends on the age of the child, his stage of development, the effect the proposed method might have on the child and others, and many other factors. To many parents this is an unsatisfactory answer; they want a prescription that will be effective in any situation, or a procedure that will always get results.

How then can a book about gifted children help you? You are concerned over your children's welfare and want to do what is best for them. You may often feel the need for support and guidance.

Perhaps you wonder whether your children are gifted, and if so, along what lines. You want to know what you can expect from them and what you can do for them. You would like to understand why a bright child does not always live up to his potentialities and how you can help him become the best possible person. Since child development takes place in a relationship, you need to look into your own motivations and feelings as they may affect your child's achievement. We offer no pat prescriptions. We hope this book will give you insights that will foster better understanding.

Much of our information about gifted children has come from research studies. The person you will most often hear mentioned in connection with the study of gifted children is Lewis M. Terman. He has briefly told the story of his life interest in this field.* It began when he was a senior in psychology at Indiana University and prepared two reports, one on mental deficiency and one on genius. His master's thesis, published in 1904, was on leadership among children, and his doctoral dissertation was an intensive study of the intellectual processes of seven very bright and seven very dull boys.

At Stanford University his first task was the revision for use in this country of the Binet scale for measuring intelligence. In standardizing his scale on a thousand children, he found that IQ's ranged from 60 to 145. This disparity in intellectual performance suggested to him an ambitious study of gifted children.

His dream was realized in 1921 when he obtained a grant from the Commonwealth Fund to begin a study of a thousand children of IQ 140 or higher. The average IQ of the group selected was approximately 150; eighty of them scored 170 or higher.

Dr. Terman's purpose was to describe the characteristics of children of high IQ and to find out what kind of adults they became. Comparing them with groups of unselected children he found that his group of intellectually superior children were, in general, superior in physical appearance, health, and social adjustment; markedly superior on certain tests of character; and vastly superior on a variety of school achievement tests. The results of follow-up studies over

* Lewis M. Terman, "The Discovery and Encouragement of Exceptional Talent," *American Psychologist*, IX (June, 1954), 221–230.

forty years showed that in general these children fulfilled the promise
of youth. As adults they scored about as far above the average as they
had when they were children. Moreover, the large majority kept on
growing intellectually. Not a single one developed "postadolescent
stupidity."

At about the same time, Leta S. Hollingworth made her pioneer
study of gifted children; in 1926 she published her classic book,
Gifted Children: Their Nature and Nurture, one of the earliest and
best references on the education of extremely gifted children.

In another part of the country, Paul Witty reported a study of three
hundred gifted children which gave a similar picture. Later he
identified many gifted children in low socioeconomic groups.

These and many other studies have given us a wealth of information about gifted children in general. Much less attention has been
paid to individual differences among these children. There are relatively few case studies or clinical studies that show the unique quality
of each gifted child. That is something that each parent may discover
for himself as he observes his own child.

Any published material for parents will be most effective if it is
introduced by a person they know and respect, and discussed after
it has been read. It is reassuring to parents to know that others have
the same problems, that their negative feelings are not unnatural,
and that they have often done the right thing intuitively. The parent-
child relation involves deep feelings. Although knowledge alone will
not change a parent's behavior toward his child, even a little accurate
information is all to the good, if the parent feels that he can take it
or leave it or modify it to fit his own situation.

Bringing up any child is a complicated business. The child's personality, the parents' conscious and unconscious motivation, the attitudes of relatives and neighbors, and the spirit and demands of the
times all enter into any parent-child relationship. But a book or a
teacher, as Kahlil Gibran wrote, can "lead a man to the threshold of
his own mind."

According to some contemporary writers, the salvation of civiliza-
tion depends upon the discovery and development of highly intelligent scientists and social leaders. Though it is, of course, essential
that we have key people of this sort, we must remember that their

achievements will be built on the contributions and services of many other people. No man achieves anything singlehanded. Even great intellectual pioneers like Darwin acknowledged the ideas they gained from people who never became famous.

Although the focus of this book is on the gifted, the principles it cites apply to the development of all children. The parable of the talents emphasizes the importance of each person's doing *his* best, whether it be a small or a great contribution. One danger of an aristocracy of intellect is that some intellectuals are arrogant and contemptuous of incompetence. The truly great are humble in spirit; they have the quality of loving-kindness, of sympathy with all mankind, of pity for the weak.

ACKNOWLEDGMENTS

Many persons have contributed to this book. Most important are the many parents of gifted children who have asked questions and written the author personal letters about their problems, and the gifted children themselves who have expressed sound ideas about their education and guidance. These two sources have been quoted freely and their anonymity has been carefully preserved. Some of the parents' questions are briefly answered at the end of each chapter. Some of these questions relate to topics already discussed in the chapter; others introduce additional aspects. The more extensive observations and case studies have been contributed by Alma Bingham, Ruth Crittenden, Erma Fischer, Robert P. Hopkins, Amelia Melnik, Marian Miller, E. Mosser, and William Wharton. Students in my graduate courses have also contributed helpful observations. To other writers in this and related fields, and to the letters referred to me by Pauline Williamson, Executive Secretary of the American Association for Gifted Children, the author is greatly indebted.

ONE

Is Your Child Gifted?

"IT IS possible," one parent wrote, "that not understanding what constitutes a gifted child, I may be upset about my child for no good reason. Can you tell me how parents can know whether their child is 'gifted'?"

Another parent went into more detail on the same question:

"How do we really know whether or not we have a gifted child on our hands? Our Board of Education does not give psychological tests to children until they reach the age of four. The Child Guidance Clinic tests only emotionally upset children. We would make any move necessary if a competent person assured us that our child requires special training, but if the decision rests on our observation, we would be prone to muddle along and send him through the conservative paths of education we followed. . . . We feel that our child may be endowed with above-average ability. Our two questions are: First, how can we tell whether our child is gifted, and second, if he is, what do we do?"

Many gifted children are not discovered. Consequently, they do not develop their abilities. Almost half of the students who are capable of doing college work do not go to college. Too many, as Terman said, "languish in idleness." In certain secondary schools, from 7 to 47 per cent of the students who are intellectually superior are under-achievers. Gifted children attract the teacher's attention less often than retarded children do. Their discovery, as Jacques Barzun said, "to themselves and by others, is not inevitable."* [1]

Plato proposed more than two thousand years ago that the leaders of the nation be selected by a series of tests, both academic and situational, beginning in early childhood.[2] On this topic he wrote:

* The quotations in the text may be found in the references under each chapter at the end of the book.

"We must watch them from their earliest childhood. We must select those who are tenacious of memory and hard to deceive. . . ."

It is natural for parents to want their children to be gifted. In fact, there is something special about every child. The diffident bachelor, when called upon to comment on an unprepossessing infant, plays safe by saying to the mother, "I'd expect your child to be exceptional." Every child has assets that can be capitalized and strengths that can be developed. Parents and teachers should "accentuate the positive" by looking for the special abilities in each child.

THE BROAD VIEW OF GIFTEDNESS

However, we must recognize that there are different kinds and degrees of superiority. Nothing is gained by calling all children "gifted." Paul Witty's definition, quite generally accepted, is broad enough. It includes not only those with high abstract intelligence, but also "those whose performance in any valuable line of human activity is consistently or repeatedly remarkable."[3] This definition emphasizes achievement as well as potential ability. Thus it takes account of character traits such as persistence, purposefulness, and a sense of responsibility, as well as general intelligence and ability in a specific field. It also rules out the use of abilities for selfish or destructive purposes; the achievement must be socially useful. In this book, we shall have this definition in mind whenever we use the word "gifted."

Within the terms of this broad definition we can distinguish many kinds of giftedness. Forty or more different definitions of giftedness have been proposed. Various words are used to describe the gifted: *infant prodigy, genius, the high IQ, the brightest, the exceptionally able, the most capable, the able learner, the rapid learner, the mentally advanced,* and *the academically talented.*

Accordingly, the question, "Is your child gifted?" should be broken down into specific questions: Is your child a prodigy or a genius? Is he highly gifted in abstract verbal ability? Is he academically talented? Does he have unusual ability in mathematics? Does he have a special knack with mechanical things? Is he talented in art, music, drama, or the dance? Is he socially gifted? These are questions that may be asked about children whose performance in any line stands out as exceptional.

DIFFERENT KINDS AND DEGREES OF GIFTEDNESS

The Child Prodigy

To the question, "Is your son or daughter a child prodigy?" most parents would reply, "Heaven forbid!"

So-called infant prodigies or *wunderkinder* are in a class by themselves, though they are far from being alike. Among them are children who perform marvelous feats of lightning calculation. These prodigies possess a retentive memory for figures. In most cases they have been given special training and practice. Many have learned short cuts to rapid computation. Frequently their parents have exploited them for personal prestige or profit. In other respects they may be quite ordinary. According to Barlow, very few of the prodigies of this kind that have been reported throughout history have fulfilled early expectations.[4] If they lose interest, their special skill tends to disappear.

Chess prodigies may be persons of high general intelligence; they may also be much less able persons who have well-developed, one-track minds. Chess calls for foresight, quickness of perception, concentration, and power of accurate analysis—all characteristics of the intelligent person.

Musical prodigies are less likely to fade into oblivion. During certain periods when musical talent was held in extremely high regard, there appeared a number of well-known child prodigies: Mozart, who composed minuets before he was four, sonatas at five, and a symphony when he was eight years old; Schubert and Mendelssohn, who began to compose by twelve years of age; Wesley, who at three played tunes on the harpsichord; Hummel and Chopin, who gave public concerts at nine; and, more recently, Yehudi Menuhin, who began to play the violin at three, and made his Carnegie Hall debut at eleven. The exceptional musical talents of Brahms, Dvořák, and Richard Strauss likewise attracted attention from their earliest years. Sebastian Bach, ninth in a line of able musicians, is said to have arrived at full artistic maturity by twenty-two years of age.

Far less common are historical records of precocious ability in acting. One of the few famous child actors was William Betty, who at eleven years showed amazing ability to play major Shakespearean roles. In our times child actors and actresses are more common; some give exceptionally fine performances.

Prodigies in literature and the fine arts are rare. Exceptional writing or painting requires experience with life as well as exceptional gifts of observation, sensitivity, and ability to organize. To Robert Barrat, the authenticity of the poems and letters purportedly written by eight-year-old Minou Drouet appeared to be doubtful; although some of the lines are childlike, others have a philosophical-poetic quality that seems incredible in a child of this age.[5]

Also included under the heading of child prodigies are children whose intellectual development has been greatly accelerated: Pascal was recognized as a great and original mathematical genius before he was sixteen; Norbert Wiener learned to read at four and from then on read advanced scientific books; he entered college before the age of twelve, and obtained his doctor's degree before he was nineteen; Fred Safier, Jr., had acquired a vocabulary of nearly one thousand words by the age of three; at five he read *The Iliad* and *The Odyssey*; he went through elementary school in three years and entered Harvard at twelve.

The home environments in these last three instances were radically different. Pascal's father apparently discouraged his son's mathematical interest. In fact, he went so far as to deprive him of books on the subject. But the boy, then eleven years old, secretly went ahead and constructed a geometry of his own. Later he made a remarkable creative contribution to the field of mathematics.

On the other hand, Wiener, according to his own account,[6] was subjected to his father's insistent, severe, and painful demands for precise and ready knowledge and hard, unceasing study. This "arduous course of training" isolated the child from companions of his own age, prevented him from becoming skillful in games, and aggravated a nearsightedness that threatened his vision. Any satisfaction he might have derived from his achievement was neutralized by his father, who continually pointed out the boy's shortcomings. Wiener's autobiography mentions many subsequent problems of social and emotional adjustment, which were gradually resolved by virtue of an understanding wife and many contacts with other intellectually stimulating people.

Unlike Wiener's father, Fred Safier's parents claimed that they never "pushed" the boy. They tried to be understanding, sympathetic, and loving. According to Hirshberg's report,[7] Safier, as a freshman at Harvard, was healthy, friendly, and interested in many things. He mixed easily with the older boys but lived with his father who came East to provide a normal home for the boy while he was in college. His father said that Fred was "not a genius but merely a normal little boy with a high capacity for learning." He was not a bookworm. He usually played with persons of his chronological age, but worked with his intellectual equals. Of the several boys who have entered Harvard at an unusually early age, including Fred Safier who is still in college at the time of writing, only one, an eleven-year-old freshman in 1909, failed to fulfill his early promise. He became embittered, and died in obscurity at forty-six.

Parents who exploit a child's mental alertness may suppress his spontaneity and thus prevent the development of other talents he may possess. No human beings are more to be pitied than so-called child geniuses or infant prodigies who have been pushed and prodded beyond their capacity by ambitious parents. These unfortunate exploited children have been deprived of the normal joys and other experiences of childhood. Any talent they have usually peters out as they grow older; they may become neurotic from constant subjection to difficulties that are too great for them.

An extreme instance of parental pressure is described in the biography of Ruth Slenczynska,[8] the strange story of a child prodigy. When she was only a few months old, her father was already planning a concert career for her. When she was two, he began his training. Nine hours a day of practice crowded out all childish play with dolls, games, or friends. When at eight years of age she won the applause of crowds and the enthusiastic acclaim of critics, her father smiled triumphantly and pushed her into further concert engagements. When, during early adolescence, her popularity decreased and critics described her playing as "immature," her father flew into a rage, and beat and humiliated her.

While she still loved the piano, she could no longer bear the thought of playing in public. Driven by her father to give a Town Hall concert, she failed miserably. The critics described her as "a burned-out candle," "a prodigy who had blazed for a while and subsided into mediocrity." She had played as her father had taught her. Her failure was his failure. Yet he completely rejected her. In lesser degrees the other members of her family also seemed to be ashamed of her. Despite her despondency she enrolled in college and gradually rebuilt her self-confidence by playing excerpts from the music she knew so well to illustrate lectures given by professors in the music department.

According to her own report she failed totally in the social side of college life. Her background, her appearance, her lack of social experience made it impossible for her to relate herself to other students. But eventually she married and returned to the concert stage. By the age of thirty-two, she had pulled herself together as an artist and had become a person in her own right instead of the automaton her father had tried to make her.

Characteristics of Geniuses

The word "genius" comes from the Latin, *genere* (to produce). "By their works ye shall know them." Persons of true genius produce great and original works; their achievement stands the test of time.

Geniuses are extremely rare. Too often a parent mistakes a bright, alert youngster for a genius. As one boy said, "My mother expects me to be a genius, which I am not." Certain feats of memory can be mastered by constant drill, but such achievement is quite different from the creative thinking and the ability to solve abstract problems that are characteristic of true genius. The genius has an abundance of good ideas; he shows unusual creativity; he has ability to solve abstract problems, to sense what is really significant, and to see new relationships among ideas. He is original and spontaneous. He has sudden flashes of insight and hits upon new ways of looking at things. At the same time he may show "a curious credulity"; this is a natural by-product of his receptive nature, and is usually tempered, after a while, by his critical keenness. To these intellectual qualities are added a high degree of concentration and persistence in a task. These unusual characteristics are shown at an early age.

The genius has a distinctive quality of mind and spirit. He is born with a nervous system that is extremely sensitive to all impressions; he is able to see things in their harmonious relations. To this basic quality, there is added an infinite capacity for taking pains and an ability to sustain intense concentration. The genius works intensively and takes advantage of his high periods of creative energy. His sudden inspirations are usually preceded by days of hard work, which may, at the time, seem fruitless. Environment, too, plays a part in the production of a genius. He should receive not only encouragement and approval, but also expert instruction in his field of special interest.

Contrary to popular opinion, the number of insane geniuses is relatively small. The relationship between exceptional creative ability and mental abnormality has been exaggerated. A study of 113 artists and 181 scientists furnished no evidence that the highest intellectual and creative ability depends on emotional disturbance or abnormality. It is probably true, however, that the extreme sensitivity that contributes to genius may also make the genius more than normally susceptible to stress and strain.

Men of genius are commonly portrayed as selfish, unconventional, immensely egotistical, and maladjusted. Actually, examples can be found of geniuses who show the opposite qualities. The large majority have been persons of integrity and good will; many have been in advance of their times. It is usually the pseudo- or quasi-genius, always striving for recognition, who is difficult to get along with and gives pain to his family and friends.

It is usually possible for an alert observer to detect exceptional talent at an early stage. From her biographical study of *The Early Traits of Three Hundred Geniuses*,[9] Catherine Cox concluded that well-known geniuses such as Goethe, Mozart, Francis Galton, and many others could probably have been identified in childhood by intelligence tests.

The later achievement of one fourth of the best known of these persons was foreshadowed in childhood interests and hobbies. At the age of six Macaulay was writing what he called a "Compendium of Universal History"; Albrecht Dürer made a famous sketch of himself when he was thirteen; the Brontë sisters wrote novels when they were children; and William Cullen Bryant wrote "Thanatopsis" at the age of seventeen.

More than three fourths of the parents questioned in Terman's study said they noted signs of intellectual superiority before three and a half years in the case of girls, and little later in the case of boys. The signs they most frequently recognized, as stated in Catherine Cox Miles's summary, were "quick understanding, great curiosity, retentive memory, early speech, unusual vocabulary, and extensive information."[10] They recognized musical ability at about five years, and other special abilities at about six years.

If you think your child is a budding genius, it would seem best to appreciate his products and not interfere with his absorbing interest. Under these conditions, it is reasonable to expect that his special abilities will unfold. However, opposition or even obstacles may only serve to spur him on. If Papa Pascal, in his effort to make his son well rounded, had not deprived Blaise of his mathematics books, would the boy have devised an original geometry of his own? Who knows!

Parents of bright children sometimes say, "I don't want my child to be a genius—just let him be a normal, well-adjusted, happy child." Very bright children *can* create problems. It is painful to take pains, and genius has been described as "the infinite capacity for taking pains." No great achievement grows out of an easy, comfortable existence. Young people today seem to cherish ease and abhor effort. The genius must take a more arduous path.

High Abstract Verbal Ability or General Intelligence: The Highly Gifted

Is your child gifted in abstract verbal ability or general intelligence? This kind of ability can be detected by a combination of observation and testing. If a child spontaneously shows a remarkable understanding of words, if he is keen to see relations and detect absurdities, if he is interested in books and reading even before he enters school, if he remembers readily and learns quickly, the chances are that he has superior intelligence.

These impressions become more certain indications if they are checked by intelligence tests, especially by individual intelligence tests given by a trained psychologist. Intelligence tests measure the child's ability to do certain mental tasks at the given time. The more intelligent child, under optimum conditions, can solve problems with greater speed and accuracy than can the less intelligent child.

If a child ten years old makes a score that is equal to the average of all the ten-year-olds tested, he is said to have a mental age of 10; if he performs as well as the average twelve-year-olds, his mental age is 12. A few ten-year-olds will have a mental age of 14 or 15.

The IQ, which you hear mentioned so often, is simply a ratio between the child's mental age as determined by an intelligence test and his chronological age:

$$\frac{\text{Mental age in months} \times 100}{\text{Chronological age in months}} = IQ$$

Giftedness is most commonly measured by the size of the IQ. We might find only one or two children in a million who score 180 IQ or above. It has also been estimated that about 1 per cent of the population have IQ's of 137 or above; these are generally designated as the "highly gifted." About 10 per cent—the "moderately gifted"—have IQ's of 120–137. The percentages vary from school to school. In one elementary school in a certain county only 7 per cent of the children scored above 125 IQ, whereas in another school, the percentage on this intelligence level was 29. The range in percentages among different high schools was similar. In a typical high-school graduation class one-fifth to one-fourth may score in the top 10 per cent of the population as a whole.

Tests given before children are two and one-half years of age often yield quite different results from those given later.[11] When children are about five, the results of individual intelligence tests become more reliable. The eight-year-old who scores as exceptionally intelligent will tend to score about the same when he is fifteen or sixteen. A test given in the eighth grade will predict college success about as well as one given in the senior year of high school.

Intelligence tests are also useful in indicating probable future educational and vocational status. Terman's gifted group were five times as likely as average children to enter the two highest professional and business groups; they were seven times as unlikely to become semi-skilled or unskilled workers. However, these predictions cannot be made with certainty in individual cases. Nor can success in college be precisely predicted by intelligence test scores; college success depends on purpose, persistence, and other characteristics.

Although the general trend in intelligence for a given individual is fairly consistent, his scores on different tests may fluctuate over a period of years. The IQ's of more than three-fourths of the pupils may vary by 10 IQ points or more; one-third, by 20 points or more; and one-tenth by 30 IQ points or more. In a few cases changes as great as 45 IQ points have occurred. There are also periods of relatively fast or slow progress; there are spurts and plateaus, and even regressions. Therefore, you cannot safely base any important decision on a single test. These changes in score from test to test were related to variations in state of health, mood, and self-confidence; to pressure of competing interests; to differences in the tests used; and to other home and school conditions.

A low score on a group intelligence test is more likely to be an accident than is a high score. Therefore, the higher score should usually be taken to represent true ability. Errors in scores are usually in the direction of understatement rather than overstatement.

School marks are less satisfactory than intelligence tests as indications of mental ability. There are several reasons for this: (1) some children of average ability get high marks by dint of great effort; (2) marks reflect the teacher's judgment, and sometimes even his favorable or unfavorable prejudices; (3) a few bright children may deliberately or unconsciously try to get low marks for various reasons, such as to be popular with the rest of the children or to avoid having to achieve up to capacity.

If you ask the school to give you your child's IQ, you will probably be told, "It is not our policy to give anyone a child's IQ." The principal or guidance director may offer you instead an interpretation of the test results. This is a sound policy. Much harm has been done through misunderstanding of the IQ. Certain parents have become unduly elated or depressed by this supposedly magical figure; they have allowed it to change their attitudes toward and treatment of their children, and have subsequently disregarded their own day-by-day observations. A more accurate picture of a child's intelligence is now being given by the percentile band, which shows the range within which the child stands in relation to others of his chronological age.

In some instances, parents have coached their children to prepare them for taking intelligence tests. Actually, general coaching seldom makes a difference of more than 6 or 8 points in the score. However, some parents go so far as to coach their children on the specific responses demanded by intelligence tests. Their motives for doing this are honorable: they want the child to have an intellectually stimulating school environment. If the child tests high, they reason, he will be placed in an advanced class or will be admitted to a special school. But this is cruel as well as unethical. For if the child does not have the intelligence indicated by the test results and demanded by the classes in which he is placed, he will constantly face challenges that are far beyond his capacity. He may fear failure and parental disappointment and become an anxious, unhappy child. Some youngsters caught in these unfortunate circumstances become overaggressive; aggression often stems from frustration. Some become nervous or even neurotic. Others, in unconscious protest against being expected to perform impossible tasks, refuse to put forth any effort. Still others resort to cheating; they feel they must get high marks by whatever means.

On the other hand, if the child is really gifted in abstract verbal ability—if he has high general intelligence—he should be challenged; and the chances are that he will be able to rank very high in his highschool class and meet the scholastic requirements of the college of his choice. His work will also have a creative quality; it will not be a mere pedestrian fulfillment of school requirements.

With these children, the role of both parents and teachers is to open new horizons, provide stimulating tasks, and create an atmosphere in which learning is exciting and rewarding.

Academically Talented

Some writers make a distinction between the intellectually gifted, as described in the previous section, and the academically talented.

The latter category includes 15 to 20 per cent of the school population as a whole. In some comprehensive high schools, this figure is as high as 50 per cent; it may be more than 90 per cent in schools that select their students on the basis of academic ability. Dr. James Bryant Conant defines the academically talented as "those boys and girls who have the ability to study effectively and rewardingly advanced mathematics, foreign languages and tough courses in chemistry and physics."[12] In other words, these are the students who have the potential ability, interest, and industry to succeed in an academic program.

Mathematically Able

Is your child gifted in mathematics? Mathematical geniuses are conspicuous by their ability to perform astonishing feats of mathematical reasoning. Children who are gifted in mathematics are best identified by their early interest in numbers, and their very high scores on the mathematical parts of intelligence tests and standardized achievement tests. In New York City there was a fairly large number of high school students whose marks on the mathematics section of standardized tests placed them in the gifted group, although their IQ's were below 130. In addition to scoring above 120 in IQ, students gifted in mathematics usually show these other characteristics: extraordinary memory, intellectual curiosity, keen insight into quantitative relations, facility in reasoning, persistent striving toward definite goals, and a knowledge of mathematics that is two or more years ahead of the accomplishment of their classmates. These students tend to be more successful in college courses in science and engineering than in the humanities.

Talented in the Arts

Is your child gifted in the arts? This kind of giftedness is the most difficult to identify. There are no completely satisfactory tests of aptitude for music, art, drama, or the dance. Intelligence tests do not adequately measure originality and creativity. In the field of art we have not obtained a high relation between intelligence test scores and achievement in art courses. It has been shown, however, that there are minimum levels of general intelligence below which performance in the arts is likely to be inconsistent and lacking in originality and organization. The best test is a sample of the child's work or an audition judged by one or more experts in the field. These are the chief bases for admission to the special schools in New York City—the High School of Music and Art and the High School of Performing Arts.

More specifically, musical ability may be identified by observing children's enjoyment of and sensitivity to the music they hear—their responses to various rhythms, tempos, tone colors; their awareness of changes in these qualities as well as of differences in pitch, key, or intensity. Memory for musical notes and phrases is another special ability to be recognized.

Children show indications of talent in art when they are asked to draw different kinds of pictures—a room, a landscape, "the prettiest spot on earth," and a picture of any kind they wish. These art products are then judged by art supervisors or competent lay people in the community.

For auditions in dramatics the child may be asked to give a pantomime, read from a play, or act out certain incidents.

Ability in creative writing becomes apparent in the imaginative imagery of preschool children, and in the vivid speech and spontaneous free writing of older children when they are dealing with something that is exciting to them. Special ability may be revealed when children are asked to write their responses to a beautiful film, in the manner described by Paul Witty. They may be asked to make barren sentences more descriptive or to write stories suggested by lead sentences or pictures. Samples of other kinds of writing may include a letter to a relative or friend, an editorial for the school paper, or a description of an exciting event. These products should be judged for their literary quality—for their originality and felicity of expression.

Mechanically Clever

Is your child mechanically gifted? Most boys, and some girls nowadays, like to tinker with cars. This does not necessarily indicate giftedness in mechanics. However, if parents or shop teachers note unusual ingenuity in solving mechanical problems, they may assume giftedness in this area. Contrary to general opinion, children who are highly gifted mechanically are often high in general intelligence as well. Observations may be checked against scores on some of the mechanical aptitude tests that are now available. It should be noted that while these tests identify those who are markedly deficient in mechanical ability, they do not necessarily spot those who are gifted.

Socially Gifted

The social environment in which a child grows up, and especially the personal relationships in the home, influence the development of social giftedness more than they affect the kinds of giftedness already described. Still, evidences of social sensitivity—ability to sense the feelings and responses of others, and ability to handle social situations —can be noted very early in life. Even babies show differences in social and emotional responsiveness. Some preschool children are natural leaders; they handle a situation with a maximum of satisfaction to all involved. One little boy who was building a house of large blocks with several other children, had in his group a clumsy youngster who just could not help knocking things over. Instead of saying to him, "Tommy, you go away. You're always knocking things over," this socially gifted child found a satisfactory solution for all concerned. "Tommy," he said, "I tell you what; you be the watch dog and stay *outside* the house, and when anyone comes along, you bark— and bark loud." This child was gifted in helping the group to achieve their goals and at the same time meet the needs of individual members.

Later on in their school years, socially gifted children show many of the following characteristics in an informal school situation:

They are chosen by others.

They help others, stand up for other children's rights, and are nice to everybody.

They think of interesting things to do and games to play.

They can take charge of a group.

They are good in games.

One may identify children who possess these characteristics by observing them in group activities. The children themselves may be asked to indicate which classmates they would like to sit with, serve on a committee with, go on a picnic with, or engage in other activities with. The children in a class may also identify certain characteristics in each other by naming the children they know who are like those described in a series of paragraphs.

Physically Gifted

Some children are gifted physically. They have magnificent bodies, well proportioned, graceful, admirably co-ordinated. These physically superior persons are most likely to find approval and recognition in competitive athletics and beauty contests.

Physical fitness should be a goal for other gifted children, too. A "brain" should have some "brawn," and vice versa. The modern physical education class should include some formalized exercise and vigorous competitive games as well as folk dancing and mildly vigorous group games. Dancing and "fun" activities have their place, as do also exercises that help each pupil to develop an optimum—for him or her—of strength, endurance, good posture, speed, agility, and balance.

Other Qualities

High moral and spiritual qualities enhance any of the kinds of giftedness we have described. These qualities involve ethical understandings, spiritual insights, and sensitivity to human relationships, as well as ability to translate these understandings into conduct. Persons with these qualities are often our outstanding religious leaders, philosophers, and thinkers. They contribute to the improvement of our ways of living together.

STRAWS IN THE WIND THAT INDICATE GIFTEDNESS

Obviously there is great diversity among children designated as gifted. Yet, although there is no personality pattern that fits them all, they are alike in many ways. The chances are that a child who is gifted in any of the special ways we have mentioned will also be above average in general mental ability.

There seems to be a hierarchy among the characteristics of giftedness:

1. An important factor of general intelligence.

2. A number of types of ability—linguistic, quantitative or mathematical, scientific, artistic, mechanical, social.

3. Many specific abilities under each of these types.

Although the gifted child is intellectually superior, he is not just "a brain"; neither does he conform to the absent-minded-professor stereotype. He is not often puny, stoop-shouldered, physically undeveloped, or socially unacceptable. Quite the opposite.

As a group, gifted children have been found to be slightly superior in physical development and appearance to other groups with which they have been compared. Age for age, their development is ahead of that of average children. Most gifted children are early starters. They tend to be ahead of other children of their age in walking and talking, in interests and hobbies, in reading and number work. They grow more rapidly physically, mentally, and academically than their age-mates.

They also tend to be somewhat alike in these aspects of their growth. Their growth curves for height, weight, development of teeth and bones, strength, mental ability, spelling, arithmetic, reading, and education in general, when put in comparable form, are much alike. The superior health of gifted children is related to their good sleep habits, success in school, emotional stability, and good social adjustment.

Their intellectual development may be in advance of their physical and social development and their social experiences. This unevenness in development sometimes makes certain gifted youngsters impatient with their lack of success in games and sports, and with the relatively simple interests of other children of their own chronological age.

We know that gifted children are able to learn more, and more quickly than the average, and that they are less likely to use the trial and error method in their problem solving. They like to figure things out and arrive at generalizations and conclusions. They become bored with repetitive drill on unrelated details; they dislike textbooks that are crammed with facts thrown together with no discernible pattern.

Of course, there are exceptions. One gifted child may, in the beginning, grow rapidly in mind but slowly in body. This happens rarely. Occasionally a gifted child is late in starting. One boy who had an IQ of 104 at age six, scored 123 at age fifteen. His later record

showed continued growth into adult life. Some gifted children surprise us by beginning to do their best academic work during their
late high school years, or even in their college years. This "late flower-
ing" occurs more frequently among boys than among girls.

Gifted children in general show certain intellectual capacities that
have already been mentioned:

A remarkable memory—they seem to retain everything they see or
learn.

A keen desire to know.

An insatiable curiosity—they continually ask "why." Their questions
are more searching, more concerned with cause-and-effect relations,
and more persistent than those of other children of their age. They
not only want to know; they have the ability to make the most of
their opportunities to learn.

Gifted children are able to solve problems without help and to
cope with unfamiliar situations. They have a capacity beyond their
years for thinking through problems and for generalizing and reasoning things out. They tend to be more concerned with abstract ideas
than are average children; they like to ponder questions of religion
and morality and problems of world peace. But although they have
the ability to see subtle relations and to think deeply for people of
their age, some of them are prone to indulge in superficial thinking.
Perhaps the school has not held these youngsters up to standards of
rigorous thinking. In some cases children are coached or overstimulated at home to acquire a superficial glibness that helps them to pass
as "gifted."

The gifted have an abundance of mental energy. Their breadth of
interest is remarkable. They often have many interests, or a broad
absorbing interest, and spend much time on their collections and
hobbies. If an activity is self-initiated and engrossing to them, they
will concentrate on it and stay with it without getting restless. They
are often self-starters. They are likely to join in more activities, both
out of school and in school, than the average.

The school achievement of gifted children, as measured by standardized tests, is often two to four years above their grade placement,
especially in the language arts, arithmetical reasoning, history, and
science. They are likely to be weakest in handwriting and other

subjects requiring manual co-ordination or dexterity. They usually read well and extensively, though recent studies have shown that their reading tastes leave much to be desired. The youngsters surveyed did not, of their own accord, read more difficult books than those read by their less able classmates. Some gifted children may be following the path of least resistance in this respect; others may be afraid of being considered bookworms or "too brainy" by their friends. Home and school share the responsibility to stimulate these youngsters, without nagging them, to reach the intellectual level of which they are capable.

Gifted children tend to be old for their age. They feel at home with older children and adults, and are able to take part in adult conversations and to participate in adult games, projects, and interests. However, they should learn to get along with younger as well as with older children. Later on, as teachers or members of other professions, or even in business, they will have to understand and deal with people of different ages and abilities; childhood is not too early for them to begin gaining this experience.

They often show capacity for leadership at an early age, although they may not be elected to positions of leadership in school. They are often modest, and show appreciation for the achievements of others. They are fun to be with; they usually enjoy playing games as much as other children. They are successful in sports, though they often avoid rough games like football and more often play games in which verbal facility is involved.

They also show superiority in character and personality. According to character tests, they are less boastful than other children, more truthful and trustworthy under stress, and less likely to cheat. They are capable of other desirable social attitudes and behavior. It is natural that they should be somewhat aware of their superior ability, and consequently more self-confident than the average. Gifted children are also distinguished by their originality and creativity.

There are, however, many different kinds and degrees of excellence. Children in the same family are different. Parents should recognize and welcome these differences. Why should Johnny be like his older brother Bill? It would be a dull world and a dull family if everyone were alike. By excelling in different ways—in art, in music, in social relations, in mechanical work, in abstract verbal ability, or in mathematical ability—children contribute to an interesting and well-rounded family life; later on, this same diversity will help them to carry on the many-sided aspects of the world's work.

Children who show any of the various patterns of giftedness in their early years are quite likely to fulfill this youthful promise. Professor Terman's follow-up studies of one thousand gifted children showed that they tended to maintain their superior character and achievement as adults. To this general tendency there are exceptions, of course. Some seem to lack the drive or purpose necessary to develop and use their special abilities.

Much depends on the guidance and education these young people receive at home. In the motivation of a child's achievement the father seems to play an important role. However, both parents play a vital role in our nation's present search for talent. Parents are in a good position to identify various kinds of giftedness in their children, and to provide conditions conducive to their development. Each child should have an equal opportunity to develop in his own best way.

NO TWO ALIKE

As you have been reading about the characteristics which you might expect to find in your gifted child, you have probably thought, "I know gifted children who are not like that." True; no two are alike. And, for the various reasons mentioned, an individual child may not have developed the characteristics possessed by the majority of the gifted children described in the studies.

Moreover, the characteristics mentioned may be combined into many different patterns in individual children. One child may possess such a high quality of verbal ability that it overshadows other characteristics. Another may have many abilities more or less evenly developed. Still another may be extremely talented in one of the arts, though of only average general intelligence as measured by the tests.

Some individuals show a combination of extraordinary abilities in several different fields. Albert Schweitzer has displayed outstanding ability in music, theology, medicine, religion, humanitarianism, and social service. Leonardo da Vinci possessed superior creativity in many fields. Gandhi, Theodore Roosevelt, Benjamin Franklin, Winston Churchill, and many others have shown various combinations of high abilities.

HOW TO IDENTIFY GIFTED CHILDREN

Identification of talent and general mental alertness begins at home.[13] Mentally superior children can usually be identified early. Before the age of five, most of them exhibit a capacity to learn spontaneously from clues in their environment. During their preschool years they are likely to show many of the characteristics already mentioned. As early as the first grade one may identify children who are outstanding in one or two special abilities, such as word meaning, manipulation of numbers, reasoning, or social leadership.

In a conference with the child's teacher or with the school guidance worker or psychologist, the parent may both give and obtain evidence of the child's capacities, aptitudes, and achievement. The most accurate appraisal is one that is based on a developmental record. Such a record includes the results of several intelligence tests and of achievement tests in reading and mathematics. It also contains the child's scholastic record from the time he entered school. Teachers should enter on it their observations of the child's performance when faced with social or intellectual problems, together with their estimates of his ability in relation to that of other children of the same age. The regular cumulative record should be supplemented by reports of interviews with the family of the gifted child. These would contain references to the family's awareness of the child's superior ability, their hopes and plans, their efforts to develop his abilities, their co-operation with the school and other agencies in developing the child's interests and talents, the child's outside interests and hobbies, and any concrete evidences of special ability that have been observed. All these kinds of information should be interpreted to the parents, so that they can help to recommend and provide the further experiences that the child needs.

Intellectual ability, as measured by various intelligence and achievement tests, is the aspect of giftedness most commonly recognized in the setting up of school programs. This practice is justified by the fact that good things tend to go together. High scores on intelligence tests indicate generally high scholastic aptitude; they are likely to forecast success in high school and college. There are, of course, exceptions to this general rule, for intelligence is only one ingredient in achievement. Home background is especially significant. Some children who come from impoverished homes, where they lack companionship and things to play with and explore, may not show their real ability on standardized tests. It may take six years or more of schooling to compensate for some of these deficiencies in early environment. We must remember, too, that it is easier to identify the able and ambitious student than to recognize the child who is potentially able but unaspiring.

Moreover, it must be re-emphasized that a single intelligence test score is not conclusive; the individual may score higher or lower on a repeat performance; occasionally there is an error in scoring. The results of two different intelligence tests may differ considerably. Accordingly, the IQ rating is not used as the sole criterion in identifying giftedness. Other evidence is taken into consideration: the teachers' appraisal of the student's ability, his school achievement, opinions of counselors and parents, reading proficiency, mathematical ability, hobbies and interests.

PSEUDO GIFTEDNESS

It is not always easy to identify a gifted child. Some glib, vivacious children give the impression of being brighter than they really are. Some children who have been coached or pushed by overambitious parents or teachers are trained to show some of the characteristics that gifted children show naturally. This kind of superiority is only temporary; it is not maintained as the child grows older and is confronted by increasingly difficult tasks. Then, too, a docile child may win a higher rating from a teacher than a child who does the unusual thing and asks questions the teacher cannot answer. Not every child who likes to draw, listen to music, or tinker with mechanical toys or gadgets is talented along those lines. Possession of two or three of the characteristics listed in this chapter does not make a gifted child. Without a basis for comparison, some parents may assume that their child is gifted, though his ability is actually only average. The entire configuration of interest, achievement, and purpose is what counts. It is important to know how a specific ability was acquired, and how it fits into the child's total pattern of behavior.

On the other hand, some truly gifted children elude identification. These are the quiet ones. For some reason they hide their light under a bushel. Only occasionally do they give parents and teachers a glimmering of their real capacity. Sometimes, too, parents who lack a sound basis for comparing their child with others, accept a superior child as average, as indeed he is—in a family of gifted persons.

Schools may make mistakes, too. Not long ago the record of a thirteen-year-old boy was presented to the admissions committee of a private preparatory school. After examining the boy's previous school record and the comments of his former teachers, the committee of twelve members voted unanimously not to admit him. It turned out, according to the account in *Newsweek* for March 4, 1957, that the record they had considered was really that of Sir Winston Churchill during his first years at Harrow some seventy years ago. The admissions committee had rejected a boy who was to become a great statesman, an inspiring leader, a famous historian, an artist, and winner of a Nobel Prize for literature. If the record had included intelligence test scores, the boy's potential intellectual capacity might have been detected—but who could have foretold the development of his other outstanding gifts?

YOUR ATTITUDE TOWARD THE TRULY GIFTED CHILD

[If you learn that your child is gifted, you may have to resist the natural tendency to boast about it, or to force him prematurely into advanced work. He needs to experience the joys of childhood. He needs normal give-and-take associations with children of different ages. Although exceptional in his mental ability or special talent, the gifted child is like other children in many respects. He may have fears or anxieties, he may feel lonely or unhappy, he may have a quick temper or some physical handicap.]

[Let him try his wings, give him opportunities to develop his interests, but refrain from showing him off. He has to be himself; he must not become a martyr to your own unfulfilled ambitions. Sometimes parents expect too much of a bright child; they hold up a goal of perfectionism which the child cannot achieve. The child never gets a sense of his real self; he is saddled with his parents' aspirations for him; he has lost himself.

The child needs approval and praise for the genuine accomplishments he makes, but he should not be given excessive or indiscriminate praise. Even though he is bright, he is not the center of the universe. Others have talents, too, and he should respect them. It is usually better for the young child not to be aware that he is exceptional. Then he will enter more freely into social relations with other children. They will be less likely to resent his superiority. If he is deprived of normal childhood play and outdoor experiences, he may protest this deprivation by resisting the learning of which he is capable.

The behavior of the gifted child may give you clues as to the ways in which you can be most helpful to him. He will initiate plenty of activities in an environment in which books and other materials are available. Your role as parent is to permit the child to follow his inventive ideas, and to carry on home projects in science, dramatics, and the like. Invite in other adults who are interested in the child's special projects. Encourage the child to visit museums, exhibits, and other places of interest. He is usually glad to have books recommended to him and made easily available. Let the child's responses be your guide. He will show you what he can and cannot do profitably. It is exciting to watch a bright child develop.

You can expect him to ask many questions. Even though you cannot answer them all, you can keep his curiosity alive. Many a gifted child began to be interested in some special field when he shared one of his father's hobbies or went with him on a tour of discovery.

If your child is highly gifted intellectually, you may unconsciously neglect other aspects of his development. He needs to have regular duties and responsibilities. He should learn to accept people different from himself.

There is also a great temptation to overschedule the time of the gifted child; he *can* do so many things. But overscheduling may defeat your purpose. The child may resent it; he may become balky or rebellious; he may have trouble concentrating on any one task. It is one thing to provide experiences that interest and challenge a child, and quite a different thing to put too much pressure on him to achieve along the lines you have laid down. Each of two extremes is to be avoided: (1) exploiting a child or pushing him too hard, and (2) discouraging him from going as far and as fast as he is able to go.

We have often heard it said that parents should accept their children for what they *are* rather than for what they do. The late Dr. James Plant made this distinction between *whoness* and *whatness*. If a parent is concerned only with the child's achievement, he may give the child the impression that he does not care for him as a person. Children sometimes resent this attitude on the part of parents. And quite rightly, if it stems from the parent's desire to increase his own prestige through his child's achievement. In its extreme form this is the attitude of parents who exploit their child prodigies with no regard for the children's rights.

To avoid misunderstanding, the above statement should be modified to read: Parents should accept their children for what they are *as well as* for what they do. In fact, we cannot fully accept the child as a person unless we are also concerned that he fulfill his potentialities—that he become the best person he is capable of becoming. Therein lies one of the sources of his happiness.

Like other children the gifted need discipline in the sense of control. A French writer has said that the trouble with American children is not that they are brought up badly, but that they are not brought up at all. The seriousness of this lack of firmness and control is now being recognized. Firm adherence to reasonable standards is part of a parent's loving care.

THE GIFTED CHILD IN THE FAMILY

The child—any child—is only a part of the family. Everything should not revolve around him. There are many good reasons for helping him to accept his appropriate role. In working out a child's routine, one must consider the needs and satisfactions of the whole family. Parents have a right to a life of their own, quite apart from their children. Opportunity for the members of a family to be themselves, even to the extent of being aloof at times, is as essential to wholesome family life as "togetherness."

Parents can be too anxious about their role of bringing up children. They do not have to assume every last little responsibility. The child, increasingly from his early years, should be led to take responsibility for what he does, what he is, and what he becomes. Since there is no one best method of child rearing, parents can take a flexible approach —which is quite different from a hesitant or inconsistent way of treating children. The ordinary devoted mother gets along very well by doing what she feels she wants to do for her baby. She watches the way he responds to varied treatment. She also considers how she feels about the whole situation. Surely her observation of the child over a period of time gives her an intimate knowledge of his needs. When a mother is doing a good job of caring for her children, it is best to leave her alone. On the other hand, parents should not consider that they are unloving because they are preoccupied and overburdened with the strain of daily living.

The other children in the family certainly influence the gifted child—whether they are bright or dull, older or younger, the same or the opposite sex. He also influences them. Certainly each of your children has some unique ability—sensitivity to people; delight in beauty; vivid, colorful language; ability to see the funny side of a situation. Awareness of these diverse gifts broadens our idea of giftedness, and helps us to avoid undue competition among children. It leads us to accept all children, regardless of special accomplishments. However, giving a child recognition for doing something special helps to build his self-esteem. The late Dr. Plant said that everyone needs to be especially good in something. Then, when he is feeling discouraged about his lack of achievement in other lines he can say: "Anyway, when it comes to playing baseball (or spelling, or being chosen as leader) I'm pretty good." What one can *do* helps to build his idea of what he *is*.

The reward that parents reap for their love and guidance of each of their children is to see them grow in independence, social sensitivity, and individuality.

QUESTIONS AND ANSWERS

1. *How can I know whether my child is gifted?*

A father put the question this way: "My daughter who was eight last month is in the third grade. Whether she's gifted or not, I do not know. However, she is having difficulties in getting the marks her teacher thinks are satisfactory for her. I think she is definitely lazy in many ways but I sense in her an understanding and perhaps a general intelligence which seem at variance with her school achievement. Is there an organization or clinic in this vicinity that could give her tests of general educational development, personal adjustment, etc.?"

These are some indications that a child is gifted: a *spontaneous* eagerness to know and to learn; a *natural* quickness to see relations, solve problems, and learn new things; originality and creativeness; earlier-than-average development, e.g., walking and talking early and being physically and socially advanced for his age. Such observations should be checked by an individual test administered by a well-trained person; such persons are usually connected with a school, university, or child guidance or mental health clinic.

2. *What is the difference between (1) pushing and pressuring a child and (2) challenging or stimulating him?*

The parent who puts undue pressure on the child disregards the child's nature and needs. The parent who challenges the child helps him to set realistic goals and standards, and provides conditions in which the child can achieve these with real but reasonable effort.

3. *How can you tell the truly gifted from the pseudo gifted?*

The truly gifted child is inner-impelled, spontaneous, and interested in his activities. The pseudo gifted is impelled by outside pressure. He is anxious about meeting the demands of his parents, and seems to find little or no real delight in his intellectual activities.

4. *Should a parent tell a child that he is gifted?*

The parent should not give the child the impression that he is exceptional or superior to other children. However, from an early age the parent can help the child to develop a true picture of himself—of his strengths and limitations, of the kinds of things he can and cannot do well, of the kind of person he is.

5. *How should a gifted child in a family of average children be treated?*

Fortunately each child in the family has some special physical, social, or intellectual abilities for which he may obtain recognition. It should be an important part of the education of the gifted child to learn how to make others feel successful and happy.

6. *How important is general mental ability?*

General intelligence is important in predicting a child's future success in school or later life. However, it is character traits that give the individual the necessary push or drive. Some able boys drop out of school by the time they are sixteen because high wages and entertainment during leisure hours have a stronger attraction for them than further knowledge and skill. On the other hand, the associations that they formed during the high school years and the habits of industry that they developed there may have engendered a morale and ambition that will eventually lead them to seek a college education.

7. *What factors explain the differences between top performers in a given field and those who perform only moderately well?*

The three factors seem to be capacity, opportunity, and personality. Superior performance also depends very often on the early recognition of potential ability, its nurture, and its utilization.

Capacity for abstract thinking and verbal fluency is especially needed for superior performance in occupations requiring many years of scientific or professional education.

Opportunity must include early experiences which predispose a child to be intellectually active and interested, to solve his own problems, to make the most of his environment, to free himself from hampering personal relations, and to think of himself as confident and competent.

Personality may either facilitate or interfere with the utilization of capacity and opportunity. Personality patterns become quite firmly fixed at an early age; however, the total pattern of potentialities may change if an unfavorable environment is improved early enough in the child's life.

8. *Why shouldn't outstanding performance in athletics be classified as one kind of giftedness?*

It is! In many high schools and colleges the star athletes get more training and have the advantage of more financial subsidization than do students who have other types of exceptional ability.

9. *Can intelligence tests identify the exceptionally creative child?*

Probably not, for our present tests give credit for the commonly accepted answer. The creative and original child may even be penalized on a standardized test if he gives a unique, rather than the usual answer.

10. *Is measured intelligence associated with success in school and life?*

Yes, though the degree of relationship is far from perfect. In some school subjects the association is fairly high while in others it is practically zero. This variation is due to a number of other factors such as health, values, purpose, drive, attitude toward himself and life, habits of work, emotional adjustment, adequate background knowledge and skill, which determine how well a person uses his native ability.

The age at which the test is given influences the predictive value. In general, tests given at an early age—before four years—tell little about the child's future school and college success. But certain tests given in the eighth grade predict college success about as well as those given in the twelfth grade.

TWO

What It Takes to Make a Gifted Child

GIFTED children are lucky. They have the advantage of being born healthy and mentally alert and being well brought up. More specifically, it takes four things to make a gifted child: a good heredity, favorable experiences in infancy and early childhood, an evironment that offers opportunities for the development of abilities, and guidance and instruction. From their parents gifted children need acceptance without exploitation, understanding without prejudice, and guidance without domination. The gifted child is a product of nature and nurture in intricate combination.

Children and young people are influenced by many persons and many events that occur in their lives. Of course, in the beginning, the mother's influence is all-important. But gradually the child's world expands to include the whole family, other relatives, friends, schoolmates, community groups, and, eventually, occupational associates. The "social atom"—the individual and his associations—gradually becomes more complex. One thirteen-year-old gifted boy described these multiple influences as follows:

"I don't think there is any one particular instance that makes me or any other person become what he or she eventually becomes. I think it is a gradual maturing and growth in the individual. I think the individual is influenced by everyone he associates with—they actually become a part of you. Of course your parents, teachers, and close friends usually have the greater influence on you. I don't think there has been any *one* experience in my life up to this date that has completely changed my outlook on life."

A GOOD HEREDITY

Even at birth babies are different. There are no two alike. One newborn may weigh three times as much as another. Some are quiet, others are restless. Some are placid, others are fretful. Some seem more alert than others. Each individual is born with a nervous system of a certain quality; some are more sensitive than others to everything that they see and hear and handle. Some are born with exceptional ability to relate and organize their experiences. These extrasensitive individuals with superior powers of organization are the potentially gifted.

We cannot sidestep the fact of individual differences. The child's native endowment sets an upper limit to his achievements. The famous scientist, Sir Francis Galton, once said, "Where the allowance [of general ability] granted by nature is inadequate, the keenest will and the stoutest industry must strive in vain."

However, giftedness is not like a fairy godmother's gift bestowed at birth. It is rather a process of becoming. Intelligence is not ready-made; it is not given, once and for all. It keeps on growing into maturity. It constantly creates, elaborates, and refines itself by selecting, comparing, and organizing life experiences. In this sense intelligence is learned.

Any seed that you plant may rot in the ground, or send up weak and spindly shoots if the soil is poor; it will come up strong and fruitful if the soil is good. A good seed that sprouts in poor soil and has unfavorable growing conditions may never develop as it should, while even a poor seed that lodges in good soil has a chance to develop to its optimum capacity. This is why parents are so anxious to give their children the best possible environment.

The relative influence of heredity and environment—the rather futile nature-nurture controversy—is still unsolved. At one extreme, environment is considered of major importance. At the other extreme, research on identical twins suggests that heredity may have several times more weight than environment in producing differences in intelligence. Catherine Cox Miles, in her comprehensive review of research on gifted children, concluded that "we must, therefore, believe that inheritance of gifted traits is individual and complex and that training can only develop, never create, gifted capacity."[1]

Our belief about this relation between nature and nurture influences our actions. If we think the child's development is predetermined, then we tend to let nature take its course. If we believe the child is the product of his environment, then we tend to try to make environmental conditions favorable. If we are convinced that the child has resources within himself, we try to create conditions favorable to active self-creation on his part. Actually, there is some validity in each of these approaches. We want to give the child certain areas of freedom to develop in his own best way. We want to facilitate his development by favorable environmental conditions. And we want to recognize the child's active interaction with external conditions.

Although most of the gifted children in Terman's study grew up in well-to-do families, with well-educated parents and an intellectually stimulating atmosphere, being gifted does not necessarily mean being born in a well-to-do family. We sometimes find dull children in wealthy families and very bright children growing up under poor cultural and economic conditions. In one city, 75 per cent of the gifted children had parents who were classified as unskilled, skilled, or "white-collar"; the number of gifted Negroes was in proportion to their number in the general population. We also find wide differences among the children of parents who seem to be much alike in ability and background. Such differences may be explained partly by the infinite variety of hereditary patterns possible in the union of the male and female germ cells.

Parents who have, as one mother said, "a gifted child on their hands" sometimes become overanxious about their responsibility for bringing him up. Everyone makes some mistakes. Everyone sometimes wishes that he had handled a situation differently. But blaming yourself or feeling guilty or anxious about it is worse than useless. No less an authority than Dr. Benjamin Spock thought that more mistakes are probably made today by parents who try too hard and assume too much responsibility than by parents who take the more relaxed approach of simply trying to understand and enjoy their children. As Dorothy Barclay summed it up: "Live the good life and love that baby."

INFLUENCES ON THE GIFTED CHILD'S DEVELOPMENT

We know that certain conditions are generally favorable to child development. First among these are constructive parental attitudes toward the child.

Parental Attitudes

Fortunately it is usually easy to enjoy and to respect a gifted child. If you find yourselves at any time resenting him, ask why. Perhaps he makes you feel inferior because he is brighter and quicker than you are. This is sometimes embarrassing, but it really should make you proud—proud that he is *your* child and has gone ahead of you. Perhaps you feel a little jealous because people respond to him more warmly than they respond to you. But he is part of you, and why should you be jealous of him any more than you would be jealous of yourself? In fact, your pride in him should crowd out any tinge of jealousy. Perhaps he just wears you out with his questions and enthusiasms and eagerness for new experiences. If you can sometimes put him in a safe place with books to read or with safe science and art materials to use, he will go ahead on his own steam. Then you can withdraw for a while to your own less strenuous occupations.

Gifted children are not likely to be rejected in the sense of being unwanted or subordinated to other children in the family. However, they may be deprived of the experiences they need because of poverty or the unwise expenditure of what would otherwise be an adequate income. If one or both parents are dead or often absent from home, or if the parents are divorced, the child may feel neglected. Such a child is often hungry for affection and seeks it in his school and other associations.

When asked what parents should do for their children, one gifted youngster said she thought "they should take more interest in the kids." Another said that the parents should know where the child is going and not just say "run along." He also thought parents should not go out at night and "just tell the kids to turn off the lights when they go to bed." A child needs a supporting relationship, a reinforcement of his goals and ambitions. Otherwise he tends to feel that what he does or accomplishes doesn't matter because no one really cares what happens to him.

Overprotection is probably more common than neglect in the case of gifted children. It is so natural for parents to want to protect the child from the dangers and difficulties of life. But overprotection limits the child's opportunities and may eventually decrease his inclination to explore and to use his initiative. The child to whom this happens tends to be afraid to grow up and accept responsibilities.

Some parents seem to be concerned primarily with the child's achievement. Naturally they want the child to fulfill his potentialities, to be a credit to them, and to increase their prestige. But this concern for achievement can go too far. The child is made to feel he is wasting his time when he plays. He is expected to do things before he is mature enough to tackle them. He is given affection solely as a reward for achievement. This attitude on the part of the parent may make the child feel that he is loved, not for himself, but only for his achievement. Consequently he may feel resentful; such children sometimes deliberately or unconsciously try to fail in school.

Possessiveness may have somewhat similar effects. When the parent shows the child's report card proudly to his friends, it may seem to the child that the parent is taking all the credit for himself.

Boasting about the child is almost as bad. It embarrasses him and may affect his social relations with other children. It may also give people the impression that he is a little prig.

The practice of exploiting a child to enhance one's own prestige has already been mentioned in Chapter One. Sometimes parents' ambition leads them into wishful thinking; they imagine that their child is more gifted than he is.

The child who is driven by his parents' unrealistic ambition is seldom satisfied with his success. He constantly strives for a perfection he cannot attain. He is often haunted by feelings of unworthiness, anger, and guilt. Even if, by dint of prodigious effort, he manages to excel in academic work, he may fail in his relations with people. His hostility toward his parents may be transferred to his teachers and classmates, and, later on, to his employers and fellow workers. Thus an individual of this sort may fail to attain the vocational success of which he is capable. A parent who superimposes an unrealistic ambition upon his child may actually be defeating his own purpose.

Many gifted children complain that their parents are never satisfied with their performance. When they bring home a report card the only comment is, "You could have done better." If it is true that "nothing succeeds like observed success," then, with most children, a word of genuine praise would spur them on to their optimum achievement. However, what really counts with most people is not the success or the praise itself, but the approval of a loved person. It is also true that when a child cannot fulfill his parents' expectations, he may tend to lose confidence in himself.

As Dorothy Barclay has said, "the relationship between parent and child is, of course, the most important factor in the development of good feelings toward the rest of the world."[2]

Parental attitudes are often affected by other persons who are brought into the family circle. This may increase the emotional complexity of the parent-child situation. To be sure, relatives often come in handy. They may supply the extra love that some children, especially the less gifted, need. They may extend the experience of the gifted child and expand his world; they may help in an emergency.

If mothers-in-law, sisters-in-law, and grandparents sometimes annoy you, you might ask why. Is it because their interference is detrimental to your children? Does it make you feel inadequate? Or is the resentment associated with some early childhood experiences of your own? In handling any difficult situation we need to identify the causes before we try to apply a remedy.

Although parental love has been emphasized as basic to good child development, love cannot be evoked at will. Some individuals have never learned to love. They cannot feel warmly toward their children. It does not help mothers to feel guilty about this lack of affection. What can they do? They can understand the child's needs. In many cases they can change their behavior toward the child—be less critical, look for things they can praise, and create conditions in which the child can feel loved and accepted.

Nothing you can *do* or *say* is a substitute for the way you feel. Your feelings shine through your actions and are conveyed to the child by your smile and tone of voice and gestures. Gifted children are keen to sense your intent. They often understand "the language of behavior" better than you do. They quickly recognize discrepancies and inconsistencies between your words and your true feelings.

Culture and Traditions

The traditions of the gifted child's family, his school or college, and the society in which he lives affect his development in many ways. In some families, the son is enrolled in an exclusive preparatory school or in one of the Ivy League colleges practically on the day he is born. Going to college is taken for granted. On the other hand, some families in low socioeconomic groups never consider the idea of sending a child to college or else they reject it as beyond the scope of possibility. In certain ethnic groups children are subjected to much more parental pressure to achieve than is the case in other groups. These parents apparently influence the child by dominating his decisions, while still allowing him a degree of participation.

We no longer think of molding a child to a pattern. We try instead to create conditions in which the child develops his individuality within the framework of what society accepts as desirable and sound.

The restrictions and limitations, imposed by the culture, are also being viewed more and more from the standpoint of the needs of the child. Children need firm limits just as much as they need a sense of security and love. Consequently we try to cultivate and encourage, rather than to pressure and push. We change our methods as the child's needs change and the demands which the culture makes on him increase and intensify. For example, we sometimes continue too long the kind of complete permissiveness that is suitable only for the infant. Sometimes, too, we expect children to make decisions that are too mature for them; children should have just as much freedom as is appropriate to their stage of development. A child who is free to make decisions should also be free to take the consequences of his decisions.

The spirit of the times has much to do with the development of talent. In certain periods of history the arts have flourished. In our time science and technology are favored. Through talent searches of various kinds potential scientists are being discovered. Equally important, Terman stated, for the welfare of the world is "the discovery and encouragement of potential poets, prose writers, artists, statesmen, and social leaders."[3]

Home Conditions and Child-Care Practices

In Terman's study a large majority—85 per cent—of the homes of the gifted children were rated *favorable*; only 9 per cent were rated *unfavorable*. The parents were in the prime of life when the children were born, and the mother's health was good. Conditions of birth were normal, a larger proportion than average were breast-fed, and the children's health during the first year was excellent.[4] Apparently these gifted children got off to a good start in life. One reason why so large a proportion of gifted individuals are found in superior homes is that superior people tend to create a superior environment and seek the best education for their children, despite difficulties.

More specifically, Alexander Reid Martin[5] found certain home conditions to be favorable to child development, whether the child is of rich or poor parentage, bright or dull, physically attractive or handicapped:

The parents expect the best of the child.

They give the child not only material things, but their own time and thought.

They do not force their ideas and ambitions upon the child.

They do not say, "You should do what I want; just look at all I've done for you."

They do things as a family group, "*with* as well as *for* the child."

They give the child real jobs to do that make him feel grown up and important.

They treat the older children with due respect.

The children in the family have some squabbles that help prepare them for struggles outside the home.

The home is not broken, and the parents enjoy doing things together.

The resiliency of some gifted children is amazing. They surmount the most adverse circumstances. For example, Marion's father died when she was a baby. Since her mother was ill, the two children were sent to a children's shelter. Intermittently they were with their mother and in foster homes. Of the second foster home Marion writes:

"It was a wonderful place. My 'Mom,' as I called her, was an understanding woman. She taught me a lot of the little I know today. During that period, my mother came to visit me every other week end.

"My mother was and still is a wonderful person. She has an outgoing and friendly nature. I think she is the most selfless person I have ever known. She is lenient to a fault. She has always "inspired" me to be good. I think it's her great courage and kindness that makes me love her so much."

This child, from a home broken into bits by the death of the father and the illness of the mother, was still cheerfully able to appreciate a good foster home and at the same time maintain a loving relation with her own mother.

Personal Relations

At any stage in a gifted child's development, parent-child relationships may confirm or deflect his developmental trend. The influence of the parents on the gifted child's development cannot be overemphasized. It is a primary influence; it is the influence exerted during the child's most impressionable years. It is an influence continuous day after day, year after year. It pervades all aspects of his life. Parental influence is further intensified by its emotional tone; anything a loved person says or does is particularly influential. However, we must remember that what affects a child's development is the way in which he perceives or views home conditions and his parents' attitudes and behavior. That is one reason why some early childhood antagonisms, jealousies, and fears are so persistent.

The role of the parents, as described by Dale B. Harris, is to facilitate the child's growth, not to push or pull him along a path preordained by them. The parents provide opportunities for the active child to explore, to discover, to develop. They encourage him. They build on his potentialities but leave an area of freedom for him to be himself.[6]

Mother-child relations—The child's first and most important relations are with his mother. During infancy the gifted child needs to acquire a sense of trust that frees him to reach out toward people and things in his environment. In these early months, lack of warm physical contact with the mother, painful illness from which no one can bring relief, or maternal disregard for the baby's natural body rhythms and needs may block the child's best development.

Evidence is available to show that infants seriously deprived of maternal affection and the normal stimulation of things to look at, listen to, and handle, may become apathetic. Even a child born with superior ability may fail to develop his potentialities under conditions of extreme deprivation. He may not acquire that basic sense of trust in his world and in himself which, later in life, would enable him to cope with his problems.

Father-son relations—The importance of a good father-son relationship has also been emphasized. Something certainly is lacking when there is no man about the house to set a good example and to guide a growing boy.

When the father is dead, or separated from the boy by divorce or other circumstances, the suggestion most often made is to find a relative, a teacher, a minister, a doctor, or a youth leader who may serve as a "father substitute." Such a man, who should be a real person with sound principles and values and a sense of humor, may give support and friendship, discuss subjects of importance to the boy, and be a good example to him. However, establishing such a relationship is not easy. It should not be obviously manipulated by the mother. Nor should the father substitute add this responsibility to an already heavy schedule. Such conditions would be likely to produce tension on the part of both boy and adult.

It is probably better for the mother to feel less concerned and anxious about her son's deprivation, and to try to make the mother-son relationship the best possible—a relationship in which the boy is neither overprotected nor pushed prematurely into the role of "the man of the family."

Complex family relations—Feelings in families form a complicated network. There may be conflicts between parents, jealousies among brothers and sisters, and, on the part of the child, fear of losing love.

Conflicts between the parents are a cause of anxiety to the child; they may undermine his security. If they culminate in divorce, the child sometimes becomes the victim of one parent's hostility toward the other. The child feels rejected. As one gifted child said to her parents after they had decided to get a divorce, "I'm sorry it has to be now, when I'm at an age to take it so hard."

The more psychologically mature the parents are, the less serious their conflicts will be, and the less arguing they will do in the home. There is nothng more comforting to a worried child than parents who have love and respect for each other and for their children.

Mary Poppins, Pamela Travers'[7] charming character, is a good example of one kind of adult who has a constructive influence on children. She is self-confident, forthright, even gruff and grumpy on the surface. Yet she creates a relationship of trust and certainty. She also makes life exciting. She sets limits. On Michael's bad day she finally says, "This is the end," and carries him off kicking and screaming to bed. But when his naughtiness has worn itself out, she resumes her close, confident, secure relationship with the child.

Sibling relations—When the parents' love is unlimited, there is usually no serious problem of rivalry among brothers and sisters. There is then no need for the older child to be jealous of the attention the mother must of necessity give to the new baby—there is love enough to go around.

To scold a child for feeling jealous of a brother or sister usually intensifies his feeling of not being loved. It confirms his fears. To counteract his fear, the mother may give him a little extra time and attention.

Gifted children often mention being annoyed by brothers and sisters. Like other children, the gifted have a certain amount of natural aggression which they take out on their siblings. For children in the same family to compete and to be somewhat jealous of one another is a common occurrence. More often the gifted child's problem is to avoid making others jealous of him.

Relations with friends—As the child moves away from the family circle, friends become increasingly important. A chum may bring out the best in a seven- or eight-year-old child. Other friends may open up new interests. Classmates and friends in high school may help a bright child to make the most of himself in spite of poor family background or financial limitations. On the other hand, in a group where intellectual interests are hooted down, bright youngsters tend to achieve below their capacity. With girls, this problem is intensified. As one girl said, "If you're taller than boys, it's bad enough, but if you're brighter, it's fatal."

The Child's Self-Concept

From very early years the child is constructing a picture of himself—

as well liked by others, as competent, as possessing special ability. Unfortunately some gifted children think of themselves as "only an average boy," or "a boy whom nobody cares much about," or "a child who can never reach the goal his parents have set for him." The way in which the child perceives himself and his world largely determines what he says and does.

Accurate self-appraisal is a process of discovering one's potentialities—recognizing one's strengths so as to build on them, and accepting one's limitations. Bernard Shaw said that his happiness began when he focused his attention on the things he could do and ignored those in which he was likely to fail. It is important that a child gradually obtain a clear picture of the kind of person he can become. This ideal but realistic concept becomes a guiding light to his path.

Memories of childhood are built into one's self-concept; they bridge the gap of intervening years. It is often true, as Dostoevski wrote, that

". . . there is nothing higher and stronger and more wholesome and good for life in the future than some good memory, especially a memory of childhood, of home. People talk to you a great deal about your education, but some good, sacred memory preserved from childhood, is perhaps the best education. If a man carries such memories with him into his life, he is safe to the end of his days, and if only one good memory remains in our hearts, even that may sometime be the means of saving us."[8]

If others recognize and accept the child's true ability, this helps the child to accept himself—his strengths and his limitations. Thus he develops his individuality. When a gifted person conforms to average standards there is a serious loss of human resources. Conforming for the sake of popularity with one's peers results in reduction to mediocrity.

OPPORTUNITIES TO DEVELOP AND USE ONE'S ABILITIES

Giftedness does not develop in a vacuum. The people in the child's environment must be interested in intellectual or other kinds of achievement. The child must have opportunity and encouragement, instruction and guidance, association with others of similar interests, and the stimulus of success.

It is not true that gifted children can always develop their potentialities despite unfavorable conditions. Some do; they make opportunities out of calamities. But on all sides we have evidence of underachievement among the gifted.

Kinds of Opportunities

Gifted children need opportunities to acquire knowledge; erroneous information can only lead to erroneous conclusions. They need encouragement to wonder, to question, to be self-reliant, to get satisfaction from the exercise of their powers. They need materials and equipment for developing special talent in science, mathematics, music, art, and mechanical work. For social development they need opportunities to play various roles in group situations.

Challenging Opportunities

The words "stimulating" and "challenging" are often used in connection with the education of the gifted. What do they mean? Adequate stimulation would imply tasks in which the child is interested, which he can handle without frustration, and which give him knowledge or skill that can be applied to increasingly complex problems. The focus is on the growth process.

All learning cannot be fun. Some tasks must be challenging, or the child will not have a chance to try his powers, to discover his potential ability, and to exercise his resourcefulness.

Fortunately the gifted child naturally enjoys being active. He likes to use his mind, as well as his body. He has an inner urge toward self-realization. He is a self-starter. This self-motivation ensures the degree of mild tension that is essential to learning.

But what about the many children and young people we see today who have such inertia, such indifference, that their only desire is to do the entertaining or pleasant things—to take the path of least resistance? To counteract these tendencies, do we not have to exert some pressure on the child? Do we not need more emphasis on objective standards of achievement, on goals to be attained, and on measured progress toward them? Should not the mother's role of unconditional love in infancy be supplemented by the father's role of discipline in the sense of helping the preadolescent and the adolescent to measure up to certain standards?

There is at present a tendency to interpret "challenging" as "getting tough with the kids"—holding them up to the most rigorous academic standards. When these are, for any reason, beyond the child's capacity to attain, he fails. Discouragement blocks progress. Failure raises doubts as to his intellectual ability, and may create undue anxiety. Heightened anxiety may interfere with learning. As a result the child conceives of himself as intellectually incompetent, and this self-concept tends further to restrict the use of his ability. Thus an unfavorable mind-set for learning is created. External pressure is not the answer to this kind of problem.

A goal is more effective than a goad. Adults should give this child positive encouragement in his intellectual interests, and provide him with opportunities to enjoy the excitement of ideas; these measures are more likely to prove genuinely challenging to him. To encourage more efficient learning we must provide conditions that reduce excessive anxiety, build on initial successes, and help the child to learn new and increasingly difficult skills.

A blend of permissiveness and control seems best. This encourages a child's intellectual curiosity, achievement, social development, and creativity, and tends to decrease quarrelsomeness, disobedience, and other negative behavior.

According to Dale Harris,[9] parents who maintain firm standards and values are more likely than other parents to help their children recognize the importance of education and honest work and the worth of achievement. When these children become adults, they are more likely than others to find satisfaction in their jobs and to be concerned for the welfare of others. They tend to be somewhat dissatisfied with themselves, but this is part of having high standards.

When a genuinely gifted child is not fulfilling his potential, the loving parent may be tempted to allow him to take the low road of easy success and carefree happiness. He may want to shield the child from pain, failure, and discouragement. He may modify rules that the child finds difficult to follow. In the child's infancy, of course, the good parent made many adjustments to the child's needs. During the preschool years he very gradually introduced the child to the world of obligation. Now, sooner or later, as Jacques Barzun advised, the child must be brought to face the reality that he has not worked up to his capacity, that he has not taken advantage of his opportunities, and that he is therefore not deserving of praise or reward. It is difficult for a parent to be sufficiently blunt and forthright in such a matter. It even seems a cruel thing to do. But it is still worse to see a gifted child falling far short of his potential ability, and to know that he will realize later what he might have become if he had been required to face the discrepancy between his capacity and his performance.[10]

How much pressure should we apply? This is an individual matter. Some children need a very firm hand. Until they have acquired more inner controls they need to be made to do what they ought to do. Others become discouraged and unable to put forth any effort when they are under heavy pressure to achieve. They sometimes find devious ways of withdrawing from the situation entirely.

The only way you can discover the right amount of pressure to evoke a child's best efforts is to observe his response to your attempts to stimulate him to higher achievement. You have to feel your way in dealing with children. A child will respond quite differently to a task that he has undertaken voluntarily than to a task that is superimposed upon him; a voluntary undertaking has the quality of play rather than work, as it is generally conceived. It is also important to remember that children need to be free from responsibility at times.

The child who has tried his best but is unable to reach an overambitious goal that he has set must be helped to face the fact that he must lower his level of aspiration.[10] Such goals are often of parental origin, so subtly superimposed on the child that he believes they are his own. It is as cruel to subject a child to continual frustration, failure, and the tension that results from parental disappointment as it is to neglect his untapped endowments.

Basic Experiences

We may expect optimum development to occur when a child is genuinely loved, when he is given experiences appropriate to his age and ability, when he finds satisfaction in using his mind and his body, and when he meets with enough success to enable him to think of himself as a competent person growing toward maturity.

Variations in Patterns of Influence

Gifted children are found in many kinds of families. Walter Barbe described a family that does not correspond to our usual ideas about the origin of a gifted child:

The parents met in high school and were married before they graduated. The father finished high school and took several evening courses, but the mother, a superior student, withdrew before graduating.

Psychological tests placed both parents in the upper 1 per cent or very superior range of intelligence. The father's father was a barber and the mother's father was a teacher with a minimum of college education. The father, though an excellent tile-setter, was intermittently unemployed. The mother was a housewife who devoted herself to constant supervision of the children. Although their income was very small, they would not accept charity.

There were eight children; the two oldest boys had superior intelligence; the second was the brightest of all the children, although the youngest, at two years of age, also gave promise of being very bright. The third and fourth children, also boys, were having difficulty in school; the fifth one, who had a hearing loss, was an underachiever; one of the two girls, at one time diagnosed as severely mentally retarded, was doing average work. Thus five of the eight children were very superior in intelligence, and the other three seemed to be at least average.

The children did not do well in school. All of them remembered the first grade as an unpleasant experience; they found it difficult to break away from the family and to conform to the demands of the classroom. It was not until the fourth grade that they began to achieve in accordance with their ability. None of them wanted to be teachers, largely because of their dislike of teachers.

An unusual amount of learning took place as a result of their home activities. Each morning there was reading and discussion of a section of the Bible, after which each member of the family talked for a few minutes on anything he chose. They also went over together all the questions in the booklet "10,000 Questions and Answers of the World Book Encyclopedia." The extent of the children's knowledge was amazing. The father and the two oldest boys played chess. When satellites were first being launched, the family constructed a telescope.

One of the brightest boys attributed his special interest in history to a fifth-grade teacher who made him the class historian; his job was to look up everything the class wanted to know in this area. The eleven-year-old child had purchased an old French-English dictionary and was learning French words.

The children were socially sensitive, tactful, and adjusted exceptionally well in social situations. Many children visited their home, including one who had no mother. The oldest boy had a clear idea of his abilities. The second oldest, and the brightest, was careful not to make the other children feel inferior to him. The mother took pride in her children's intellectual achievement and "knew where they were at all times." The parents had practically no social life outside the home except in some church activities.

In the junior high school they were getting A's and B's, though they were obviously not being challenged to do their best. They would not be able to obtain a college education without financial assistance.[11]

This exceptional family demonstrates how much intellectual stimulation and social education may take place in a home of low socioeconomic status; there was more challenge in the home than in the schools which these children attended. Despite their very small income, these parents provided an excellent environment for gifted children. They respected each child whether he was bright or average; they enjoyed intellectual activities together; they helped the friendless; they maintained a close family solidarity. The mother might have facilitated the children's transition from home to first grade by visiting the school before a child entered, and preparing him for some of the adjustments he would have to make.

REINFORCEMENT OF POSITIVE GROWTH

There is, as the poet Housman said, "much of good and much of ill" in every individual. Our task is largely to help children reinforce their good tendencies and, if possible, help them to modify their bad ones.

Nature of Learning

Children tend to keep on doing whatever brings them satisfaction. If the situation arouses fear or anxiety or is otherwise unpleasant or painful, they try to modify it. Thus they learn. Of course, learning is not so simple as this statement implies. There is, for example, an infinite variety of rewards. Even pain is sometimes rewarding. What is a reward for one child may be punishment for another. A private smile of appreciation may be highly rewarding to a child, whereas outspoken praise before a group may discourage him from further efforts along that line.

It is wise for the parent to reward the desired response immediately; otherwise the child may associate the reward with some subsequent action. It is also better to reward progress in the right direction than to wait for the finished product. Conditions conducive to learning were briefly summarized in *An Introduction to Child Study* as follows:

"Children learn best when they are mature enough and ready to learn; when they feel confident that they can learn; when what they are learning is meaningful to them, i.e., has functional significance to them. Also essential to learning are suitable equipment, materials, and companions, freedom to select and use them, and skillful guidance in learning."[12]

Goals of Learning

What we reinforce is exceedingly important. We should guard against encouraging intellectually gifted children to use their special ability as a means of dominating adults or other children. Teachers and parents too often encourage gifted children to be intellectually overaggressive—always wanting to answer the teacher's questions, dominating discussions, calling attention to another person's errors in order to put him in his place. Adult approval, admiration, or even acceptance of such behavior unduly encourages it. It requires considerable restraint on the part of the gifted child not to criticize others and not to deny other pupils the chance to participate.

Gifted children, like other individuals, need approval, but we must be careful what we approve. We must not encourage superficial glibness and mere speed of response. We must reserve our appreciation and genuine praise for evidences of originality, imagination, and creativity, of honesty, courage, and patience, and of social responsibility. Dr. Albert Schweitzer expressed the obligations of giftedness in this way:

"Whatever you have received more than others in health, in talents, in ability, in success, in a pleasant childhood, in harmonious conditions of home life, all this you must not take to yourself as a matter of course. You must pay a price for it. You must render in return an unusually great sacrifice of your life for other life."[13]

For the sake of society as well as for their personal happiness, it is necessary for gifted children and youth to use their special abilities in the service of others.

Reinforcement of Sound Values

The development and reinforcement of values loom large in the education of a gifted child. One parents' group, quoted by Dorothy Barclay, listed the following comprehensive statement of values:

" 'As a family we will work to help every member develop: A security that comes from belief in himself; insight into his own strengths and weaknesses and those of others; ability to think straight and honestly; good health and interest in conserving it; intellectual curiosity, variety of interests, a striving to learn; goodness and respect for goodness—honesty, friendliness, moral courage, compassion; appreciation of beauty; acquisition of knowledge and skills for present and future use; self-reliance and the ability—and willingness—to take responsibility; ability to get along with, enjoy and help people of all ages, races, economic and educational levels.'

"Some family discussion, some quiet list-making, some review and evaluation of where family time and money go—and why—will help parents toward a clarification of values that can help to make big decisions easier. . . . ."[2]

Merely refraining from imposing our own values on the child does not make it certain that he will develop his own. Parents should clarify their own values. If they never express their convictions or take a firm stand on an issue, they actually make it difficult for the child to develop his own values. Children learn decision-making as much by observing the example of their parents in making wise decisions as by making decisions of their own and taking the consequences of their choices. Parents can also help by setting appropriate limits within which a child of a given age can make decisions. Too often children are expected to make decisions that demand more knowledge and capacity than they possess.

Growth of the Spirit

Children's spiritual experiences are personal and fleeting. They are difficult to reinforce. About all we can do is to accept and encourage them when they occur—the tenderness a child feels toward a wounded animal or a troubled playmate, or the indignation he feels when he sees injustice or cruelty. When he has a moment of wonder and an overwhelming sense of the beauty of the world or of a noble action, we can let him express it in his own way. A church school group who had an experience of awe and wonder expressed it in an original song. Each verse described the wonder they had felt in the stars, the sprouting seeds, the pattern of snowflakes. The refrain was, "We can but watch and wonder." The gifted child often feels intensely about his experiences. Our part is to respect and delight in his joy. As the child grows older, we can help him to acquire skill in writing, drawing, painting, rhythms, or other forms of self-expression.

QUESTIONS AND ANSWERS

1. *Is mental ability inherited?*

Mental ability is inherited to the extent that it depends on the structure and quality of the nervous system. It may be inherited in somewhat the same way that color of hair, stature, length of arm, shape of nose, and other physical characteristics are inherited. However, it is subject to change as the child interacts with the environment.

2. *What is the relative influence of heredity and environment?*

The relative influence of heredity and environment on a child's intelligence is still a controversial question. It cannot be answered in general. Undoubtedly the intellectual stimulus in the home and the educational opportunities in the school affect a child's performance on the ordinary type of intelligence test. Home and school background, and parental aims and aspirations, may also exert an influence on the child's interest in intellectual things. In a few cases, illness or malnutrition of the mother during the prenatal period or of the child in the early years may permanently impair the development of the nervous system. By the age when intelligence can be measured, it has come under the influences of the child's environment.

Specific abilities and disabilities—artistic, musical, numerical, and so on—seem to be inheritable. Certain temperamental qualities such as tendency toward general emotional stability or instability also seem to be inherited in some cases. However, these so easily come under the influence of early home conditions and relationships that no clear case for their biological inheritance can be made. As a child grows older his mental ability becomes more and more specialized.

If all infants were exposed from birth to favorable emotional, educational, and cultural conditions, there would be a larger percentage of gifted children in our population.

3. Is a child's position in the family related to giftedness?

The gifted child's position in the family—whether he is eldest, middle, youngest, or only child—may have a special influence that parents should recognize. Contrary to general opinion, the eldest child seems to have more difficulties in adjusting than the only child— at least a somewhat larger proportion of eldest children are referred to child guidance clinics. Some of these referrals no doubt indicate not so much maladjustment on the part of the child as exaggerated concern on the part of the inexperienced parent.

There are, however, certain advantages in being the first-born. He is usually most fondly welcomed by parents and relatives; in some cultures he is given special privileges. Nevertheless, he may be burdened with many responsibilities: he may have to help care for the younger children, he may be prematurely held up to adult standards, he may be subjected to pressure by his parents to perpetuate their name or fulfill their own unrealized ambitions. It is not easy for him to share his parents' affection with younger brothers and sisters after he has been the sole object of their concern.

If the eldest child must devote much of his time to taking care of younger children, he may not be able to pursue his own interests, make friends of his own age, or do the reading and study necessary to achieve up to his intellectual capacity.

The other extreme is no more desirable: overindulgence of the eldest gifted child would tend to make the other children resentful toward him, and to give him an undue sense of superiority.

It seems that the larger proportion of gifted children are first-born or only children. This tendency is apparently to be attributed more to the parents' socioeconomic status and their high ambitions for their first-born, than to the possible biological advantage of childbearing at an earlier age. However, the child's position in the family—whether first-born, middle, or youngest—is not nearly so important a factor as complex interrelations among the members of the family.

4. *As a parent, what can I offer in the home so that the child does not become dull mentally?*

Although neither the best home nor the best education will make a child gifted if he has an inferior quality of mind in the first place, superior home and school opportunities will help the child to develop whatever ability he possesses. In a good home there are affectionate relationships and lively conversation among all the members of the family. There is plenty to do and see; there are responsibilities appropriate to the ability of each individual. The child is offered opportunities to develop special talents and explore the environment with as much freedom as is commensurate with his sense of responsibility. The key word here is "offered"; the child should not be artificially stimulated or forced into activities beyond his normal range. Professor Terman's study reported that 70 per cent of the parents said they "had allowed the child to go at his own pace."

5. *If a mother cannot stay away from her job indefinitely, when does her child need her most?*

Although the little baby cannot show his need for mothering, this need is in fact very great during the first year. It is difficult indeed to find a mother substitute—someone who will give the baby as much warmth and devotion as his own mother. The first year is of first importance because it is during this time that the baby is building basic attitudes toward life—attitudes of trust and self-confidence, or distrust and self-doubt.

6. *What kind of families have gifted children who get along well at home, at school, and with themselves?*

All kinds of families—rich and poor, professional and unskilled workers, college graduates and those who have not completed their high-school education—have gifted children who are making good progress at home and at school. But these families seem to have certain things in common: *All* their children are loved, wanted, and appreciated; trusted, respected, and accepted as persons. The parents are proud of their children and treat children's problems as part of the process of growing up. The parents get along well together. Children and parents read, play games, entertain friends, sing or play musical instruments, and take trips together.

7. How soon should a parent begin to teach a gifted child?

The time to teach a child is whenever he needs help. The activity itself is important, but the child also needs to get a sense of achievement, of mastery. He will not get this sense of accomplishment if he merely plays aimlessly, without the knowledge or the tools necessary to do the job well. When a child never puts forth real effort in work and play during the early years, and when he does only what he wants to do, he is not likely to develop his potential ability. Work habits developed with satisfaction during preschool years help to prevent underachievement later.

THREE

The Gifted Preschool Child

"I AM sure," said one mother, "that my five-year-old is a gifted child, and I want to do what is best for her. I do not want to push her ahead nor do I want to do anything to hinder her development."

Another mother wrote: "My little son is four and a half and is the joy of my life. He is quick and bright mentally and beautifully co-ordinated physically. While, of course, I don't want to *push* him, I certainly want to help develop his potential."

These quotations express the desire of many parents to help their children develop in the best way; to help them maintain their own momentum of growth.

"AS THE TWIG IS BENT . . ."

In a very real sense these early years, so important in and for themselves, also forecast the future: "The child is father of the man." "Well begun is half done"—some would say, much more than "half done."

Of pervasive importance are the emotional experiences of infancy. Many predispositions acquired during the early years persist and tend to determine for some time the way in which the child perceives new situations. Once the individual has established certain ways of feeling and acting, he tends to resist change. This is a kind of psychological predestination. A child who is born bright may become slow and unresponsive if the conditions of his infancy fail to foster self-confidence, discourage normal independence, or cause inner conflict.

However, we should not take a fatalistic attitude toward the effects of early experiences. They are not absolutely irreversible or irrevocable. The favorite influence of teachers, chums, and other persons in the child's later environment may partly counteract unfavorable parental attitudes and correct personality fault lines. For example, a child may outgrow an immaturity that stemmed from early overprotection or domination, if his later environment rewards his efforts to be independent and to take initiative. On the other hand, the most favorable early environment is not proof against the effects of subsequent adverse conditions.

At any age or stage, however, we must remember that personality reorganization is limited by the child's previous developmental history. Personality modification depends on the child's natural or acquired resiliency or plasticity in the face of new environmental influences.

TWO DEVELOPMENTAL TASKS: TRUST AND INDEPENDENCE

The first year has much to do with a child's outlook on life. If he is fed when hungry, comforted when lonely, relieved when in pain, he builds a basic sense of trust. This is his first developmental task.

During the second year the child becomes more independent. He takes advantage of more and more opportunities to learn from his environment. His intellectual capacities develop through looking, talking, listening, and handling different kinds of things. The child who is too docile and dependent does not reach out to things and people, or profit by these new experiences.

To gain a reasonable amount of independence is the child's second developmental task. Although from infancy on, he naturally shows a gradual growth in independence, he needs, at every stage of his development, to achieve a balance between independence and dependence. To be willing to ask for help and accept help as needed, Margaret Fletcher wrote, is a sign of maturity.[1]

Extreme independence may take the form of aggressiveness; sometimes the child shows this at home, sometimes in permissive play, sometimes in both situations. Independence has different meanings for different children. Some children may feel guilty about it; others find satisfaction in aggressive behavior; still others appear to conform, but harbor a strong desire to destroy property or to injure people.

Real independence is different from isolation. Ideally a child accepts a dependent relation with those whose help he needs. But he is also beginning to take responsibility for what he says and does and is. He is growing toward self-responsibility. This is a very important achievement for the child.

Occasionally a mother resents having her child move away from dependence on her to enjoyment of new friends and new experiences. This attitude is bewildering and confusing to the child.

THE PROCESS OF "BECOMING"

Children's attitudes toward achievement begin to form also from their earliest years. "Becoming" is an active process. Being born is not easy. Taking the first breath is an achievement. Probably at no time in life does the individual achieve as much as he does in the first two years. He learns to walk, to talk, to cope with his environment, including the people in it. His achievements give him great satisfaction.

Even though a child is precocious intellectually, he still faces many problems in the process of growing up. It is no easier for him to learn the ways of civilized life than it is for other children. Settling down to regular mealtimes, toilet training, motor co-ordination—none of these jobs can be hurried with any child, however advanced he may be in talking and reasoning. Competent handling of the normal difficulties of the first few years prepares him for the tasks of later life. It is impossible, and undesirable, to make all the hard places artificially smooth, and the rough places plain.

WORK AND PLAY

A gifted child wants to be physically and mentally active. In fact, physical and intellectual activities are interrelated. Children learn a great deal from play—activity carried out for its own sake. The earliest form of play is delight in the practice of newly acquired abilities, such as putting a peg in a hole or repeating a newly learned sound. The child's play is purposeful; it is the source of much of his learning during the preschool years. We should always try to preserve the play element in the work that we expect of children—the element, whatever it is, that causes children to put forth effort consistently and enthusiastically. One important aspect of play is that it is self-initiated: it is the child's idea; he wants to do it; he has in mind a definite goal.

We should avoid associating work with drabness or drudgery. At the same time we should help the child to realize, even in these early years, that any kind of achievement requires effort.

Like other children, the gifted child may be discouraged by the complex appearance that a task often presents at first view. It is wise to show him how to tackle it step by step, the easier parts first, so that he will be stimulated by success. Still, though he may begin on its simpler parts, the gifted child likes first to see the task as a whole. He likes to do difficult things that are within his capacity. He gets satisfaction from a task well done.

GETTING TO KNOW THEM

It is difficult to tell parents what to expect of gifted children at different ages. There are often marked differences, even with respect to interest, among children in the same family. Differences in temperament are still greater. Children in the same family, who are equally gifted, show different emotional traits, despite the apparent uniformity of their environments.

There is therefore no substitute for observing the individual child. We learn by watching. Before a baby begins to talk, we can only infer how he feels. Observation of the baby's behavior and the situation in which it occurs suggest that he is experiencing certain feelings such as we ourselves may have experienced under somewhat similar conditions. But we can never be sure whether we have made the correct inference about another person's thought or feeling.

With older preschool children, dated verbal snapshots and candid photographs are useful in deepening our understanding. They record the language of behavior. A young child expresses himself spontaneously in action more than in words. The way he walks, the way he talks, the expression about his mouth, his anxious or laughing eyes, the tone of his voice—all are clues to his thoughts and feelings.

Occasionally it is wise to make notes of these observations. Arranged in chronological order, they may show trends in the child's physical, intellectual, social, and emotional development. They may suggest desirable qualities that need to be reinforced, or fault lines that need to be corrected before they eventuate in an eruption. When a problem arises, these recorded observations may give perspective on its origin and nature. Such a record may also show that temper tantrums, fights with other children, or refusals to co-operate may not actually occur as often as the worried parent thinks they do.

When a new and strange type of behavior occurs, observation may help a parent to answer the question, "Why?" For example, fear of the dark may occur only under certain conditions; or it may prove to be decreasing in intensity as the child's competence increases. Getting a clear picture of a difficulty is the first step toward correcting it.

With reference to any aspect of the child's development, a parent may observe what the child does, how he does it, the conditions under which the behavior occurs, and the way in which the child handles the situation. From the actual observation of the behavior the parent may infer what satisfaction or dissatisfaction the child is getting from the experience.

There is a common tendency to focus attention on troublesome behavior. However, it is also wise to record observations of the child's spontaneous expressions of interest, enthusiasm, eagerness to find out, co-operation, friendliness, and wonder. These observations give parents an understanding of the child's potentialities for growth along positive lines.

To record observations, have a small pad and pencil handy with which to jot down what you see and hear. Dorothy Cohen and Virginia Stern note that colorful words help to make the child come alive as one later reads the notes. To say a child "whirled into a group of playmates" or "bolted out of the room" is more vivid than merely to say that he "ran." Similarly, the tone of voice may be described precisely as "subdued," "high-pitched," "shrill," "lilting," or "raucous." As older children say when they are asked to keep diary records of their daily activities, it is a "nuisance" to make written records; however, notes of this kind give you an excellent opportunity to view a child's behavior objectively and steadily.[2]

GLIMPSES OF GIFTED CHILDREN

You cannot expect your child to be just like a generalized picture of "the gifted child." He may not walk early or talk fluently or learn to read before he goes to school, or be physically and socially superior to other children of his age. Every child is unique. The following glimpses of gifted children highlight their individuality:

Bright Babies

One father was worried because his baby looked so intently at each new object. He was taking it all in. This child, who at six scored very high on an intelligence test, later showed a similar concentration in his work and play.

When Anne was only six weeks old she followed with her eyes a fly that was buzzing around, and tried to catch him when he flew within reach. This showed an unusual eye-hand co-ordination for her age.

Two- and Three-Year-Olds

John is now two years old. From birth he has been strong willed, cheery, open, smiling, and happy. He has yet to act shy when meeting a new person. He has always been highly energetic. His physical development has been normal—first teeth at nine months, creeping by ten months, walking by thirteen months in spite of a physical defect in one foot and ankle. He goes "all out" in everything he does: when he first got to his knees to crawl, he crawled the whole length of the room; when he learned to climb the steps on hands and knees, he climbed the whole flight at once; when he pounded the pegboard, he pounded in all the pegs, and then turned over the board and pounded them all back; when he takes apart the "take-apart" toys, he takes them apart completely, and when he puts them together, he puts back all the pieces.

His vocabulary development has been fantastic. At seven months he started with the word "Daddy," pointing to his father. By one year of age he used twenty to thirty words which he comprehended. At eighteen months, he began to use three- and four-word sentences, and counted the steps to twenty. At twenty-two months he knew all of the verses in his Mother Goose book and repeated them as he turned the pages. He knows all the words to the songs his parents sing for him, and those they have made up for him. He knows the alphabet from beginning to end without mistake.

John is now passing through the "what's that?" stage with every new object he sees. He loves to be given directions and will carry them out to the letter, for example, "Take Daddy's shoes to the closet, please."

This child certainly seems to be precocious; he is highly active, if not overactive. His accomplishments are far in advance of his age. The question is: How were they acquired—in response to a natural curiosity and mental alertness, or as a result of constant parental stimulation and instruction?

Three-year-old Claire, according to her mother:

"has a remarkable memory which was noticeable at a very early date. She reads, prints quite well, spells, can do simple arithmetic. She has an extremely inquisitive mind. Her favorite pastimes are reading and listening to her extensive record collection. I know this is not the average behavior for a three-year-old.

"Her physical development has also been advanced. At the age of two she was swimming across a public pool and jumping from a diving board. She started dancing lessons and seemed to do as well as most of the older students, and to remember better. I am trying to give a rounded picture of the child—an almost impossible thing to do unless you meet and speak to her."

One wonders how spontaneous and free from anxiety this little girl is. It is important to know how the child "got that way." Was she free to explore her environment; was she given help in order to do better the things she wanted to do; or was a rather rigid training program imposed upon her?

Fours and Fives

A father who is obviously well read in psychology described his four-year-old daughter as follows:

"Jill is an exceptionally brilliant child. When she was less than one year old we discovered one day that she knew all the letters of the alphabet at sight. Then with amazing rapidity, she taught herself to read. (Oh, we certainly encouraged her, but we actually had little to do with her learning.) First it was a word at a time, then a sentence, and finally paragraphs and pages. Besides this she absorbed knowledge like a blotter. Tell her something or explain something once or perhaps twice, and she never forgets it. Right now she is learning how to write, that is, print, for she does not have enough motor control to write in script.

"Emotionally she fluctuates between behavior characteristic of her chronological age and that more indicative of an eight-year-old than a four-year-old. Our greatest satisfaction is derived from the fact that, despite the unavoidable fuss made over her, she remains sweet, uninhibited, and completely natural. Although she is aware that she has unusual talents, she accepts this very matter-of-factly.

"We recently had her tested by a psychologist who reported that her over-all intelligence score was in the upper 1 per cent of children of her age. A reading test placed her among ten-year-olds in reading ability."

This description might have been taken directly out of a book on the psychology of gifted children! But again we need to know more about how the child acquired these achievements so far in advance of her chronological age. Undoubtedly the obvious delight of her parents and their friends at each evidence of progress spurred her on to greater achievement.

Dorothy will soon be five. She is large and husky for her age and has the mind, ability, and comprehension of an adult in many ways. She won't play with children of her own age—says they are babies. In Sunday school the teachers have put her in a class of second-graders because they say she belongs there—is too advanced for her age group.

This brief description suggests the difficulty that highly gifted children have in making social adjustments, and in adjusting themselves to a school where individual needs are not recognized and provided for. Such a child should have special help in learning to get along with other children. She would "catch on" quickly to the idea of looking below surface behavior both in herself and in others.

The Case of Kim

The following is the story of how a gifted child grew during the preschool years under conditions that would generally be considered unfavorable. How do you account for her apparently good development? What were the favorable elements in this case? The information here presented was obtained from the following sources: interview with the mother, interview with the nursery school teacher, interview with other nursery school workers, association with the child, and observation of the child. At the time this record was made, six-year-old Kim scored, on the Stanford-Binet Intelligence Test, around 130 IQ.

Family background — Kim is a "middle child," with two sisters aged ten and three. Her father has a responsible supervisory position. Her mother, an outgoing, friendly person who obviously enjoys her children, works for a printing company and has her children with her only on weekends.

The father and mother have been separated for two years, and the children have had no contact with the father during this period. The mother says that the children never had a close relationship with their father (he looked on them as a responsibility only) and rarely mention him. Until the separation, the home life was beset with many difficulties, including financial troubles. The mother worked most of the time, leaving the children with their maternal grandmother.

At present, Kim and her younger sister live in a nursery, while the older sister is in an orphanage.

Appearance — Kim is a nicely proportioned child, measuring 46½ inches in height and weighing 48 pounds. She has blue eyes, a perky nose, and blond hair which frames a finely featured, alert face. Her delicate lips part easily into a winning smile. She is physically well co-ordinated; moves with grace, assurance, and purpose; does not tire easily; and participates enthusiastically in active games, although by nature she is quiet.

General personality — Kim is friendly, generally quiet, thoughtful, and unassuming. She is described by her mother and the nursery school workers as lovable, contented, even-tempered, and possessing a good sense of humor. Nursery school workers find her very understanding and responsive to other children. She mothers the younger children, is always ready to assist them, seems to sense their feelings easily, and has gained recognition as a peace-restorer. She is quick to seek causes for upsets: "Why is Tommy crying?" "How did Susie get her feelings hurt?" Kim is the most mature child in the nursery, and sometimes becomes annoyed when younger or less perceptive children consistently interfere with her activities or invade her privacy. She is quite likely to comment, "You're spoiling it," or "Don't do that." Often when children are not carrying out in an acceptable manner a game or activity that she has set up, she tries to reorganize the activity or withdraws from it to play with her dolls or look at a book. She is a strong leader, but also a good follower.

Recently Kim was in the hospital with an infection. She adjusted to hospital routine exceptionally well, and became the darling of the nurses. Although she was confined to bed for quite a period, she never complained, and the hospital staff were astounded by her patience and cheerfulness. She is able to explain many of the activities carried on in the hospital. She told her mother that the doctor "used a drug called penicillin to cure the infection," and commented on how wonderful it is to have hospitals to help sick people.

Kim's mother said that Kim was never a feeding problem, slept well from a tiny baby, seldom cried, and always seemed able to amuse herself. "She was such a good baby that we didn't even know she was around most of the time." From the time she was small she seemed to want to do things for herself. She started feeding herself very young and tried to dress herself at a much earlier age than the other two children in the family. Kim was very easy to toilet-train, and was completely trained at about twenty months.

Kim is very persistent and persevering in the face of problems. She is self-reliant and does not seek help until she has tried several avenues herself with no success. She analyzes situations before making moves. Her mother reports that from two years up she enjoyed jigsaw puzzles. At first, she would remove the pieces systematically and place them in sequence on the floor. Then she would return them to the frame. Her mother would take the pieces out, mix them up, and then tell Kim to put them back. She would study the pieces before attempting to insert them, and rarely tried to put a piece in the wrong place. Nursery school teachers report that she does quite complicated puzzles with assurance and deftness in a short period of time.

Kim is sensitive to the demands of situations, and does not like to be told what to do. She automatically proceeds with cleaning up, taking her bath, and other appropriate activities. Being told seems to take some of the pleasure out of doing the thing. However, she does accept criticism and does not hold a grudge. When she is angry she never says, "I don't like you"; but she will say, "I hate the whole world now," or "I don't like the nursery any more."

Speech — Kim began talking at about ten months. She started putting words together prior to her twelfth month, and was using simple sentences at a little over a year. She picked up new words readily, using them accurately and without hesitation. At two and three she used words like "dictionary" and "encyclopedia," and at four could spell "encyclopedia." She learned to spell "encyclopedia" from a television program. At four she liked to help her older sister with her homework.

At six years of age Kim has an extensive vocabulary, is using lengthy sentences and complex constructions, and seems to express the essence of a situation with a few words. Her talk is purposeful and expressive, not rambling and desultory. She carries on a sustained conversation easily. She can explain games, situations, or activities in a concrete way. She listens attentively, does not need even long or quite complicated directions repeated. Nursery workers report that she readily understands verbal instructions and rarely has to be shown how to do anything.

Interests and activities—Kim loves literature and has shown a keen interest in books since she was a year old. Her mother reports she would look at books contentedly for hours. Nursery school teachers indicate that she recognizes some words as stories are being read, reads signs, reads and writes her name, and interprets pictures in books adeptly. She is very observant, seeing even the most insignificant parts of a picture and relating them to the whole.

Kim enjoys telling stories; after once hearing a poem, story, or song, she can very often repeat it meaningfully. She leads the other children in singing or reciting poems.

No one has made an attempt to teach her to read, although the teacher in the nursery school has shown her the letters in the alphabet. She will say "A is for apple," and so forth. (The four- and five-year-olds have two hours of school five days a week at the nursery.)

The teacher reports Kim is the best pupil, the quickest to catch on, asks the most penetrating questions, is the most neat and orderly. She is good at creative art, and often draws pictures of people. Sometimes she omits a vital part of the person, such as a hand or foot. She frequently tells a story about her picture.

The teacher feels Kim is definitely ready to read; she displays a keen interest in books, recognizes some words, follows story sequence well, notices likenesses and differences in words.

Kim associates details or episodes from stories with daily living experiences. On a trip to the zoo, the children were told to look carefully along the road for a castle that they would pass. Kim said, "There is a castle in the story of Sleeping Beauty." Upon seeing the castle she said, "If it were bigger and had more towers it could be the castle of Sleeping

Beauty." On the same trip, a sign reading "New Zoo" was being sought. Kim inquired, "How would it look? How do you spell zoo?" After hearing the spelling of zoo she said, "I can find the sign now." She did.

Kim enjoys the sound of words and will say over and over certain words that give her pleasure. One of the words she particularly enjoys is "Cadillac."

Kim's mother has a typewriter which Kim loves to use. She types her name, copies words from books, or types single letters.

A year ago, some of the children from the nursery were used as models in a fashion show. Kim relives this experience by organizing fashion shows periodically in the nursery. She shows the little models how to walk, pose, execute turns and bows. She can take a shawl, hat, or some other article from the dress-up box, and use it in many different ways. Sometimes her creations reflect the latest styles.

Nursery school workers report Kim has a good conception of time. She distinguishes morning from afternoon, today from yesterday, and seems to sense the time for routines. Often she asks, "What time is it?" She comments, "It's time for Wunda Wunda." Her mother reports that at three years old Kim would say it was time for a certain television show, and would seldom be more than fifteen minutes from the correct time. In the nursery she frequently stares at the clock, but there is no evidence of her being able actually to tell time.

She knows that Saturdays and Sundays are weekend days. She remembers she is to go to the beach in July and says, "But that is not until the summertime." Nursery school workers have commented on her excellent memory.

For over a year Kim has been talking about being a ballet dancer. She loves to make up little dances and has good rhythm. In snapshots, she poses often in the stance of a ballerina.

Kim enjoys dolls. She reads and sings to them, and frequently plays with them.

Behavior problems—Kim has an occasional tantrum. The nursery workers think these tantrums are justified in many instances. She does not go into a tantrum unless provoked by someone or something over a sustained period. During a tantrum she hits or kicks furniture, never people. She gets over them quickly.

Encouragement: experiences provided—The mother says she hasn't given Kim any special attention or experiences. She was always too busy working, and actually has not had much time to spend with her children.

Too, the mother has had many problems to face. She did buy books for the children, allow them to watch certain television shows (which the mother reports have always been especially interesting and meaningful to Kim), bought puzzles for them, and occasionally took them to visit relatives.

At four years of age Kim traveled with her mother and two sisters half-way across the continent by bus. The mother reported Kim was always observing things on this trip and asking about them. "She seemed to see more than her older sister." She also talks about things that happened on the trip and amazes the mother with the details she remembers.

Kim has probably had richer experiences and more adult attention since she arrived at the nursery. She is included in frequent trips to various places—the beach, fire station, planetarium, amusement parks, near-by cities, zoo, and so forth, as part of the nursery school program. In the nursery school there is a wealth of materials, such as puzzles, clay, books, blocks, art supplies. The children are encouraged in their creative efforts, invited to ask questions, helped to think for themselves and be independent. The nursery school teacher specifically relates past experiences to new ones, and encourages the children to use their past experiences in various kinds of situations.

The head of the nursery is a dynamic person, interested in diverse things, and has a wonderful personal relationship with each child. She is anxious for the children to have many kinds of experiences and encourages frequent trips. She encourages the adults in the situation to listen attentively to children, to fondle them, and show love for them in many ways.

We do not, of course, know all the subtle influences that affected this child's development during her preschool years. However, of those we do know, two stand out: a continuing affectionate relationship with the mother; and the perceptive efforts of the nursery school workers and teachers, which apparently reinforced the child's positive behavior, both intellectual and social. There is also mention of a wealth of educational materials, trips and excursions, and companionship with both children and adults.

WHAT MAY BE EXPECTED OF GIFTED PRESCHOOL CHILDREN

It will be noticed that gifted children in the above accounts are frequently described as having certain characteristics. Achievement looms large; a good memory is recognized; reasoning ability is mentioned less often; favorable attitudes toward oneself and others, originality, and creativity are seldom named.

Specific Achievements

Prominent among the achievements mentioned for gifted preschool children are specific learnings—the language arts, rudimentary arithmetic, and factual information. With skillful teaching, these learnings could be acquired by not-so-gifted children. Therefore, in judging whether a child is really gifted, it would be necessary to know *how* he learned to talk, or read, or count. It makes a big difference whether he did what came naturally to him or whether he was trained; whether he took the initiative or whether it was his parents' idea. Any measure of child development becomes inaccurate if the child receives special practice and instruction on the test items.

Quite often a parent does not realize how much teaching he really does. A conversation between a mother and a teacher illustrates this difficulty of accurate reporting:

Teacher: You say Charles has been reading phonetically since he was four and one half—how did he learn the sounds?

Mother: He'd ask us how a letter sounded and we'd tell him.

Teacher: He knew the letters of the alphabet?

Mother: Oh my, yes—I guess he knew them since he was a year and a half.

Teacher: How did that happen? Did you teach him?

Mother: No, he just picked it up.

Teacher: But he must have seen them some place—can you think of any way? What toys or—

Mother: Well, I guess the first ones were on his blocks. You know some sides have letters and some sides have pictures. We used to show him how to spell his name—and how to spell "cat" and "cow" and things like that. We never used "moo moo" for cow the way some people do with babies. We just tried to talk sense right from the start.

Gifted children tend to be somewhat more precocious in talking than in walking and the other motor accomplishments of this early age.

A bright five-and-one-half-year-old boy could count up to one hundred by three's and seemed to understand something about fractions. When he was told that there are four quarters in a dollar, he said, "Then if you have six quarters, do you have a dollar and a half?"

This same boy also drew a diagram of a rocket and constructed it according to his specifications, criticizing his errors as he went along and continuing to work on it over several days until it was completed. In explaining his diagram he said, "There's a small pipe going down to the floor, and there's another pipe going out the back. When you light it, that makes the rocket go—zoom!"

Special Talents

Children may evince an early interest and ability in the arts by making early efforts to draw and paint, showing skill in drawing pictures of animals and people, or appreciating color and design in their own and in other people's drawings and paintings. They may be unusually interested in pictures and picture books or in museums and exhibitions, and may show originality in finger-painting, clay modeling, or other arts.

Children make rhythmic responses to music as early as two years. The child with a gift for dancing and appreciation of rhythm may show this interest in his response to recordings. He may invent rhythms of his own and learn rhythmic skills rapidly. Similarly, a child may indicate musical talent by his early enjoyment of rhythm, melody, or singing, or by developing skill on a musical instrument.

No one characteristic or group of characteristics, however, distinguishes the child who is highly creative in any of these artistic fields from children who are average or below average in creative ability.

Verbal Ability

At an early age gifted children usually delight in repeating familiar sounds and trying out new sounds and words. They begin to use words earlier than the average. At any given stage of development they will surpass the average child in use of complex sentences, accuracy of diction, and expression of relationships.

Girls usually begin to talk earlier than boys, and achieve a greater fluency, although there does not seem to be much difference in the general intelligence of girls and boys during the preschool years.

The size of children's vocabularies at various ages is significant. Children understand words before they are able to pronounce them. One investigation reported that the number of words understood by two-year-olds of average ability was 272; at three years, the number was more than three times as large; at four years, it had almost doubled again; and at five, it was over two thousand words. The corresponding numbers for gifted children of the same ages would generally be still larger. The number of words actually spoken varies greatly with the individual child.

Children's precision in the use of language also varies greatly. A bright three-year-old spoke very clearly and precisely: "That is dangerous," she said to her little brother. A verbally mature child five years old objected to attending gym period with his class. He said, "Sometimes you let us choose. Can't I choose whether or not I want to go to gym?" The teacher said, "Not this time. Today we all go." Danny sighed philosophically. "Choices are luxuries, aren't they?" he said. This same child could talk fluently about motors and could construct an electric magnet.

There is a difference between real verbal superiority and a superficial kind of fluency. Some children use many words, but do not use them accurately. They chatter incessantly but do not say much. This kind of language facility is often mistaken for a sign of high intelligence; careful testing may prove otherwise.

In an atmosphere of trust and confidence little children, Hughes Mearns says,

". . . speak out of their hearts in their native language. [Their speech] has a rhythmic cadence, a sense for the right word, and an uncanny right placing of that right word for just the emphasis intended; and yet it rarely ever rhymes. To me, and to many others, this language is too worthy to be neglected; we feel that it should be encouraged, brought out, allowed to grow in strength, beauty, and power."[3]

Some mothers have recorded the casual language of their gifted children. For example, a mother took down the words of her five-year-old daughter, weary after a long day of play:

> "I'm tired:
> Tired as the lazy stones
> That are always sitting down;
> Most tired as the sky
> That stays up all night and day,
> Whether it's early with spider-vines
> Or late with frogs singing."[3]

General Mental Ability

More important than specific academic accomplishments are evidences of mental alertness, ability to see relations, exceptional memory, creativity, and delight in mental activity. Christine, a highly gifted child of two years and three months, showed many of these characteristics.

When shown pictures for small children, instead of simply naming objects in the pictures as average children of this age do, she showed an awareness of the feelings of the people portrayed; for example, "The little girl's crying" (rather than merely saying "girl").

When she was three and one-half her father was reading aloud an article he had written, which repeated the word "comprehension" several times. Christine sat on the couch listening. When he had finished reading he turned to the child, amused at her attentiveness, and said, "Well, how does it sound?" "Daddy," she replied quite seriously, "there's too much 'comprehension' in it."

At about the same age, Christine pointed out the window on Christmas Eve. The evening star was very bright in the sky. With a kind of joyful wonder she said, "Daddy, come see where the star lives."

At Christmas when Christine was three and one half, she recited from memory, of her own accord, all of the poem "The Night Before Christmas"; she had heard her parents read it several times, and had played a record of it by herself a number of times.

That same winter, Christine had a little white muff and wore it quite a bit, feeling very grown-up. One cold day a neighbor said, just making conversation, "Why aren't you wearing your muff today?" The child paused in her play for a second and held out her hands saying, "I've got my mittens on."

When Christine was just five, she was given a children's book that had directions for teachers printed on the jacket. Her father heard her reading, half aloud, to herself: "Do not make the child read before he is ready . . . , etc."

At five years two months, following a conversation about a muddy creek near their house, Christine said, "Daddy, I did a 'speriment, and now I know why the creek is muddy." "What was the experiment?" he asked. "I dug a little hole in the yard and the rain filled it up," she reported, "and I scraped some of the loose dirt off the sides of the hole into the water, and that water got muddy, too." "Good!" her father said. "And so?" "So," she said, "I think that's how creeks get muddy—from the banks."

Christine's parents provided the best possible conditions to nurture her high native intelligence. Four things they considered most important:

1. They demonstrated, by example, that they set a high value on the things they wanted her to learn: reading, an analytical approach, reasonableness, kindness.
2. They timed their responses to suit her needs. For example, if she asked a question about sex, they would answer it, but tell only a little more than she asked. They stopped when she showed boredom or lack of comprehension.
3. They stressed self-reliance; they allowed her to handle each situation and solve each problem that lay within her ability.
4. They used very little pressure on academic matters, but stood by to give help if needed, and to broaden her experience.

Curiosity

One of children's greatest assets is their curiosity—"an exploring drive," it has been called. It leads them to find out about all sorts of things. It is especially insatiable in gifted children when they are three and four, or even younger. They will ask questions about everything; each question is followed by a chain of related questions.

Among the subjects they ask about is sex. Naturally they are curious about where babies come from and why girls are different from boys. If their curiosity is treated in a casual way, it is satisfied without any accompanying feelings of guilt or shame. Conversation about sex organs can be conducted in the same tone as conversation about clothes or books. It is the exceptional preschool child who shows intense concern about these matters. Since they understand the explanations accurately, gifted children are likely to accept them in a matter-of-fact way.

Imagination

According to Terman's study, gifted children have more imaginary companions than do children in general. Although this tendency can lend itself to a certain amount of withdrawal from reality, and though it does appear in some maladjusted children, it may also indicate a healthy imagination that finds pleasure in indulging its creativity.

Children like to dramatize themselves. One very bright four-year-old came home from nursery school one day, playing the role of an adult. She talked to her mother like a visiting teacher, asking about her mother's problems and her children. Her mother went along with her in this make-believe, which continued until bedtime. Then came a perplexing predicament. The child had to make the choice between retiring like a grownup or going to bed like a child with the cuddly toy that had comforted her during many dark nights. Her mother noticed the child's distraught expression when, still play-acting with her, she said a formal "goodnight." A few minutes later, the child called downstairs: "Madam, there's the doorbell. Your little girl has come back." Thus she solved her dilemma.

It is incidents of this kind, far more than specific achievement in counting or reading, that indicate true giftedness. Reasoning, imagination, and creativity may all be noted by observant parents in the daily activities of gifted children.

Social Relations and Social Sensitivity

Gifted children should be helped to cultivate social sensitivity. Their capacity to sense the feelings of others—to laugh with them and to help them when they are in trouble—can be recognized early. Babies respond to laughter in the first few months. Some even stop crying when someone laughs with them. Responsive laughter paves the way for further good relations. Similarly, babies will often cry when they hear another child crying.

Older preschool children have various ways of showing sympathy with distress. Their sympathetic responses are especially aroused by the weakness or need of younger children. They often try to comfort or help a hurt or crying child.

One four-year-old gifted child, seeing her little brother crying, trotted off and came back with her own favorite toy that had comforted her: "Here, Johnnie, you take it."

Another child, only three and one-half years old, was told that some children had no shoes or stockings; realizing how cold they must be, he wanted to buy them shoes and stockings and other things.

Such generous impulses should be encouraged, and, when feasible, acted upon.

Some of the ways in which children express sympathy were described by Lois Barclay Murphy:

By defending the rights of a smaller child.
By spontaneously sharing materials or toys.
By trying to comfort another child with caresses of various kinds—patting, kissing, putting their arms around him.
By telling a child, "I like you."
By getting a toy to give to another child.
By reflecting the emotion of another child. [4]

Curiously enough, some children, especially those who are generally active and sociable, may show both sympathetic and aggressive behavior. But sympathetic responses are usually more frequent in preschool children than are unsympathetic ones. Sympathy for others may also exist along with a stoic endurance of one's own pain. Even when a child has quarreled with another child, and hurt him, he often feels guilty or sad about it. Of course, it is the quarrels that most often attract our attention. Adults should pay more attention to the child's expressions of sympathy and kindness.

Concern for another child is related to leadership. Children who are chosen by many are usually those who help others to succeed and be happy. In small groups of preschool children there are many opportunities to show sympathy and to take leadership responsibility. Given opportunity, natural leaders emerge.

A child's kindly feelings are reinforced by the approval of others, and by his own satisfaction in having been of help. Sometimes children have found that it pays to be helpful; sometimes they are merely following the suggestions of a loved person.

The gifted child who seems to be lacking in sympathetic response may be shy; or he may be afraid to approach a strange child who is in distress. His apparent coolness is not often due to lack of imagination as to how the other person is feeling. This quality of being able to sense and respond to the feelings of others is of great importance in many professions as well as in family life.

It is important that gifted children learn to love. This ability stems from the child's early relation to his mother. Even little children show tenderness toward babies and animals. Parents should play

with the child, in the same spirit in which the child plays; this tends
to increase the child's affection for his parents. During children's
third, fourth, fifth, and sixth years, according to C. W. Valentine,
"fathers become more instead of less popular with boys."[5] A heightened sense of companionship between the father and his maturing
son is one explanation for the father's increased affection for the boy.
Children are more often jealous of another child than of the father
or mother.

As Nelson Foote defines it, love is "that relationship between one
person and another which is most conducive to the optimal development of both." Many a child has had a profound influence on his
parents' personality and character development; the parent-child
relationship exerts a two-way influence.

Self-Assertiveness or Aggressive Behavior

When self-assertiveness makes its appearance, it should be recognized as a tendency to be directed in constructive ways, rather than
an undesirable trait to be suppressed. Around two or three years of
age, the child is very likely to show a drive or "mastery motive" to
do what he wants to do and do it without help This drive does not
usually show itself in hostility toward others; the competitive urge
has not yet begun. It is a desirable tendency to strive for the attain-
able and to be independent; it should be reinforced by approval so
long as what the child wants is good for him and others. It is strength-
ened by the satisfaction that comes from overcoming a difficulty, or
from making or doing something on one's own.

Rebellious self-assertiveness, especially its antiparental phase,
seems to reach a peak between the ages of two and four or five.
During these years, occasional outbursts of rebellion are normal, or
at least common, to all kinds and conditions of children.

Perhaps they are less frequent among gifted children, who may
suffer fewer frustrations than less able children. However, any child
who is sociable is likely to have some contacts that produce conflict.

Some children who were more aggressive than average during
their preschool years turned out to be more friendly than average,
according to a follow-up study made eight years later. A certain

amount of rebellious behavior during the middle preschool years would appear to be a good sign.

At the age of four or five, competition takes various forms. The child often says, "Watch me; see what I can do," or "I can do that, too," or "I can do that better than Billy," or "I did it better this time." Two of these comments, you will note, relate to competition with oneself—the kind of competition that the child should be encouraged to develop, beginning in these early years.

In judging the outcome of either aggressive or submissive behavior, we draw upon our social philosophy. The more aggressive children may be more successful in a competitive society. Yet those who are less "pushy" may also attain worthwhile ends. Better than either extreme is moderation—aggressive behavior tempered by social feelings. We may help the child to achieve this balance of impulses by avoiding extremes both of permissiveness and of restraint in our treatment of him.

Anxiety and Fears

The child may develop a deep, pervasive anxiety, according to Harry Stack Sullivan, even before he learns to talk. This arises from maternal behavior that is forbidding rather than accepting; that is tense rather than tender. Anxiety is second only to loneliness in being totally unwanted. In its milder form, it motivates learning: the child learns to do the things that reduce his anxiety and to avoid behavior that increases it.

Fears are less difficult to cope with. Gifted children may be expected to have fewer fears than the average insofar as they are more able to discern the causes of fear, and more resourceful about doing what is best in a fear-provoking situation. In some cases, curiosity or interest keeps the child from abandoning a frightening activity despite his fears.

Strange objects and persons, strange situations and noises evoke fear in the majority of children under four. It may be the strangeness of the sea that some children fear on their first visit. Fear of the dark is not common during the first year; it arises later from the images with which some children people the dark.

It is natural to be afraid of anything that may cause pain or injury.

Gifted children, with their keener insight into the consequences of certain conditions, may have more anticipatory fear than less sensitive children. Whether or not a child will fear a given situation depends on his understanding of it, his physical condition, his familiarity with this kind of situation, the degree of his security and trust in the persons whom he is with, and his ability to control the situation. "Fear is in our bones"; it serves as a natural alarm bell to warn us of danger.

Caution is to be encouraged, and fear should be decreased by knowledge. In her effort to protect her child a mother may induce fears; the child catches her anxiety.

Personality Development

Regardless of changes in the child's behavior patterns as he grows older, a certain core of personality persists. The individuality begins to form very early. The behavior patterns of about 18 per cent of more than one hundred children who were studied over a period of twelve years showed a consistent direction of development. These "pervasive, persisting qualities of personality" come about largely through personal relationships—through the social interaction of the child with his parents, and later with his friends in school and with church experiences.

CONDITIONS CONDUCIVE TO THE CHILD'S DEVELOPMENT

The concern of most parents centers on providing a stimulating or challenging environment for their gifted child. This concern is well expressed by one mother whose child, barely three years old, "takes thirty books to bed with him." She goes on to say:

"We try to give him the materials he needs and likes: maps, globes, crayons, records, clay, blocks, tinker toys, letter and number puzzles, map puzzles, and of course stuffed animal toys, too. Outside equipment includes a play yard with swings, slide, pond, and seesaw. He seems happy with all this, but bored at times. It is hard keeping up with him, that is, trying to keep him stimulated."

One wonders whether this three-year-old, surfeited with so many stimuli, may not be confused rather than "bored." Generally, you need not worry about "challenging" the preschool child. He is inner-motivated. Let his curiosity be your guide.

The basic importance of constructive personal relations has already been emphasized. What else can you do to provide a favorable environment?

Safety First and First Things First

A safe environment is one that contains no harmful things that the child can swallow, burn or cut himself with, fall from, or push over on himself—until he is of an age when he can be taught to avoid these dangers. The child's environment should contain as few things as possible about which you have to say "don't." By noting how many times you have to say "don't" in one day, you can discover what changes should be made in your home and yard. For the child's sake, too, your home should be simple enough so that it does not wear you out just keeping it in order. A simple home may have much beauty of line, form, and color, even though it may look bare to some friends and relatives.

Many a mother knows what would be good for her gifted child, and would do it if she were not caught in a squirrel cage of household routine, the care of her other children, and obligations she has assumed outside the home. If she could apply some of Mrs. Lillian Gilbreth's efficiency measures, described in *Cheaper by the Dozen*,[6] she might find life a little less hectic. It would help if she could reorganize her schedule, list the things that have to be done in order of priority, and try to follow her schedule. Then she would see more clearly just what needs to be done, and when she should and can do it. With routine matters under control, she would be in a better position to meet the children's needs for attention and to have some time to herself.

Conditions Conducive to Language Development

Language develops *as part of* the child's total development, not *apart from* it. Nothing is gained by overemphasis on language per se. Play and social experiences stimulate language development rather than interfere with it. Therefore, adults who neglect other aspects of a child's activities to focus on speech and reading in these early years are likely to defeat their own purposes. If the parent anticipates the child's every want, this delays his language development; he has no need to learn to talk.

If a child does not begin to use words between one and one half and two years of age it is well to raise some questions: Is his hearing normal? Have the persons in his environment provided interesting things to see and do and talk about? Do they listen to him? Do they tell him the names of things he is concerned with at the moment? Do they repeat correctly a word or sentence he has mispronounced? Did he have a serious illness at about the time he would normally begin to talk? Is something troubling him that distracts his attention from learning the language? Does he have association with other children in his home, in neighborhood play groups, or in a nursery school?

Storytelling and reading aloud—In primitive tribes storytelling is one of the most ancient arts. It was the main means of educating children. In Ireland, Phyllis Fenner tells us, in the early days, the story teller would come to the door at evening to earn his lodging by telling tales for the whole family as they sat around the fire. Story-telling was an important part of people's lives.

One of the most enjoyable ways of enriching the environment of a gifted child is by telling stories—stories that delight and amuse; stories that help the child to interpret his experiences and to clarify his thoughts; stories that help him to understand himself, his world, and other people; stories that give him glimpses of the spiritual world.

For the youngest child, it is best to tell very simple stories comprising only a few short sentences about himself, his pet, or his toy. Simple Bible stories and folk stories of the repetitive type can soon be introduced. Perennial favorites are *The Pancake, Three Billy Goats Gruff, The Old Woman and Her Pig*. Folk tales are easy to learn and easy to tell. They have a simple plot; they are dramatic; they have stood the test of time. Some modern stories such as Wanda Gag's *Millions of Cats* have a folk-tale quality.

During the preschool period nonsense rhymes and stories, puns, and other kinds of humor help to improve the child's pronunciation and increase his sensitivity to words and language patterns, as well as give him enjoyment. The words and phrases that make him laugh attract his attention. Poetry, too, makes the child aware of the wonder and beauty of language.

Even before the child can understand all the words he hears, he may get a feeling for language as he learns to listen while someone talks, reads, or sings to him. Lullabies and nursery rhymes are good to begin with. Christopher Robin has delighted many children.

The stories you select should be appropriate to the age of the child. A group of five-year-olds described some kinds of stories they liked or did not like to have read to them:

"Sometimes they read my older sister's books and I don't like it because I can't understand."

"I don't like it when they read stories about witches. I dream about them. I'm afraid. One night I was so afraid. I was sure there was a witch right in my room talking to me."

"I don't like it when my mother goes off to talk on the phone right in the middle of the story."

"I choose a long story unless it's very late. Then I have to have a poem or a very short story. I like poems all right. I learn how to make my own."[7]

You can tell whether the story is appropriate or not by watching the child's response to it. A story should be good literature. It may also be a story that you enjoy, too. Stories like this are easy to learn and easy to tell.

After finding a suitable story, it is a good idea to read and reread it until you can repeat much of its original language. This does not mean that you should mechanically memorize it; you should memorize enough of it so that you can convey its spirit and excitement without losing the beauty and precision of the original language. From this kind of experience children acquire language patterns which become unconscious influences upon their future speaking, reading, and writing. You may have to jot down certain phrases and sentences and repeat them until you can reproduce the author's exact words. This takes time and effort. But if you learn one story every two or three weeks you will build up a repertory of stories that can be told again and again.

For suggestions on the art of storytelling any of the following references would be helpful.

Sara Fenwick, *Story-telling*. Reprint of an article available without charge from the American Educator Encyclopedia, Publishers House, Lake Bluff, Illinois, 1956.

Ruth Sawyer, *How To Tell a Story*. Written for Compton's Pictured Encyclopedia, 1000 North Dearborn Street, Chicago 10, Illinois, n.d.

Ruth Sawyer, *The Way of the Story Teller*. New York: The Viking Press, Inc., 1942.

Gudrun Thorne-Thomsen, *Story-telling and Stories I Tell*. New York: The Viking Press, Inc., 1956.

Elva Young Van Winkle, *Story-Telling Time*. A useful pamphlet on how to tell stories. Distributed by the General Federation of Women's Clubs, 1734 N Street, N.W., Washington 6, D.C., n.d.

To supplement your own storytelling, you may use some of the records of Bible stories and other tales made by great storytellers such as Gudrun Thorne-Thomsen, Marie Shedlock, Ruth Sawyer, and Frances Clarke Sayers. These records introduce the child to a wider range of plots and personalities, but they are no substitute for mother's or father's own storytelling. This sharing of stories with mother and father is something for children to remember; many adults cherish this experience as the happiest memory of their childhood.

Sometimes, however, the child's desire to know what "lies between the covers of books" is so completely satisfied by listening experiences that he has no incentive to learn to read. This happened to Agnes Repplier;[8] she had not learned to read by the time she was eight years old. Recognizing the problem, her mother issued the edict that no one should read to her. Then, finding the world of books suddenly closed to her the child of her own accord, though not without effort, learned to read. Similarly, the son of a college president, who was the pet of the campus, did not learn to read because he could always find someone, usually a friendly student, who would read anything he wanted to hear.

Reading aloud to a preschool child also makes for character and personality development. In addition to communicating affection between child and parent, books help the child interpret his feelings and his world.

In Joseph Longstreth's story *Penguins Are Penguins,* many a little child has identified himself with the little penguin, Perry, who wanted to be a polar bear, not a penguin. He ran away from his family and was lost in a wide, white world. After many adventures, he decided that he was glad to be himself, not someone else. Perry, the penguin, may start a preschool child on the road toward self-acceptance.

Many preschool children feel mystified when their good intentions do not turn out the way they expected. This happened to another of Mr. Longstreth's characters, "Little Big Feather." Children often want to prove they are independent. "Little Big Feather" eventually solves this dependency problem after doing a number of silly things that children enjoy reading about.

Prereading and reading experiences—Gifted children teach themselves to read in various ways. They are curious about the words on canned goods, frozen food packages, cereal boxes. Walter B. Barbe, Director of the Reading Clinic at the University of Chattanooga, Chattanooga, Tennessee,[9] told of a very bright child who reported that he had learned to read "from the cereal box, like everyone else learns to read." Another child, who traveled by car a great deal, said: "To pass time, I learned to read road signs." Others pick up words that they see on television.

Many begin to associate printed words with their sound and meaning as they look on while someone reads from one of their favorite books. Madame Curie is reported to have learned to read fluently, without anyone's knowing it, as she sat beside an older sister who was beginning to learn to read. Apparently these children remember the sounds of words they see in books, on labels, and on signs, and develop their own ways of recognizing them and distinguishing them from other words. They are not *taught* to read; they are not even conscious of learning to read. One bright boy said, when asked how he learned to read, "I got interested in books and read them; that was all there was to it."

Other children remember being taught to read at home by their parents, by a teacher who was a friend of the family, or by an older brother or sister. One girl described her preschool reading experience as follows:

"My earliest memories are of my mother and father helping me to read. My father showed me how to break up a word into syllables and how to use the dictionary. As I grew older, every now and then I would get out the dictionary and try to find out what a word meant or how it was pronounced."

Other bridges or blocks to reading—Long before a child comes to school he has built either bridges or blocks to reading. If he has seen members of his family enjoying reading, has spent many hours listening to stories, has used books in his play, and has pored over his own picture books, his attitude toward learning to read will tend to be eager and happy. If, on the other hand, his parents have conveyed either by word or action an indifference or dislike toward reading, or older children have told him of unpleasant school experiences, then he may approach reading with indifference or dislike.

The following are some of the reasons why gifted five-year-olds want to learn to read:

"When you grow bigger you have to know how. You can't even drive a car unless you can read the signs."

"I want to learn how to read so I can send a letter to Granny."

"So I can read letters I get from people myself—birthday cards, Valentines."

"So I can read notes when I get them and not have to ask my Mommy. So I can read for my Dad."

"I want to learn to read so I don't have to pester others to read books to me. Sometimes they're busy." [7]

Conversation—Conversation is important, too. It is one of the best preparations for reading because it makes the child familiar with ideas and words that he will later meet in books. Talking things over with the older preschool child enriches the meaning of words and gives him a chance and a stimulus to explore new ideas and to distinguish between facts, opinions, and fantasies. Through repeated experience, he will begin to see the difference between "I know . . .," "I think . . .," "I guess . . .," "I fancy. . . ."

The parent's speech, of course, is important. Children catch the cadence and construction of the speech of those around them. Repeatedly interrupting a child to correct his grammar and pronunciation may give him the impression that it is dangerous to be spontaneous. In time children will become conscious of correct form, and will want to master the mechanics of language.

Between the ages of two and three, when children are learning words rapidly, parents need not hesitate to tell them the exact word for something. Long words and strange words continue to delight them throughout the preschool period. A five-year-old was heard gleefully calling a playmate, "You old prehistoric dinosaur!"

Some children have a gift for language. This is reinforced as we show pleasure in their original and vivid expressions.

Opportunities for the Arts

Children's interest in art, music, and dramatic play can be stimulated by opportunities and appropriate material. Children have more latent artistic talent than is generally recognized. However, it will not develop without opportunities. Practice in music at an early age seems to be of more value than practice in motor skills or language. In one experiment, children under three improved greatly in the singing of single tones and intervals when they were given special practice over a six-month period.

A wealth of recordings such as Benjamin Britten's *The Young Person's Guide to the Orchestra* and Joseph Haydn's *Toy Symphony* introduce children to the sounds of different instruments. There are also many records of children's songs, nursery rhymes, and classical music. Listening experiences may interest a musically gifted child in learning to play an instrument. But genuine interest may be nipped in the bud if we constantly keep the child's nose to the keyboard.

Play and Work Activities

Preschool children need to participate in a variety of activities. Some of these activities provide for social contacts: attending a nursery school, visiting friends and relatives, playing with neighborhood children, enjoying story hours at the library, attending Sunday school, and learning folk dances.

Some activities develop facility in language: playing word games, making collections of labels on cans, making picture dictionaries or scrapbooks on subjects of special interest, singing about one's work in the manner of a light opera, and collecting words that have different meanings but are pronounced the same, like "meet" and "meat."

Some activities develop habits of helpfulness and a genuine feeling for the worthwhileness of work, as when the child washes the spinach, leaf by leaf, or makes thimble cookies while her mother bakes big cookies.

Inexpensive art materials and boxes of "treasures" of all kinds—bits of cloth or fur, buttons, pins, colored paper—all may be used imaginatively. Simple playthings like these are much more stimulating to the bright child than expensive mechanical toys.

Working or playing, the child is learning. The problem—and it is a real problem calling for more alertness than a tired mother is sometimes capable of mustering—is to reinforce the child's desirable attitudes, his generous impulses, his satisfaction in finishing a task, his worthwhile achievements. As Anatole France put it: "I would make lovable to her everything I would wish her to love." This is a most important principle of learning.

Detrimental Conditions

Conditions that may prevent a gifted child from using his native ability have already been mentioned. They may be briefly summarized here, as they apply to the preschool years:

1. Deprivation of a normal mother-child relation in infancy.

2. Separation from the mother; this may be particularly disturbing to the child between two and three years old. To him, his mother's absence for days or weeks means loss of love and security. If the mother knows beforehand that she is going to the hospital or will have to make a long journey or visit, she may find a mother substitute before she leaves. This provides a continuity of relationship for the child. A gifted child, even as young as two or three years, can be helped to understand that while mother is going away she will keep on loving the child all the time she is gone, and that she will come back. While she is away, a daily picture card or toy from her will help to reassure the little child that "Mommy's coming back." Hospitalization can also be a disturbing experience to a young child, especially if he is under three or four years old. The older gifted child can be

helped to understand the hospital experience and why it is necessary. The scientifically oriented preschool child may come back with much fascinating medical information!

3. Overdependence on the mother, or overprotection by the parents, who solve all the child's problems rather than letting him solve those that he can handle. The other extreme is to give the child no guidance in learning, and no time to succeed in a task he wants to accomplish.

4. No limits or control—this may arouse anxiety in the child, and may help to produce an aimless, indecisive kind of personality.

5. Lack of companionship; this may impoverish the child's vocabulary as well as depriving him of social experiences.

6. Excessive hostility which the child must suppress. In doing so, he may suppress his normal curiosity and thereby limit his intellectual development.

7. Lack of suitable play material and other appropriate environmental stimulation.

The case of Alex, as reported by Leland H. Stott in the *Merrill-Palmer Quarterly*,[10] illustrates the importance of home influences on a child's social and emotional development:

Alex was obviously a very bright child—alert, quick in comprehension, and equipped with an excellent memory. During his babyhood he was quite healthy. He was overactive, excitable, and emotionally unstable; he needed consistent, firm, calm, and affectionate treatment during his preschool years.

Instead, he was subjected to an unfavorable home atmosphere. The parents quarreled a great deal and were inconsistent in their methods of treating him. They set standards of conduct that were impossible for him to follow. From the very early years both the parents and the grandparents made an issue of his thumb-sucking. When he was about two and a half, he became very negativistic. He was constantly scolded and punished by his grandmother; his father was harsh with him because he feared Alex would hurt his baby sister, who was the father's favorite.

From this family background, Alex developed the domineering, hostile pattern of behavior that characterized his preschool years and persisted through his tenth year, when the intensive study of the case was closed. His record in nursery school and early elementary school contained many instances of bossy behavior. If he could organize things himself, he enjoyed being the center of attention. He had many good ideas but, if he could not have his own way, he became destructive, hurt other children, or went off by himself. This behavior was not a passing phase, nor was it easily outgrown. However, he submitted to authority when it was sufficiently firm, often accepted correction and used it constructively, and was responsive to approval. These positive characteristics give clues as to the treatment the child should have had.

Here was a potentially gifted child whose patterns of social behavior, acquired during the preschool years, prevented him from using his real intellectual capacity.

Pros and Cons of Nursery School and Early Entrance to Kindergarten

Whether nursery school is of value depends upon whether it gives the child the kind of experience he needs. One boy, now thirteen years old and in the ninth grade, realized the importance of getting off to a good start in school. In his own words:

"At age three I started in at nursery school. I feel that the teachers there made a great impression on my outlook on school. Had my early school experience been bad, my whole outlook on school would be that it is a 'stupid' place. Now that I have come through elementary school and enjoyed it and I am finishing junior high, I am looking forward to the rest of my education."

It is difficult to know whether a child who has attended nursery school has an advantage in social development when he enters kindergarten or first grade, because children are sent to nursery school for such different reasons. Dr. James R. Hobson has studied this question in the Brookline, Massachusetts, public schools for twenty-five years. During this period all educable children who were four years nine months of age by October first of the school year, and even younger children who passed an individual psychological and medical examination, were admitted to kindergarten. This is an unusually early age for kindergarten admission. Following these children through high school, Dr. Hobson found that twice as many of the boys and almost twice as many of the girls, as compared with pupils who had entered kindergarten later, obtained all B's or A's for the last two years of high school. Moreover, they were also more active in high school extraclass activities, except for sports like football. He concluded that early entrance for bright children seems, in general, to be an advantage. However, decisions in individual cases should be made on the basis of a study of the child and of the opportunities available at home and in the community.

The following comment presents one father's view of the problem:

"Many people have advised me to do something about my gifted three-year-old child, but no one really knows what to do. The Board of Public Education in my city is only interested in mass education and in assisting retarded children. Their advice seems to be to discourage her interest in scholastic achievement and see that she has more opportunities for social development. But, as far as I can see, the child is not inhibited or emotionally disturbed. She is happy, disciplined, and gets along with children of her own age or older. She was an easy child to teach.

"It seems a shame to waste time in developing her potential ability just because our public education system demands that she wait until she is six before she enters school to learn the things she already knows very well. I foresee a bleak, boring period spent in classrooms where she will be forced to slow down to the speed of the average student and where she will quickly lose interest in learning."

This parent's complaint, though perhaps somewhat exaggerated with respect to the child's ability and the policy of the school, nevertheless has a great deal of truth in it. Many other parents have described similar situations. There is a real problem in bridging the gap between an intellectually stimulating home and a school that caters to average ability. One aim of the next chapter is to give some suggestions for dealing with this dilemma.

Although modern educators have faith in the inner resources of parents and encourage them to think through their own problems, a little advice now and then is relished by the most self-reliant parents. To parents of gifted children who ask, "What can we do to help our gifted child develop his potentialities?" Garry Myers has given the following sensible advice:

"If you suppose your child, at two, three, or four, is more than usually gifted, check with a psychologist and the school to help you know if you have grounds for your supposition. Convinced that he is gifted, resolve to enjoy him as a person and let him grow up without becoming conceited or feeling queer, but to have normal enjoyment with children of his age. Guide and discipline him in good ways of health, self-reliance, responsibility and due regard for the rights of the rest of the family and other persons he is most often with. See that he learns effectively some early limitations but has ever so many outlets for his interests and energies. Listen to what he has to say and answer his questions. Talk with him companionably. Encourage his exploring and inventing with playthings and his surroundings. Provide him with ample tools and materials for creative fun. Most of all, appreciate and enjoy what he achieves with such, especially when done with noticeable concentration, persistence, and effort. Go exploring with him. Keep learning with him and searching for added information from books in order to answer his questions and stimulate his further curiosities.

"Read to him fanciful stories to stimulate his imagination. Enjoy his own yarns when he spins them from his head. Read to him also from illustrated books of interesting facts and their explanation, including some of the wonderful books of elementary science." [11]

GUIDANCE OF PRESCHOOL CHILDREN

Guidance implies a goal. In the complex daily routine of child care, parents sometimes lose sight of long-distance goals for the child. These goals have to do with character and personality development—recognition of and respect for the rights and feelings of others; ability to make, carry out, and accept the consequences of decisions; satisfaction in success, and willingness to try again in the event of failure or disappointment.

To Help or Not to Help?

To help the child gain that nice balance between dependence and independence previously mentioned, you can steer a middle course between forcing help on him and insisting that he accomplish the task all by himself, regardless of its difficulty. If you give unnecessary help, the gifted child may accept it when he has to, and try to avoid you when he is engaged in some absorbing problem that he wants to solve and can solve successfully. If you neglect or refuse to give him help when he needs it, or if he is made to feel that any aid will be given with disapproval, he may become disgusted with the whole situation, and resist help later when he needs it.

If he is constantly belittled, even a gifted child may acquire a sense of unworthiness. If he is excessively coerced, he may become either hostile or oversubmissive.

If he makes a mistake or does not do the job perfectly, he should not be made to feel that he has failed. "That's all wrong; let me do it for you," is the kind of response that makes a child unwilling to tackle a new task. "You did it a little better this time; soon you'll learn to do it all by yourself," is the kind of comment that stimulates a child to further effort.

If a two-year-old child says no to reasonable requests, it helps a parent to know that this behavior is characteristic; children of this age are trying to become more independent. Encouraging him to do as many things as he can without help gives him the learning experiences he needs. Protecting him from repeated failure in impossible tasks prevents him from feeling afraid to venture on anything new.

Threats act like a wet blanket on a child's natural initiative: "Mommy won't love you if you do that." "You'll get sick if you don't wash your hands." "Look out; you'll fall." Instead of using threats of this kind, it is much better to distract the little child from the forbidden activity, and then help him do the right thing by making it so attractive that he wants to do it. It is important for him to learn to substitute with some feeling of satisfaction a socially accepted activity for one that is not approved.

If a child seems to be handling a situation effectively, let him go ahead. If he seems eager to read or to do things you think are too difficult for him, let him try. Following his lead is quite different from forcing him into activities for which he is not yet ready. Gifted children will often surprise you by the things they are able to do when opportunity is provided and the decision is left to them.

Accentuating the Positive

Children see themselves through others' eyes. Scolding, criticism, and disparaging remarks give a child the impression that he is stupid, bad, or a disappointment to his parents. The self-concept affects his behavior and prevents him from realizing his potentialities. Of course, a child must be restrained at times, and his mistakes must be corrected, but the emphasis should be on what he does right, not on what he does wrong.

A certain amount of tension, frustration, and conflict is inevitable. Children as well as adults have to learn to tolerate these feelings. But excessive fear and anxiety destroy self-confidence and make it impossible for the child to reach out to new experiences. Intellectual ability does not blossom under these conditions; it is nipped in the bud. Absence of excessive fear and anxiety gives the child a feeling of security, and the confidence that he can cope with a situation, with or without help.

Nonverbal Communication

How does a baby acquire that basic sense of trust that is such an important accomplishment during the first year? How does a mother communicate with the baby who has not yet learned the language? The earliest communication between mother and child is nonverbal. It takes place through physical contact, facial expression, tone of voice, and gentle, confident handling that makes the baby feel secure.

The mother reads the baby's language of behavior. When she offers him an unfamiliar food, she is asking him whether he is ready for it. The baby may answer no by refusing to open his mouth, pushing the food aside, or spitting it out. At the time, the mother accepts his answer and will try again later, when he is likely to answer yes.

Effective Suggestion

The feelings and behavior of a small child fluctuate rapidly. His aggressive attack on another child may suddenly shift to sympathetic solicitude; his rebellion may quickly change to co-operation. The preschool child also has lapses in which he reverts to earlier types of behavior. The older child gradually learns better co-ordination of his impulses. The adult can help him build attitudes and values that guide his actions. Once a relationship of respect and affection is established, the adults' suggestions and example become influential. "The greater the child's affection or admiration for the suggester,"

C. W. Valentine concluded, "the more likely is the suggestion to work."[5]

Sometimes suggestion does not work because self-assertiveness sets in. This self-assertiveness stems from the child's self-concept and his "own self-determined plans of action."

As the child grows older, his peers tend to supersede his parents in influence. In fact, he may show an active resistance to his parents' suggestions, however reasonable they may be. This drive for independence crops up again in early adolescence, or even before, in the gang stage.

When You Appeal to Reason

In understanding children's behavior, you can often help to straighten out their feelings. Teddy may say he doesn't like Mrs. White who is visiting his mother. Actually he doesn't like being "left out" while his mother is talking to Mrs. White. But his mother may say, "I know how you feel—Mrs. White and I *have* been talking a long time, but I'll have time just for you pretty soon." Thus reassured, Teddy may be more able to accept the visitor, and may understand his own feelings and behavior a little better.

A simple comment may help children to solve their problems of school relations in the nursery school. When a child is helpful, a parent or teacher may say, "How good of Jean to do that." This comment may stimulate the other children to be kind, as well as reinforcing Jean's tendency toward kindliness.

Earlier than most children, the gifted child will accept the reasonableness of a rule or request if it is explained to him. If disciplinary action is necessary, he will often understand when the parent explains the reason for his action. If the parent can show that the necessary discipline is in line with something the child himself wants—for example, to feel grown-up or to keep his best friend—then the adult becomes the child's ally.

Lois B. Murphy gives an example of the way a child was helped to understand a situation that was disturbing her:

"Cathie was restless and couldn't go to sleep the night her mother left for a brief trip; finally she began to cry, and to whimper, 'Maybe she won't come back.' When I went to her and held her hand and asked, 'Are you afraid she won't come back because you were naughty today?' she nodded her head silently while the tears kept rolling down her cheeks. 'But all little girls are naughty sometimes, even your mommy was naughty sometimes when she was little, and she knows that you want her to come back; she will come back.' Cathie's tears stopped. 'What did she do when she was naughty?' From here on we talked a little about the things that happen to everybody—sometimes they break things, sometimes they get angry at their mothers. Cathie squeezed my hand very hard and held it tightly for a few moments, until soon she was sound asleep and her whole body was quiet and relaxed and her hand loosened its grip."[12]

Helping a gifted child to understand is often an effective method of helping him to cope with his emotional disturbances.

Individual Differences in Children's Response to Guidance

All we have to do is to watch and listen in order to become aware that gifted children differ with respect to the things that disturb them. They also express their feelings in many different ways. Some become angry, some cry, others withdraw within themselves and move away from people. Some are disconsolate.

They also respond in different ways to our attempts to help them. Some children derive comfort from talking quietly with an adult about the situation that has bothered them; others need the physical comfort of a mother's arms. A pat on the head comforts one child, while another child will seem to resent any physical contact. What helps one child may have no effect or the wrong effect on another. There is no way of knowing what to do except by noting how the child responds to the treatment we think will probably be best.

The way the child expresses his hurt feelings influences our attitude toward him. If he cries we may either think he is being babyish, or we may feel tenderly toward him, recollecting our own childish sorrows. If he strikes out against persons or things, we are likely to react with counteraggression. If he loses his appetite, we may become worried—for several reasons. If he refuses to be comforted we tend to feel frustrated and helpless.

Self-Guidance

We often learn a great deal by observing the way children help themselves and one another. Intuitively, they often do just the right thing. Lois B. Murphy, of the Department of Child Psychiatry, Menninger Foundation, tells how:

". . . a lonely little girl who had not yet become at home in the nursery noticed an unhappy little boy lying on the floor, miserably banging his head on the floor. She went over to him and lay down on the floor, banging her head along with him. Soon he turned toward her and they smiled, then giggled at each other and the ally in misery became an ally in fun."[12]

Earlier than most children, gifted children begin to help themselves. They learn to cope with stress and emotional pressure. We can help them when they are distressed by reminding them of something that comforted them on a previous occasion—for example, playing a favorite record.

Gifted children often find a satisfactory solution to their problems of social relations without adult help. If justice seems likely to prevail, the parent need not interfere. The children will learn more from each other's actions than from parental interference. Children derive satisfaction and a sense of competence from working out their own solutions. Timing is important. If the parent waits too long before taking action in a situation where one of the children might be badly hurt, the other children may feel a deep sense of guilt; they may even blame the parent for not helping them handle the situation more satisfactorily.[13]

Reasonable Control as Guidance

Gifted children are quick to learn when they can "get away with" refusing to go to bed, or defying other rules and regulations. Parents who see the results of too much indulgence tend to swing to the other extreme—rigid control. Neither extreme is desirable. Excessive permissiveness represents a failure to help the child meet his most important need—the need to develop his potentialities. Undue strictness, on the other hand, deprives the child of the necessary chance to be himself, to take initiative, to be spontaneous and creative, to become more independent as he grows older. "Love them and leave them alone" is not the answer, as Dr. Frederick Allen has recently pointed out.[14] Discipline, in the sense of order and reasonable control, is an important need of childhood.

Indirect Guidance

Much guidance is indirect—guidance through the environment and guidance through example. Many attitudes are caught. This is especially true of qualities such as genuine courtesy, consideration, and understanding of others. A mother who herself was gentle, spontaneous, and skillful in finding opportunities for delight and enjoyment in daily life, had a three-year-old who showed the same qualities. The persons who mean most in a child's life tend to shape his personality.

QUESTIONS AND ANSWERS

1. *How can preschool children be tested to obtain evidence of their mental ability? And how should the results of the tests be used?*

This is a task for a trained psychologist. Even though he uses the best test available, the results he gives you are not "the last word." If he were to give a test to your child six or seven years from now, the IQ might be 15 or 20 points lower or higher.

However, Dorothea McCarthy concluded, it is possible in nursery school to predict "fairly accurately which children will be ready for first grade at age six, and to aid in their school placement well enough to avoid some serious misplacements."[15]

Test results may be used to confirm or modify your own observations of your child's intellectual ability. They are also useful in suggesting the kinds of experiences most suitable to him.

2. *Does a preschool child profit by special training in motor skills, language, or numbers?*

During the preschool years there is little or no advantage in special training. In an experiment, one twin at about one year of age was given special training for six weeks in climbing stairs. The other twin received no training during the same period, but was then given two weeks' training. The second twin, who had received his shorter training at a later age, climbed better than his brother who had had six weeks of training earlier; he walked upstairs, while the first twin continued to climb upstairs on all fours.

Similar results were obtained from experiments in the teaching of language. The twin whose training was begun five weeks after the first twin, quickly caught up with his brother and went ahead of him. There is enough evidence to convince us that premature attempts to train a preschool child do not pay. When a gifted child shows an interest in any particular skill and a readiness to learn it, that is the best time to give him practice and instruction.

3. *How important is reading aloud in developing a child's interest in books and in reading?*

Reading aloud is one of the first things a parent can do to build a child's interest in reading. By this means the child learns about "the delight that lies between the covers of books."

When the reading time seems too short, he becomes eager to read the books himself. He gets used to handling books and "reading" the pictures. If parent and child are attuned to each other, this shared experience brings them closer together.

Children often perceive others as being unwilling to read to them. Five-year-old-children said:

"My Daddy reads the newspapers and I don't care about it and besides, he just wants to read to himself. Maybe what he is reading is important."

"My father wants to read to himself about his business and he doesn't want me to be around to bother him when he's reading. He might skip a line and do it wrong."

"My mother reads big grown-up things. My father reads work things. He has to."

"They won't even read the funnies to me . . . Daddy and Mommy won't. I say to them, 'Aren't you going to read to me?' They say, 'Later. I don't feel so good.'"[7]

Reading to a preschool child is a direct path toward the more systematic instruction he will receive in school; it is a prelude to his school success in the language arts. Listening to stories builds his vocabulary and gives him a sense of language patterns. This helps him to anticipate meaning when he begins to read. The first-grade child who has been read to at home is usually eager to read in school; he is already familiar with books and finds them fascinating.

4. *What type of home training should a bright preschool child have in a community where unfortunately there are no nursery schools for gifted children to stimulate them, and at the same time to give them the opportunity of playing with children who are intellectual equals and whose interests should be similar to theirs?*

A child of three or four years shows his ability in many natural ways such as seeing relationships, working out original and effective solutions to his everyday problems, and finding a way to reach a toy he wants. A firm foundation of physical, social, and emotional development ensures that the child will be free to learn later on. Today's ordinary home environment should supply enough intellectual stimulation—unfortunately, it may supply too much of the wrong kind. The right kind of personal relations with parents, other members of the family, and friends are more important stimuli to learning than a multiplicity of things.

5. *Jane is four years and eight months. Our schools do not enroll children in the first grade until they are six—six as of September first. This is true for public as well as for private schools. I am very concerned that Jane will be almost seven before entering school. For quite some time she has shown the desire to read. Would you recommend my teaching her? If so, what books would help me give such instruction and what books would you recommend for her reading?*

Other parents have the same problem of what to do about children whose birthdays come one or more months too late to permit them to start school at what seems the logical time. These children are ready for school. Some of them have started reading on their own, and are taking books from the library.[16] They can tell time and have basic number concepts. They are also well adjusted socially, and get along with other children. What can parents do to prevent the child from merely marking time while he waits another year to enter school, and an additional half year before his class starts reading?

Many of these parents have given their children opportunities at home to develop their intellectual interests without hampering their physical and social progress. They have encouraged their children to engage in the spontaneous experiences of childhood and have given them opportunities to play normally with other children of different abilities and backgrounds.

Whether it would be desirable for a bright child to enter school before reaching the specified age would depend on a number of factors:

1. Whether he is equal to other children of his chronological age in physical and emotional, as well as intellectual, maturity.

2. Whether the first-grade teacher is sympathetic and understanding and willing to make special provision for the able learners in her class.

3. Whether he lacks suitable playmates in his neighborhood.

4. Whether he need to develop more independence and wider casual contacts with people.

If these conditions exist, then it would seem wise for the parent to see if the child can be admitted on the basis of a readiness test, or transferred from the kindergarten or a private school as soon as he demonstrates that he is making a good adjustment to the group situation.

When such a child is admitted to the first grade, it would be well to get in touch with the first-grade teacher and work with her to provide some special individual activities, such as reading on a subject and reporting in an interesting way to the class, writing plays, and taking a certain amount of leadership in groups of children working on different projects. The gifted child may even help a group that is rather slow in learning to read. With the co-operation of the teacher a variety of experiences may be provided in an ordinary first-grade class.

If the conditions mentioned above do not exist, or if the school is unable to make an adjustment, then the alternative would be to furnish the best possible home environment and make it possible for the child to participate in neighborhood play groups.

6. *My five-and-one-half-year-old son has just started kindergarten in a public school. The few weeks he has attended classes have left him completely bored and disillusioned. His inquisitiveness and alert manner have disappeared. At home, before he started school, his*

thirst to know, to question, to learn, was constant. He learned to read, write, tell time; he learned games like checkers—all this by questioning and perseverance until he mastered what he started out to learn. He used his reference set to find out so many things he was curious about. Starting school was a tremendous excitement for him. Seeing how he reacts to kindergarten, I don't know what to do. He is an outgoing child, quite popular with his friends of all ages, and very sports-minded. My fear is that his capacities not being used in school will be dulled and just disappear.

Apparently in this case there was a marked discrepancy between the kind of experiences this child was having at home and those he had in kindergarten. It would be helpful if the mother could visit the kindergarten some day and see what kinds of activities the children are engaging in.

A number of parents have been concerned that their kindergarten-aged children were too advanced for the regular kindergarten activities. It should be possible for the kindergarten teacher to encourage the child to engage in all the activities that are appropriate for his chronological age and physical development—games, outdoor play, and similar activities. The gifted child needs to choose his activities and to learn to play happily with other children. But it is possible also to include planned work periods and some definite instruction in the kindergarten program.[17] Doing some things he is expected to do and learning to do them well gives the child a sense of growth and achievement. He is praised only when he has really shown improvement. During kindergarten days he should realize that school is not all play; that there are many things to know and to learn here. He should look forward to these special work periods. Although emotional problems may interfere with a child's learning, the sense of having accomplished something worth while tends to decrease a child's feelings of anxiety and frustration. The bright child should have the opportunity to look at books from which he can learn something, to do creative drawing and painting, to give puppet shows and dramatize a story, to set up and label science exhibits and to do simple experiments, to help the teacher write names and signs, to make little books and newspapers, to engage in other projects of interest and value to him, and to be allowed to finish a task without being distracted.

7. *What are some causes of retarded language development, when there is no physical defect?*

The most obvious cause is lack of need to learn the language—the child gets everything he wants without asking for it; adults do his bidding, and he has little contact with children. Jane Beasley emphasizes the influence of personal relations on a child's growth in language. The parents' expectations, anxieties, and disappointment in the child's lack of progress in speech tend to make him anxious, and may aggravate his difficulty in learning to talk. Indifference on the part of the parents between the twelfth and eighteenth months may prevent his learning the sound combinations usually acquired during that stage of development. Parental rejection or too much pressure on him to speak may interfere with his freedom and spontaneity in talking.

FOUR

The Gifted School Child

"Our son, who will be eight years old in January, is thought to be a gifted child. His IQ rating on a Stanford-Binet test given last September was 167. At the time the test was given he was in second grade, but it was decided after the test that he should try third. So far he has done well scholastically, but, as we were totally unprepared for this problem, we wonder how well other children have adjusted to this situation. We have had to rely on the teachers he has had and they have been wonderfully helpful, and we are certainly grateful for the help already given.

"We want very much to have our son use his full potential, but do not want him to be overdeveloped mentally to the detriment of his social and emotional development. Thus far he seems to be well balanced and we hope he stays this way."

This parent's attitude toward her very bright child is all that could be desired—it shows warm acceptance, concern with his total development, appreciation of the help his teachers have given, and eagerness for more understanding.

Parents are rightly concerned about the school years of a gifted child. During these years, when the child is so eager and quick to learn, it is tragic to waste his precious time and to run the risk of his becoming indifferent or lapsing into the habit of working below capacity. During the elementary-school years the child builds study habits, and attitudes toward school and toward learning. Under unfavorable conditions he may experience emotional difficulties that block his learning.

GLIMPSES OF GIFTED SCHOOL CHILDREN

Each child develops in his own unique way. One may grow more rapidly than another. Some gain certain skills ahead of others. Some make a happy adjustment to school; other do not get along at all well. Some of these individual differences in ability, behavior, and background are illustrated in the following descriptions written by parents and teachers.

A Charming Gifted First-Grade Child

Katherine is the third child in the family. The two older children have IQ's of 146 and 150+. Her Stanford-Binet IQ, after she had been in first grade for three months, was about 146; her mental age was eight years eight months, when her chronological age was only five years eleven months.

The family give their children many opportunities for learning. They are taken on educational trips. They are made responsible for doing certain chores and for assisting their parents around the house. One child is responsible for making the salad, another for setting the table, and so forth.

Katherine is the tallest child in her first-grade class. She is sturdily built and enjoys good health. She is also the youngest in the class; she was six only last January. She has abundant energy, a fine flair for the dramatic, and a good sense of humor.

Unlike many children, who are very dependent when they enter the first grade, Katherine was a great help during the first days of school. She was able to follow directions and also to find her way around the school by comparing the numbers on the doors with the numbers the teacher had written for her. In a short time she recognized the numbers when they were given to her verbally.

She has a very good vocabulary and likes to take part in the "Show and Tell Period," when the children talk about things that they have seen and done. She is friendly and talkative. On the Metropolitan Readiness Test, given in September, she scored higher than all but 3 per cent of all the children of her age who had been tested. However, she was not reading words when she entered the first grade.

She began her preprimer in September and by midyear was reading in the first reader. The words she has learned by sight she reads very well; now she needs phonics to help her sound out new words.

When Katherine has completed her classwork in writing and numbers, and in her reading group, she studies the library book she will later read to the class or tell them about. Sometimes she is assistant teacher and helps others in their reading and numbers. Many gifted children do not like to be teachers—it bores them—but Katherine is most helpful and enjoys it. Sometimes the teacher asks her to go to the library and get a book on a topic in which the class is interested.

When the class made hand puppets and used them in plays, Katherine was a leader in this project.

In the second half of the first grade, after Katherine had learned the basic skills, the teacher obtained some supplementary books, both story and informational, on the second-grade level. She also had Katherine help her in building up a picture file and making scrapbooks for the class library. Katherine enjoyed using the art materials for creative work. By now she could write several sentences on a given topic, and was beginning to dictate poems.

This seemingly rather ideal picture of a gifted child is actually very accurate and realistic. She was the product of a fortunate combination of heredity, home experiences and relationships, and school conditions. We can infer that the parents were more concerned during her preschool years with fostering basic attitudes of good will, helpfulness, and delight in physical and mental ability than with striving for specific achievements in reading and numbers.

The teacher, within the limitations of her responsibility for the entire first-grade class, enjoyed the child and welcomed her assistance without depriving her of necessary instruction and practice in the basic skills. She also provided opportunities for Katherine to engage in special projects, many of which were of a social nature and involved service to other children.

A Bright Second-Grade Child with Social and Emotional Problems

Donald is seven years and ten months old. He has two brothers, one two years younger, the other one half year younger. His father, an engineer, and his mother are college graduates. His forebears on both sides are professional people. Both parents are young. They feel that they make only a few demands on Donald, and that these are reasonable; they believe that Donald should meet the demands. At times they are at a loss to know how to handle him.

The mother seems to be most impressed with two of Donald's characteristics: that he is a happy child and that he is strong-willed. However, she questions the quality of his happiness since he is not willing to give up anything or "share himself." He plays after school with one child exclusively, and Donald is usually top man.

When he has temper tantrums at home, his parents leave him alone; they have found that he will straighten out.

Donald is slight of build, and his facial expression is keen and alert. Although he is a well-co-ordinated child, he is more interested in reading than in athletics. He has double vision and must wear glasses all the time.

In school he is among the younger members of the second-grade class. He seems to have little in common with the group. He participates in group discussions and activities when they interest him, when they are carried out according to his ideas, and when they are not of too long a duration. He seems to enjoy letting his classmates share his information about the Civil War, but in the daily give-and-take his mental processes are likely to be so different from theirs that there is no meeting of minds. If he drops a project before finishing it he comments, "That is just the way I want it." He learned to read early, and reads widely. His unusual command of language skills was noted by the first-grade teacher, who reported that he had independently read 108 books during the year, and was interested in books far in advance of his age—the Bible, *Robin Hood*, and so forth. His writing is very careless.

At home he reads only the books that appeal to him. He reads all the books he can get on a given topic, even though some of them are beyond his comprehension.

The second-grade teacher noted many incidents such as the following:

When the teacher tried to help him select a book he countered every suggestion with "No, no, not *that* one." He finally agreed to take a book without really looking at it.

He becomes almost hysterically angry if other children touch his things, even when they are genuinely interested in them.

His relations with other children seem to be short and casual. When another boy who lived near him asked him to walk home with him, Donald said, "If I happen to be going that way."

One morning he brought a book, suggesting that the teacher read it to the class. When she had not read the book by noontime, he said in a belligerent tone, "If you don't read that book today, I'll take it home tonight."

When the teacher suggested that he think more about his writing, and showed him a better way of making his p's, he emphatically said, "No, no, I don't want to. I like *my* way."

One day another child took the book he was reading while Donald was cleaning up in art class. The teacher suggested that Donald explain to the other child that he wanted the book and request him nicely to give it back. Donald placed his hands over his ears as he does when he hears anything that does not please him, stamped his foot, broke into uncontrolled sobbing, and sat down at his desk, overcome by frustration.

Donald's arithmetic papers are carelessly written, and the computation is very inaccurate, though he shows that he knows the answers when the teacher goes over the problems with him. One day he said, "I learn them so quickly." When asked how he learned them he said, "Oh, I guess, and learn them bit by bit, but I'll tell you one thing—I don't want too many problems. I just won't do them."

One day he refused to take part in a class project that involved writing a letter to a popular teacher who was absent. He said he wasn't going to write, didn't like to write. Ten minutes before the end of the period, Donald was still reading instead of writing the letter. When the teacher was firm about his staying after school until he had written the letter, he at first said his mother was waiting to take him for a haircut. When the teacher said she would call his mother and explain why he would be delayed a few minutes, he pounded on his desk, and screamed, "I can't write; my hand shakes too much. I tell you, I can't!" (Trying a little) "There—don't you see? You shouldn't make me—I can't do it." He sobbed and yelled loudly. After trying to talk with him and vainly offering to help, the teacher left the room. After a while he was quiet. When the teacher returned, Donald was relaxed and smiling; he had written an adequate letter.

The report from the psychologist showed a mental age of twelve years four months and an IQ of 157. His listening comprehension was on the seventh-grade level, his reading comprehension on the fifth-grade level. He seems unable to accept failure in tasks such as writing and number problems that he cannot master as quickly as he does most things. Failure to achieve quick success may represent a threat to his self-esteem. His apparent need to be omniscient may also account, in part, for his refusal to accept help or suggestions from other people, his poor relations with other children, and his attitude of "I want what I want when I want it."

The next year Donald was skipped to the fourth grade. There he made friends, gained in self-control, and won the genuine appreciation of his classmates.

These desirable changes cannot, of course, be attributed entirely to skipping a grade, although acceleration in this particular case seemed to be a sound move. During his second-grade year he probably discovered that his temper tantrums, his brusque treatment of other children, and his refusal to meet accepted standards did not bring him satisfaction. The apparently wise way in which his parents and teacher treated him during this period of negativism helped him to outgrow his immature ways of behaving. It would also seem possible that during this negative period he was under some kind of pressure, or was emotionally disturbed by his lack of achievement in sports and skills involving motor co-ordination. His reactions were nervous and highstrung, and these qualities are often signs of over-stimulation or frustration.

An Eight-Year-Old with Special Talents

Doris has an IQ of 139, as tested when she was five and one-half years old and again when she was six and one-half. Her special interests are creative writing, composing (she has had two years of musical training), and memorizing parts of plays such as *Romeo and Juliet*. She engages in imaginative play with a Robin Hood castle and houses.

Having skipped the second grade, she has successfully found her place now in the third grade. For her reading she chooses such books as Dickens' novels. We wonder whether these are too stimulating for her.

According to the mother's report, this child is very much advanced in her musical and reading interests. It would be important to know what she is really getting out of the adult books she reads, apparently of her own accord. Books that were better suited to help her understand herself and her present world would probably contribute more to her personal development. She should be encouraged to explore other interests—to take trips and excursions, and to make other friends than the two she has selected. Later, her interests will tend to become less diffuse, and it will then be time for her to pursue them more intensely.

A Sixth-Grade Boy, Bright, but Lacking in Initiative

David was described by his mother as follows:

"He is not a child of much initiative, although we've tried every way we know to develop it. Neither does he read as much as we'd like him to."

"On the Stanford Achievement Test he made a score that placed him at the eleventh-grade level, far above his present grade placement. He has many talents and interests which are not being developed, and I hate to see him waste himself. Our school does have some special classes for above-average children, but as we live outside the city, there is a problem of tuition and transportation."

In this brief description there are indications that the parents are putting too much emphasis on school achievement. They have been successful in helping the child attain a high achievement test score, but in doing so they may have aroused a resistance to learning and a dislike for reading. Obviously the knowledge he has gained is not worth this price. If we knew all about this case, we might be able to discover quite reasonable explanations for David's lack of initiative and for his resistance to his parents' pressure.

An Exceedingly Gifted Child Frustrated by Her School Experience

Sue, a fourth-grader with an IQ of 185, did a tremendous amount of reading. She became interested in China, but received little encouragement to follow this special interest. Serving as a monitor did not appeal to her. She developed headaches—probably a psychosomatic expression of her distaste for school and the "babyish" things she had to do.

Children with IQ's over 180, as Leta S. Hollingworth[1] suggested, may have special difficulties in adjusting to people and to the ordinary school. They have such quick insight, so much initiative and originality, and so great an ability to predict outcomes that they find it difficult to slow down to the tempo of the usual classroom and to enjoy conversation with average persons—unless they take pains to develop special sympathy, understanding, and interest in helping others to be happy and successful.

These glimpses of gifted school children merely suggest the manifold patterns of development that may be found among children of superior mental ability.

WHAT TO EXPECT OF GIFTED SCHOOL CHILDREN

With so much variation among gifted children, what can you expect of your school-age child? What abilities and characteristics is he likely to show? How can you expect him to behave? We cannot say exactly, but you may expect him to have many of the characteristics summarized in this section.

Physical Appearance

Like Katherine, the child described on pages 105–106, many gifted children are superior in appearance, physique, strength, energy, and health. They tend to have fewer than average physical defects. Although they show a fairly average incidence of colds and other contagious diseases during the school years, the gifted are reported to have fewer headaches, fewer symptoms of nervousness, and less malnutrition than the average. Their better health is partly accounted for by their reportedly good habits of eating, outdoor play, and sleeping.

You would expect a bright child to be reasonable about health habits. Good health frees him to explore his environment and enjoy his experiences more fully. Some of these qualities you may expect to find in your child, even though he may vary quite a bit in size and appearance from the "typical" gifted child.

Play Activities

Gifted children between the ages of six and thirteen are generally just as keenly interested in play as are other children of their age. Their range of play interests is quite as wide. At these ages they tend to spend more time in playing than in reading and studying. In Terman's study the gifted children mentioned ninety different games that they enjoyed. The list included bicycling, skating, and ball games, as well as parlor games and puzzles. They preferred, a little more often than did children of average ability, quiet activities that required thinking. Although the boys were less interested than average boys in competitive games, they were not effeminate in their play interests. Beginning at the age of eight, they tended increasingly to prefer games that were popular with other children—another manifestation of their concern for conforming to their age group. Co-operation in group play may be expected to increase after the age of seven or eight. Instead of merely kicking a ball around, older children organize into baseball or football teams.

The gifted are quick to understand the rules of a game, and to follow directions. They are also likely to settle quarrels quickly and amiably. When a gifted child is not interested in the games of his age group, he often improvises or invents new games.

Occasionally we find a gifted child on the sidelines. This reluctance to participate may stem from a feeling of awkwardness, or from annoyance that he cannot learn physical skills as rapidly as he acquires verbal knowledge.

It is unusual for a child of these ages to play always by himself. He may be too shy or too timid to play rough games, or too bossy to be chosen by others. Or his intellectual interests may cause his classmates to shun him. The parent or teacher who knows the reason for the child's rejection is better able to help him. If he is helped to choose games or game positions in which he will not appear awkward, and if he has some special instruction and practice in the necessary skills, he usually enters wholeheartedly into the play activities of children of his own age.

The mentally superior child needs physical exercise and recreation, not only for better health, but also for the social contacts, self-esteem, and group acceptance that come from participating in games and sports.

Collections and Hobbies

The large majority of gifted children—about twice as many as the average—make collections of some kind. The peak of interest in this activity occurs between the ninth and twelfth years. The gifted are likely to make collections associated with scientific interests. Stamps, historical objects, and geological and botanical items are also commonly collected.

Some collectors' items such as old matchbooks, pictures of baseball players, bottle caps, and other things whose value is incomprehensible to adults, may be important as part of the child culture during the early school years. Collections represent one means by which the child identifies with his age-mates and establishes his status away from the family group. This is a necessary step in establishing his own identity.

According to a study by the home economics department of the United States Department of Agriculture, the American people are spending more and more money on wholesome hobbies—musical instruments, boats, bicycles, sporting goods, flowers and seeds. Children's leisure time is being filled with dancing classes, music lessons, sports, arts and crafts, swimming, tennis, horseback riding, and modern dancing. However, informal and unscheduled hobbies seem to have been neglected. As Dorothy Barclay pointed out, overorganization of children's time endangers the recreations and hobbies that "combine a high level of spontaneity, a sense of unforced effort and an enjoyment of the work involved for its own sake."[2] Children should choose their own hobbies. Parents may help them get started and encourage them, but they should not push them into certain hobbies against their will. Nor should they make a fetish of the child's having a hobby.

Mental Alertness and Reasoning

You may expect your gifted child to pick up and remember information of various kinds and to use it accurately when needed. Gifted children's accuracy and precision in the use of words shows most vividly if we compare some recorded responses of a bright, an average, and a below-average child.

Question: Who discovered America?

B (male, age 10-9, IQ 141): I guess you want me to say Columbus. He didn't actually discover the coast of America. He discovered Cuba and the islands which are now Haiti and Puerto Rico.

A (male, age 10-9, IQ 108): Christopher Columbus.

BA (male, age 10-9, IQ 78): Eisenhower?

Question: In what way are a cat and mouse alike?

B: They are both warm-blooded animals. They don't lay eggs.

A: They're animals.

BA: They've got tails, and fur, and ears.

Question: In what way are paper and coal alike?

B: Well, they're both made from trees. Paper is made right from trees today. Coal is also from trees. Back in the time of the dinosaurs, trees were pressed down, and the Ice Age came, and all the pressure and the time turned the trees into coal deposits.

A: They both can burn.

BA: I don't know—(brightly) you can make marks on paper with coal.
Question: What is a diamond?
    B: It is the hardest known and next to the most valuable substance. It
    is pure carbon. Volcanoes erupt and the smoky carbon is trapped.
    After hundreds of years of pressure—[examiner's hand gave out].
    A: It's pretty and shiny and costs lots of money. It comes from mines.
    People wear it in jewelry.
    BA: A diamond ring.

Puzzling questions appeal to bright children. They often like to
work on tasks which are relatively difficult for them. They may speak
contemptuously of the "baby stuff" they are given in some classes.

Ability to see relationships is one common characteristic of gifted
children. You can observe this ability in many kinds of situations. For
example, when the first-grade teacher was telling the class how
scarce books were when Lincoln was a boy, Danny commented, "But
that was long, long ago. Today we have many libraries with thousands
of books." Another child volunteered to find out more about Lincoln's
mother. "Oh," said Danny, "Jane's going to do an historical study."

The same youngster was conducting an experiment "to get a
carbon sample for my collection"; he held a metal cap carefully over
the flame, putting it down every few seconds. Several children asked
why he kept putting it down. "Well," said Danny, "you see, metal is
a good conductor of heat and it would burn my fingers if I held it
over the flame too long."

Increasingly, as gifted children grow older, they need tasks worthy
of their best efforts—tasks that require thinking and reasoning. Critical thinking is the process of recognizing a problem in a fresh and
open-minded way, and systematically trying to solve it. It may be an
arithmetic problem, a fable to interpret, or a problem in human relations—any of these would appeal to bright ten-year-olds.

Rather than always telling children how a problem was solved, we
can present them with a problem as it presented itself to pioneers in
the field. As they think through such problems as how to make fire, or
the invention of the airplane, they have the thrill of discovery. They
feel that *they* are pioneers, and experience the joy of thinking and
reasoning.

School Achievement

You may expect your gifted child to do well in school. The gifted children in Terman's study were rated superior both by teachers and on achievement tests. The achievement of gifted children is often two years above their grade placement.

However they do not necessarily do equally well in all subjects. In general, they tend to do better in English, history, mathematics, and science than in subjects requiring manual skill such as writing, sewing, and art. Some youngsters become so absorbed in a certain subject that they neglect other aspects of their schoolwork. The gifted child is often a poor speller and dislikes to write. He would rather talk. Because some of these children will later be handicapped by their poor handwriting and spelling, they should be persuaded to try to bring these accomplishments up to par.

Interest and ability are certainly related. Doing well in a subject increases the individual's interest in it; interest in a subject evokes effort to learn it. Some pupils find science exciting and history like "a long true story." Others are as interested in arithmetic as they are in puzzles, and some enjoy the sheer mental activity involved in mathematics—when they solve the problems successfully.

Gifted children between ten and fourteen are usually keenly interested in science. In addition to their natural curiosity, they are probably stimulated by the popular emphasis on science in newspapers and magazines and over radio and television. They delight in experiments; they will spend many leisure hours at home in following through the simple experiments described in such books as:

Larry Kettlekamp. *The Magic of Sound.* New York: William Morrow and Company, Inc., 1956.

John Lewellen. *The Boy Scientist; A Popular Mechanics Book.* New York: Simon and Schuster, 1955.

Nina Schneider and Herman Schneider. *Let's Find Out.* New York: William R. Scott, 1954.

Although mathematical ability is related to general intelligence, some children show special ability in adding, subtracting, and other mathematical computations. Practice in these operations obviously affects a child's performance at any age. When interest, high general ability, and special number ability are combined, a mathematical genius sometimes results. It is said that Gerhard Gauss, at nine years, took only a few minutes to solve correctly the first long-addition sum given to the class, while the other pupils took an hour and then arrived at the wrong answer.

Children's interest in school subjects may fluctuate for various reasons. The personal appeal of the teacher and the way in which the subject is taught have a great deal to do with the pupil's interest. Gifted children often dislike history when it is taught as a collection of dates and unconnected events, but are enthusiastic about it when they see how the present grew out of the past and how the lives of great men have helped to shape the course of events. In the early stages of learning a foreign language, too much mere memorization may prevent gifted children from enjoying insights into other lands and people. Arithmetic seems to stand either very high or very low in children's subject preferences.

Underachievement, which may be owing to many causes, is likely to block the development of self-confidence and security. A child may not receive enough appreciation. As one parent said, "When a child accumulates knowledge on a topic from many sources, parents and teachers should show appreciation of what he finds out." On the other hand, if parents overemphasize achievement per se, the child may conclude that achievement is the price he must pay for his parents' continued love. If he loses their love, there is no longer any need to try.

Reading

You may expect a gifted child to learn to read early and easily and to read more than the average. He is also likely to read on a wider range of topics, and to read more nonfiction than the average child. Gifted children often become completely absorbed in a book. One girl said that when she was reading *Heidi*, she shut out everyone until she had finished it.

The majority of gifted children read more than the average child. In their elementary-school years, Terman's group of gifted children spent, on the average, twenty hours or more a week in reading. A two-month record that these children kept showed that the seven-year-olds read, on the average, ten books during this period of time; at age eleven, they read fifteen books. From then on there was little increase in the amount of voluntary reading, although they still enjoyed reading. As one youngster said, "Now in the seventh grade I belong to a number of clubs . . . and take piano and oboe lessons, so my interest in reading is slowing down. But I still say, give me a good book any time."

Values of books—Parents of gifted children are right in recognizing the importance of books in the child's life at every stage of his development. Books bring delight. They expand and enrich the child's interests and experiences. They help him to interpret life situations, and gain appreciation of the beauty of the world. They make it possible for him to gain insight into human characteristics and relationships, as he sympathizes with the characters and lives through their vicissitudes. When life is good, books add to its significance; when life is difficult, books make it bearable or give insight into its problems.

Real literature arouses noble emotions and stimulates the mind. An absorbing book has an integrating effect on a child's personality— it helps him "to pull himself together." Books build values and standards; they help to shape the way a child perceives the world. They help him to achieve emotional independence, as Elizabeth Enright's Melendy children did; to find sound values, as did *Sensible Kate* in Doris Gates's story (Viking, 1943), and to learn to work for the things one wants and not be cast down by failure, as in the case of the heroine of Mary O'Hara's *My Friend Flicka* (Lippincott, 1941). When values and standards are reiterated they are unconsciously built into the child's thinking and feeling. And "as a man thinketh in his heart, so he is," and so he acts. That this idealistic statement of the possible value of books is not just wishful thinking is indicated by children's own statements about the influences they have received from certain books.

Reading interests—Children's reading interests change with age, and become increasingly complex and specialized. The little child's world is a composite of the familiar features in his environment. He is curious about this world and wants to read stories about real children like himself. Such stories help him to feel secure, because in realistic books the child finds a world he can understand, problems he can solve, and conclusions he can anticipate. He likes simple, obvious humor like that in the Peter Rabbit stories. Certain folk and fairy tales, though quite unrealistic, also fit his primitive conceptions of the world.

Gifted children between nine and eleven tend to be keenly interested in realistic animal stories. They find prehistoric animals particularly fascinating. In this day and age children acquire an early interest in space travel; they like stories about the scientific wonders of the future. For informational books, children of these ages are likely to be most fond of those that describe the dim, distant past of prehistoric animals, or the unexplored future of space travel and visits to the far reaches of the universe.

Children tend to do more free reading during preadolescence than at any other time in their lives. They can be encouraged to choose a wide variety of books: animal stories, factual nature stories, science, science fiction, pioneer adventures, biography, tales from other lands. They read for information as well as for entertainment; they like to read about how to make and do things, hobbies, and scientific experiments. During the primary grades the interests of boys and girls are similar; later they diverge. Girls are more interested than boys in stories of home and family life and in fanciful tales. However, they will choose "boys' books" more often than boys will choose "girls' books."

Biographies are especially appealing to gifted children of both sexes. The *American Adventure Series* published by Wheeler Publishing Company, and *The Childhood of Famous Americans Series* published by Bobbs-Merrill make excellent supplements to the second- and third-grade readers of which many gifted children make short work.

Gifted children show about the same patterns of reading interest as do other children, but show them one or two years earlier. At any age the reading matter of bright children is likely to be of better quality and reflect more interest in the real concerns of the world than that of less gifted children. Their intellectual maturity shows up in the maturity of their reading interests.

These group trends in reading interests that we have briefly described may or may not apply to your child; only your own observations can discern his particular interests. If you do not help him find the books that are "right" for him, he may turn to comics or other reading of inferior quality. To explore his interests, you can offer him a number of choices, some of which he will refuse; thus you will have an opportunity to learn what he likes and why he likes it.

In the middle grades your gifted child will probably want to read whatever series is popular at the time. Some of us remember being absorbed in the *Little Colonel* series and waiting eagerly for each new volume. Children often read what their chums are reading, be it comics or classics. However, one bright youngster said, "I read the *Bobbsey Twins* because all my friends were talking about them, but I disliked them so much I got new friends."

Although the course of reading does not always run smooth, the attitude of bright children toward reading is, in general, similar to that expressed in the following quotations:

"I think reading is one of the best pastimes because it never ends."

"I love to read and I think, given the chance, I could read for hours at a time, but of course there are other things to do."

"I would say I spend about one-fourth as much time reading as I spend in sports. I read quite slowly when I am reading for pleasure, although I can increase my reading speed if I must."

Despite the attraction of social activities, radio, television, and auto-riding, gifted children find considerable time for reading. This is because they find reading an enjoyable and rewarding experience which challenges their active minds and satisfies their desire for knowledge.

Creativity

Most characteristic of the highly gifted person is the ability to create something that never was in the world before. "Creativity" is a magic word. You are delighted when your child comes out with a fresh poetic expression, is keen to see a relationship, paints an original picture, or finds a new or simpler way of solving a problem. You have noted many examples of creativity in children: the three-year-old, looking out of the window and seeing a tree uprooted by the hurricane, said, "Oh, Mommy, see the tree with its feet sticking up in the air!"

These are some of the signs of creativity which parents and teachers should recognize and encourage:

Eagerness to look and listen; to take in and relate new sensations.

Curiosity about things and people.

Interest in unsolved problems.

Wholehearted absorption—sometimes they don't even hear you speak, they are so engrossed in what they are doing.

Fluency of ideas, but not with the attitude that "everything goes"; true creativity requires a critical and selective approach.

Happiness in creative activities.

Persistence and purpose in pursuing one's goal.

A conception of himself as a person of ingenuity and originality.

Obviously the child is much affected by the responses that his creative efforts evoke from others. These responses affect his self-concept and the effort he subsequently puts forth to achieve his goal. Even though there is no substitute for the satisfaction he himself feels in the creative process, he can hardly help being influenced by the way his poem, his painting, or his new idea is received. Herein lies the secret of fostering creativity—to show genuine appreciation for the rare expression of individuality, no matter how crude or feeble its first manifestation.

Dominating adults tend to suppress the constructive and creative thoughts of children. The least we can do is to refrain from interfering with the child's creative efforts. In drawing or painting, for example, we should not impose our ideas of reality on the child. The child sees things differently from the way we see them. To maintain his integrity, he must present them as he sees and feels them; he must be confident of the validity of his own kind of expression. If we express preference for the more conventional work of another child, we may cause the original child to imitate the conventional child just to please us.

Some gifted persons have overcome physical handicaps to make outstanding creative contributions: Helen Keller, who has been an inspiration to many, the blind pianist, Alec Templeton, Greg Rice, the miler, and Teddy Roosevelt, to mention only a few. Within the realm of character development many handicapped people have given to the world the inspiration of creative lives. Accepting the limitations of their specific handicaps, some of these people have explored new areas of creativity. Some have even made creative use of the handicap itself. Would Beethoven have heard the unearthly harmonies of his last quartets if he had had the use of his physical ears?

Music and Art

Almost any normal child can appreciate music. Some gifted children are talented in music. All would profit by a variety of musical activities: participating in family singing of folk songs, great melodies, and hymns; playing some simple instrument or keeping time with a drum or bell; listening to fine records and freely interpreting the music in bodily movements.

There seems to come a time, perhaps at about twelve years of age, when children lose interest in their music lessons because they have so many other things to do. One boy described the way his parents helped him at this critical point:

"When I lost interest in piano lessons and felt that I couldn't put a lot of effort into practicing, I went to both parents for help and we discussed the problem together. I've always gone to my parents for help before anyone else.

"They made me realize that I shouldn't drop piano lessons now after I'd already put so much effort into them. If I continued, they told me, pianoplaying would become easier and I would get pleasure and profit out of it later on in life.

"I followed my parents' advice and now I think that was the wisest thing I could have done."

A child's growth patterns in drawing and painting may become apparent if we collect dated samples of his art work over a year or more. One boy whose drawing of himself at the beginning of his first year of school looked like an elongated worm with a large head, drew himself at the end of the year as a recognizable young cowboy.

Some children with high general ability lack the co-ordination and "sense of proportion" necessary in drawing a man or a rabbit. Other children show remarkable draftsmanship at an early age. We should be careful not to confuse representational drawing with creative expression.

However, even representational drawings and paintings may reflect feelings, though interpretations of this kind should be made very cautiously. A bright seven-year-old girl who was proficient in academic work but very retarded in social relations, drew precise, conventional pictures of her family in which she never included herself. When she finally did draw herself, the figure was so small one could hardly find it among the others. After her parents modified her rigid schedule and gave her more recognition for her good work, her drawings became freer and less indicative of tension.

Practical Ability

It is not generally true that the gifted child is lacking in practical ability. Skill in shopwork or any other kind of handwork involves ability to perceive present relations among objects and to project a variety of possible new relations. It also involves ability to find out why certain things do or do not fit together. It is more than mechanical manipulation. This ability is evident in the preschool years; it becomes more evident in older boys than in older girls.

Its further development depends a great deal on interest, experience, and training. Persistence, too, is important. A gifted child often becomes impatient with the mechanical manipulation involved. As one mother said of her gifted child: "His mind tells him to build a certain structure, but his fingers fumble. Feelings of frustration and inadequacy are the result."

As the gifted child grows older, he is likely to show more interest in reading and other abstract activities, and to have less time for handwork or drawing—which he could do well if he were so inclined. Some of these manual interests may persist as hobbies.

Social Relations

Your child may not be popular, but still he may be well adjusted socially. He may not hold a position of leadership, but still he may have a great deal of influence for good in the group. He may not be active in many children's groups, but still he may not be disturbingly shy or withdrawn.

His relations with other children depend on a number of factors; among them are his intelligence, his verbal facility, his social attitudes and behavior, the attitude the others have toward gifted people.

If a child is exceedingly intelligent, he is likely to be lonely. He has little in common intellectually with companions of his own age, and finds it difficult to relate himself to them. Nor do they understand him or seek his company. A child with very high intelligence may lack the corresponding social and emotional maturity.

A child of superior character who finds himself among companions with low ideals may become an isolate if he insists on maintaining his standards. It takes courage to resist an undesirable type of conformity.

Language development is closely related to social development. The child who can communicate freely and effectively tends to be friendly and outgoing. Shyness and timidity sometimes arise from not knowing what to say. Withdrawn children should have opportunities for spontaneous expression and creative writing.

Gifted children are sometimes regarded as "queer" or "different" by other children. They are sometimes actively disliked by their classmates. This dislike may stem in part from fear and jealousy. The bright child is a threat to the others; he makes them feel inferior.

What happens to the gifted child's friendships when he is placed in a special class is not clear. Gifted children who spent half the school day in a special class with other gifted children chose most of their friends from the special class. According to another study of thirty-five gifted children distributed in regular classes in grades three to five, all with Stanford-Binet IQ's of 150 or over, over 80 per cent were in the top half of social acceptance as indicated by their being chosen as best friends by their classmates. It is quite possible that gifted children find more ready acceptance in the elementary school than in the high school.

Animosity toward the gifted on the part of other children is intensified if the teacher singles the bright child out and gives him special privileges and recognition. Some socially sensitive gifted children avoid arousing the unfriendliness of their classmates by deliberately refusing to put themselves forward. They will not report that they have finished first. They are glad to furnish information when it is needed by the class, but they do not volunteer information just to show their superiority or increase their prestige.

These reticent children are generally well liked by their classmates, and sometimes not identified as especially bright by their teachers. One teacher did not identify a gifted boy in her class until one day he asked a very searching question. This alerted the teacher to his exceptional ability, which became more evident as time went on.

There is justification for other pupils' antagonism toward some gifted children. Some have personality traits that evoke dislike. They are always pushing themselves forward, usurping a disproportionate amount of class time with their questions and comments, insisting that others do everything their way, saying sarcastic things that make others feel inferior, and boasting about their accomplishments. The responses they evoke from others intensify their need to do the things that made them disliked in the first place. Since they are bright and quick to understand, such children often profit when a teacher or parent points out the effect their behavior is having on others. When such a child realizes that certain things he does make others feel uncomfortable or angry, he may be able to change his behavior if the problem is not too deep to be understood verbally.

The children most likely to be chosen by others are those who are considerate without being subservient, and skillful at helping others to be successful and happy. They are usually candid, cheerful, enthusiastic, good humored, resourceful, and willing to do their share, or more than their share, of the hard work.

During the intermediate grades, chums, or best friends, are of great importance. They give the child his first experience of real intimacy with a person outside his own family. A high-school boy described an experience of this kind that took place when he was about eleven years old:

"When my best friend and I were together, we would spend hours discussing each other's problems and trying to solve them. This was the only time that I could explain my problems and the only person I could speak of them with. A boy of eleven cannot discuss things seriously with his parents because his problems seem humorous to them. My friend and I discussed the virtues of our girl friends and also constructively evaluated each other's personalities. These evaluations still hold true in most respects."

Most parents worry if their gifted child makes no friends over a period of a half year or more. There are many patterns of friendship, any of which may meet the needs of a child at a particular time.

There is such a thing as being overpopular. The child who is always in the limelight, always chosen as team captain or leading lady in the play, may be upset if he is not, for once, chosen as the top person. Such a child may be striving for admiration in order to make up for a lack of real affection at home. It is also possible that he has been so praised at home, so often set on a pedestal, that he has become incapable of making normal childhood friendships. Or he may have sensed that his parents have high ambitions for his social success; he may be striving too hard to fulfill them.

Another thing parents worry about is the wrong choice of friends. Unless a friendship involves physical or moral danger, it is usually unwise to try to break it up. The bright child will usually find out for himself whether the friend is the right one for him. It is difficult for parents to be hospitable to their children's friends when the friends seem unattractive to them. But it is partly by being hospitable that the child learns to become considerate and generous toward many kinds of people. Parents can help their children to appreciate the good qualities of all the children they know. They can help the children discover something of interest in each one, something each one can contribute to the group. In this way, Mary Northway[3] says, children learn to love their neighbors, as well as to have their own special friends.

Fear and Anger

Fears are likely to trouble many children, probably including the gifted, between the ages of five and seven; they are common to the large majority of children between eight and ten. Children fear animals, often ones they have never met. Girls mention their fear of cows and of robbers and drunken men.

Children of eleven and twelve reported that their chief worries were being scolded by their parents and "having a poor report card."

"Being alone in the dark" was regarded as frightening by about two-fifths of both boys and girls. Less frequently mentioned were fears of dogs and ghosts.

A fear that is established in childhood may be very persistent. Even though the child intellectually recognizes that it is silly for him to be afraid, the feeling may still persist.

Temper tantrums and angry or aggressive behavior probably occur less often among gifted children than among others. Though the gifted have special causes for anger, they also have special resources for finding solutions to their problems. The little boy Donald, whom we have described on pages 106–109, had some problems of social adjustment during the second grade. In an admiring group he was very affable, but when the other children criticized his work or were indifferent, or did not understand, he became angry, even to the point of hitting them. During the following year, he was placed in a more congenial group and the outbursts of anger subsided. It takes time to grow emotionally.

Moral Development

Gifted children may be expected to have reached a stage of moral development three or four years in advance of the average child. They are more likely to be trustworthy, to report events honestly, avoid overstatements, express socially acceptable moral attitudes. Superior cultural advantages in the home and generally superior personality—as well as high intelligence—probably account for this advanced moral development, as measured by various ingenious tests.

In Terman's study the gifted children surpassed the average group in prudence and forethought, self-confidence, perseverance, sense of humor, desire to excel, conscientiousness, and truthfulness. They were not much different from the average group in popularity, sensitiveness to approval, sympathy, and generosity. From these findings it would seem that the gifted group should be helped to develop a more sympathetic and co-operative attitude toward others.

Of course, these characteristics do not appear in all gifted children. The gifted are not free from faults; in fact, Terman has pointed out that "at least one out of five has more" faults than the average and "perhaps one out of twenty presents more or less serious problems."

Girls are generally considered somewhat superior to boys in character traits; however, this difference was not nearly so marked as the improvement that occurred at about the beginning of adolescence in both boys and girls.

In a study of cheating, it was found that children from the higher socioeconomic homes became more honest as they grew older, while those from poor homes became less honest. However, certain children from exceedingly poor home environments did not cheat even in classes where more than half of their classmates did.

Improvement in moral behavior may often be attributed to the influence of a loved or admired person. Children choose their first ideals or heroes from the immediate family or circle of acquaintances. After the age of seven they begin to choose persons outside their immediate environment. Although choosing a fine person as one's ideal does not ensure living up to his standards, it seems obvious that children's heroes or ideals affect their character development. We should give serious thought to the effect of the rather shoddy ideals now presented to children through newspapers, magazines, motion pictures, advertising, television, and radio.

As with learning of other kinds, improvement in moral behavior depends a great deal on whether the child has had many previous experiences in which socially accepted behavior proved rewarding. With children who are above average in intelligence, a verbal statement of a principle or standard often serves as a guide to behavior in the immediate situation. By the time they have reached a mental age of thirteen or fourteen, they are able to define clearly such abstract words as "kindness," "justice," and "charity."

Moral behavior involves the making of decisions. Decisions require knowledge of pros and cons, possible consequences, advantages and disadvantages. Without such knowledge, the child does not make a decision; he is merely forced to make a choice. Actual experience is necessary to test the soundness of a decision, once it is made. Parents may give children freedom to make their own decisions so long as these are not detrimental to health, safety, or moral welfare. They will learn by their mistakes. Gifted children often win the right to make many decisions for themselves by establishing a record of wise choices.

HOW PARENTS CAN HELP

"The best gift Bill could receive from his parents," one father said, "is a really normal childhood. I want to help him build as broad a base of real boyhood as possible, so that if the promise of his potential ability ever produces a pinnacle, it will not topple." A wise parent that!

Preschool and elementary-school years should build a broad base of health and vitality, confidence tempered with caution, joy in work and play, knowledge and skill, creativity, and character. What can you do to nurture these home-grown virtues?

Most important, perhaps, is to have confidence in your child's capacity to grow. He will tend to take what he needs from the favorable environment you provide. This confidence in the child's inner resources is prerequisite to respect for him. The adult is a facilitator, not a pusher or puller.

Next in importance is that the parents share some of their interests with their children. Parents often do not realize how much their companionship means to a child.

When one group was asked to draw pictures illustrating how their parents helped them, a ten-year-old boy drew a picture of an auto parked by the bank of a river, with a boy fishing and his father standing behind him with his hand on the boy's shoulder. Both are smiling, and several fish are swimming toward the hook. In explanation of the picture the boy said, "I think my father helps me most when we can be together."

Other ten-year-olds felt that their parents helped them when they:

explained that work should come before play,

told the child not to do things that might hurt him,

explained what would happen at the doctor's or dentist's so the child could be braced,

let the child watch them and help them at their work.

When ten-year-old Christine's father asked her if she could think of anything he had done to make her more interested in learning, she said, "Well, you've taken me to places with you and you've helped me with my homework if I needed it."

What can parents do when the school situation seems unsatisfactory to them? This problem was well stated by the father of two young gifted children:

"The public school they attend is said to be a very fine one. Yet it has no particular program for gifted children. If the teacher in a certain grade happens to be oriented toward the gifted child, she does what she can. If not, nothing is done, except perhaps to give the child more of the same work to do.

"We do not want to skimp our children at this time. Rather we would like to help them by enriching their programs. We would be very happy to participate in such enrichment. Yet we feel at a loss where to start."

Building Self-Confidence

Why do so many gifted children feel inadequate? It may be because their special achievements are not recognized. Some parents criticize their children constantly; "You could have done better" may be the only reward they get for their good work. Other parents set up standards that are too high even for gifted youngsters. If a child's planning and purposing are taken over by adults, if his learning is directed by an alien will, his natural initiative and originality are of no use.

We build a child's self-confidence by bestowing discriminating praise and recognition, giving him responsibility, and helping him find activities in which he feels secure enough to participate. By asking for his suggestions and advice on matters in which he can really be helpful we give him a sense of importance. By helping him only when he needs help, and letting him see his progress, we also facilitate the building up of a self-reliant personality.

Stimulating Thinking

Parents may encourage a child to think and read critically by helping him to build sound concepts. Many such concepts are the result of firsthand experiences. Excursions and trips furnish a foundation for many new concepts. Pictures, television, and other audiovisual aids, if used selectively and skillfully, enrich the meanings of words and strengthen basic concepts.

When the child talks about something he has read or seen, the parent can encourage him to do more than give a bare rehearsal of the facts; he can ask questions that require thinking: "*Why* did that happen?" "*How* do we know?" "*How* can we find out?" "*How* might the boy have solved the problem?" "*What* was the relation between what he said and what his friend did?"

In family discussions, too, thought-provoking questions may make the table conversation more interesting, as well as stimulating the children to think. Parents, too, have to think in order to ask such questions!

In helping a child to judge an author's contribution, the parent may raise questions such as these:

"What do you think the author is trying to do?"
"Do his ideas follow one another logically?"
"Does he give facts to back up his statements?"
"Do other authors agree with his conclusions?"

Parents may casually ask questions like these about a book both they and the child have read, without giving any impression of being pedantic.

For most families mealtimes are the main conversation times. Grace is said. Topics of family interest can be brought up, experiences of the day are related, choice bits of humor are shared, and public affairs are discussed. Children and adults listen to one another; self-discipline is maintained. Even the youngest child is encouraged to contribute to the general conversation. Occasional guests contribute new interests.

It is obvious that intelligent mealtime conversation can have a favorable influence on the development of gifted children. They can match wits with adults and with older brothers and sisters, and profit greatly by participation in stimulating conversation.

Assisting in the Gaining of Knowledge

Parents can help children acquire wide knowledge of the things they themselves are interested in. As one eleven-year-old boy expressed it:

"When something is dim in my mind, I always go to my parents for help. For my parents' knowledge extends farther than mine. One subject I knew almost nothing about was electricity. I went to my father and he explained many things and answered many of my questions."

Even though he has an exacting job, the father can find some time in which to share his major interests with his children. Arnold Toynbee is one of many notable people who trace their interests in a special field to associations of this kind with an able parent.

Parents can familiarize children with new scientific words by explaining and illustrating each word the first time it occurs, and then using it repeatedly in their conversation for several days.

Evoking Effort

The acquisition of knowledge and skill requires effort; it cannot be accomplished without a certain minimum of tension or pressure. This pressure is inherent in the difficulty of the task itself. If the task is a little above the gifted child's present competence, he has to reach in order to accomplish it; his "reach exceeds his grasp," as Robert Browning said. A certain degree of difficulty makes for a progression of experience. The problem is: how much difficulty, how much mind-stretching, how much pressure is desirable? There is no way of knowing except by observing the child's response. If the task is too easy, its accomplishment does not give him a feeling of success. If it is too difficult, he abandons it after a period of frustration. If the task is reasonably difficult and the goal is clear from the beginning, the child is stimulated to master the simpler aspects and go on to the more complicated. Dale Harris, Professor at the University of Minnesota and Director of its Institute of Child Welfare, while discounting any "inherent virtue in toughness," believes that the normal youngster, secure in his parents' acceptance, can tolerate a considerable amount of "the discomfort which may come from being held to high standards."[4] To help each child acquire a desire to do his best and a "habit of sustained excellence," Dr. Harris offers these suggestions:

Help the child set a goal or standard of performance which is the best he can possibly achieve.

Help him to see this goal clearly from the beginning.

Arrange the learning sequence so that it proceeds from the simpler to the more complicated aspects of the task.

Let the child see whether or not his performance is successful.

Ensure by these measures that he will get satisfaction in dealing with more complex problems, even though they cause him some discomfort and tension.

Understanding and skill in a given area often arouse interest. We usually like to do the things we do well. Interest evokes effort: we learn more rapidly the things we enjoy. Thus a beneficent circular response is set in motion.

Encouraging Growth in and Through Reading

Example is important. Attitudes toward reading are caught. If children see their parents reading for pleasure and profit, they tend to imitate them; eventually they will get interested in reading for its own sake. As you read to yourself, you can often share an interesting detail or verbal picture with the children. From your comments and your conduct they get the idea that reading is really worth while. It should be a part of family life and a part of the child's world.

It is well to continue reading aloud to a child once in a while, even after he has learned to read. This will help him to become more familiar with book language and with new words. More important, his delight in reading will grow. If you start to read him a story that captures his imagination, he may finish it himself.

Perhaps the best way to acquire sensitivity to words is to listen to poetry read aloud. As children grow older they may become restive when parents attempt to read poetry to them. In this case their craze for records offers an entering wedge. Why not give them some of the excellent recordings of poetry that are now available? For example, a series of records entitled *Many Voices*, produced by Spoken Arts for Harcourt, Brace and Company, 383 Madison Avenue, New York, includes such poems as Ogden Nash's "The Rhinoceros," Alfred Noyes's "The Highwayman," and various sonnets by Shakespeare.

As the child becomes more proficient in reading, the parent will make suitable books (see Appendix D) easily available. The mother may exchange books with friends whose children have the same reading interests. Her weekly shopping trips will include shopping in the library for books to bring home. The gifted child will pick up these books if they are left lying around, and before he knows it he will be deep in a story or a book of fascinating facts.

A good home library includes reference books—a dictionary geared to the age of the child, an up-to-date children's encyclopedia, an atlas; picture books for enriching children's experience, stories and informational books, homemade scrapbooks on topics of particular interest, and a filing case for clippings, magazine articles, and pictures. A bulletin board for pictures and other clippings of special interest has many uses at home as well as in school.

Children should be introduced to the local library at an early age; they should participate in the activities it provides for children of various ages.

Some books you will want to give the children as presents. They will treasure books that are their very own.

It is always helpful to have personal recommendations of books that are likely to appeal to a child's interests and suit his needs. For example, a boy named Arnold spent many hours at the museum—museums were his hobby. Recognizing this special interest, his father consulted the librarian. She recommended *How to Make a Home Museum* by Vinson Brown. Arnold was immediately interested in reading it and in starting his own home museum according to the directions in the book.

It is a mistake, especially when children are in the lower grades, to give them books that are beyond their present ability, interests, and emotional and social development. Trying to read at the frustration level takes the joy out of reading.

When the child asks for information, you can often encourage him to look things up in the dictionary or encyclopedia. This is an especially important habit for the bright child to acquire; it enables him to be on his own in his search for new knowledge.

Home reading sparks the pupil's interest and enthusiasm and leads to more rapid learning in the classroom. To encourage home reading among elementary-school children, a number of children's book clubs have been established. (See Appendix C.) These clubs provide a low-cost program of reading the year around. The books are usually carefully selected on the basis of the following criteria: variety, literary quality, moral value, and children's interests and reading ability.

How to keep children reading through the summer? This is a problem to many parents. Here are golden days for exploring the world of books, for enriching experience, for increasing vocabulary and fluency of reading. Librarians and teachers help by urging children to read at least a half hour each day. They prepare reading lists to help parents solve the problem of "the wrong book"—the book that is uninteresting, too difficult, or too easy for the child's stage of development, or just plain trashy.

For more help, parents may suggest that the local community follow a plan developed by Ruth E. Oaks that worked well in Oneida County, New York.[5] Certain schools were open for specified times each week; the Language Arts consultant supervised periods of silent reading, gave children opportunity to borrow books, and held a story hour each day.

If your child seems backward in reading, consult his teacher, the reading specialist, or the psychologist. Unless something is blocking him, the bright child usually reads earlier and better than the average. A wise parent will seek help to discover the causes and correct the difficulties. These may be physical—poor vision or lack of sleep; or emotional—unsatisfactory relationships with persons who are important in his life; or the trouble may be due to poor initial reading instruction.

Combating the Comics

If your child is in a comic-book stage, you can at least help him distinguish between different types of comics. Some are better than others. Although some children weather even the pathological type of murder-violence-horror comic, these books may be bad medicine for youngsters who are emotionally disturbed to begin with.

If the child's interest in comics continues beyond ten or eleven years of age, you can provide him with books that have some of the same qualities—fast action, suspense, fearless heroes. Children climb ladders of reading interest: from the comics they are reading to *Bugs Bunny, Woody Woodpecker,* Walt Disney's *World of Nature, Trip to Mars,* and so on, to *Treasure Island,* to *The Raft,* and eventually, perhaps, to *Moby Dick.*

The following are some of the reasons why a child may retain his interest in comics: (1) lack of other interests appropriate to his stage of development, (2) a difficulty in making friends, which throws him back on books for companionship, and (3) antagonism toward persons who forbid him to read comics.

Probably most gifted children pass through a stage of comic-reading, and then go on to other types of reading of their own accord. A gifted high-school boy described his experience in this way:

"I used to read comics. I would get money from my mother or father and get, on the average, one a day. Then I went into partnership with my sister and of course we would have little fights over which comics to get, but usually it turned out to be the science fiction type. But then all of a sudden, for some reason, I stopped reading comics—abruptly, not just easing off; I just stopped reading them. I think it was about the seventh or eighth grade, perhaps because more interesting things were happening in junior high school."

For many gifted children, the comics do not provide enough opportunity for creative thinking or exercise of the imagination.

Appreciating Creativity

All children need opportunities to be creative. To this end they should have not only suitable materials, but also adequate time and space. They need both quiet solitude and stimulating society. Many children today are overscheduled. Something is planned for every hour. They have no time, as the poet said, "to stand and stare," no time to work intensively on tasks that enlist their wholehearted interest. Many of them live in an interminable scherzo. Their minds are occupied with the trivialities of radio and television. Excessive group activities crowd out solitary pursuits. These are not conditions conducive to creativity.

A normal environment provides children with many stimuli to creativity. We can provide suitable materials for different kinds of creative expression. For example, water color lends itself perfectly to the twelve-year-old's search for new discoveries. For children of all ages, books, films, and many of their normal life experiences serve as stimuli to creative writing. Many art activities are possible in the home. A fancy painting set is neither necessary nor desirable. All a child needs is large sheets of Manila or wrapping paper, inexpensive jars of tempera paint, crayons with good strong colors, fingerpaints perhaps, an easel, and some large brushes. Water clay or plasticene has infinite possibilities. We should avoid giving gifted children the usual "coloring books," or encouraging them to copy pictures. We may encourage them to talk spontaneously about a picture they have drawn or painted; we should not ask them to tell us what it represents.

By making a scrapbook of good reproductions of works of art clipped from various magazines, the child may unconsciously acquire a feeling for color and design. We may purchase good reproductions to hang up at home, or borrow some from a local museum; these can be changed from time to time. As children grow older, trips to museums and art galleries extend their power of appreciation.

Gifted children need activities that release imagination and emotion, and provide outlets for intelligence and skill. They can become interested in creative work of all kinds: painting in unusual ways such as by the "drip" method; carving in soap; decorating cans and bottles; making block prints from prominently veined leaves, carving designs on a half potato, or cutting more permanent wood or linoleum blocks; fashioning sculptures from play-dough made of three cups of flour, two cups of salt, and about a cup of water. Some goal or purpose such as an "art exhibit" or the preparation of Christmas cards or presents gives additional impetus to these activities. A summer theater in which children and young people put on their own plays, rather than merely attending as spectators, offers many opportunities for creative writing and for ingenuity in devising scenery, costumes, lighting, and sound effects. A parent who has enthusiasm and special knowledge can get these projects started; they will then go forward mostly on their own steam.

Most important of all is our recognition and appreciation of the child's genuinely creative products, however crude. We should express our appreciation to the child, and show him the progress he is making. He should be aware that he has created a unique thing, or at least something that is original for him.

Decreasing Conflict

When children are young, we tend to control them by scolding, coaxing, telling them what to do, or punishing them. As they grow older these procedures become less effective. Then we tend either to become more severe, or to leave the child to work out his own salvation. If he has no help in learning how to meet his problems, even a bright child often fails to find acceptable solutions.

How often do we try to understand a child's behavior—to discern its underlying causes? How often do we try to help the child understand a little better why he behaves as he does? A gifted child can understand. This kind of understanding helps him to meet his problems with greater satisfaction to himself and to us. For example, if a child understands that his impulse to push and fight and dominate other children may stem from a feeling of inadequacy, and if he is helped to trace some of the origins of this feeling, he may be able to overcome both the inadequacy and the aggressiveness.

As Ralph H. Ojemann, Director of the Preventive Psychiatry Program of the State University of Iowa, has demonstrated, if we changed from "a surface approach to an approach that takes account of the dynamics of behavior, the chances of blocking strong motivations in the child (and also in ourselves) would be lessened."[6]

As we acquire more insight into children's purposes, worries, and interests, conflicts tend to become less frequent and their attitudes tend to become more favorable. A child learns from the way we act toward him. Whenever we seek the underlying reasons for a child's behavior in everyday social situations, we are demonstrating this method to the child. For example, Johnny hit Jane for no apparent reason. When he was out of the room the third-grade class discussed why he might have done it.

"He got a low mark on his arithmetic test, just before recess," said Betty, "so he was mad when he went out."

"Have any of you hurt someone else when you were angry because you yourself had been hurt? That sometimes happens," the teacher said.

"Then he should learn how to do his arithmetic better, not take it out on Jane," said Bill.

This is a simple illustration of the "causal approach" to understanding behavior. Other effective methods of teaching children to look below the surface of behavior are to discuss stories in which the characters exemplify both surface and causal approaches; to analyze, in social studies and other classes, ways of solving social problems such as delinquency by means of the causal approach; and, most important of all, to give them practice in solving their own daily problems in this way.

Fostering Moral and Spiritual Values

The moral and spiritual values of the parents rub off on the children. What the parents do speaks more loudly and effectively than what they say. Both sound and unsound values are caught. Children acquire attitudes and behavior patterns by example much more than by admonition. If we respect our children and treat them courteously, they will learn to respect us and other people, and treat us courteously. How many times have we seen our behavior, and even our very words, reproduced by our children!

Parents can help children become sensitive to the feelings of others. One gifted high-school boy showed real understanding of the feelings of a poor reader who had been in his class in elementary school:

"I remember a child who was particularly slow in reading and I think now it must have been a horrible experience for him. He would start to read a sentence and would come to a word he couldn't understand and just look at it. Then more than half the class would shout out the word at him. The first time this happened the teacher wouldn't say anything, and after the class had told him the word, he would go on again until he came to another word or group of words he couldn't understand, and the class would shout out again. Then the teacher would tell them it wasn't nice to shout out the answer, and would say, 'I know you know the word, but let Johnny get it for himself.' This went on for a while and the child got more and more upset."

This kind of empathy in an able child is certainly something that should be fostered.

In helping children to develop spiritual values, it is well to start with their unworded philosophy of life. They have already acquired an attitude toward life, a way of perceiving their world, that influences their activities. The best foundation for religious instruction is the experience of loving and being loved.

Gifted children, often spontaneously, reach out to the unseen world. This sense of wonder should be fostered before scientific or theological explanations of the universe can be understood. The eight- or nine-year-old boy who wants practical and matter-of-fact answers can be helped to realize that there are things that "no man knoweth." But certain values such as loving-kindness are real, because they produce real results in the lives of people.

HOW TEACHERS CAN HELP

If you are dissatisfied with the provision that is being made for your gifted child in elementary school, it might be helpful if you would pass on to the teacher some of the following descriptions of the ways other teachers have tried to meet the needs of gifted children in their regular classes.

Ample Opportunities To Read

In the first grade, a gifted child will usually learn very quickly to read the basal readers the class is using. Fortunately there are many other books on about the same level of difficulty that he can read with profit and enjoyment—books that are sheer fun, books about space travel, prehistoric animals, cars, hobbies, kind and courageous people, and other things boys and girls of this age are interested in today. Similarly, in the higher grades the gifted child should have special library privileges. Some gifted sixth-graders especially enjoyed a reading-discussion group that was held in the library every week. With a sound foundation in reading, the child will soon begin to read along the lines of his special interest, and will become a discriminating as well as an enthusiastic reader.

Enriching Experiences

Although children are motivated first of all by their own curiosity and their desire to be active mentally and physically, they are also motivated from without by materials, people, and group interaction.

Living things seldom fail to interest children. Farm animals, animals at the zoo, a pet, or an aquarium will arouse interest and questions, stimulate curiosity, and generate ideas.

Experiments of all kinds fascinate them.

Field trips give them the feeling of being explorers and discoverers, clarify and enrich their concepts, and make them want to know more. Selected radio and television programs can be used to stimulate their interest in current events, and to enlarge their world, even into outer space.

Children's relationships with one another and with their parents, teachers, and other adults may be a strong motivating force. Members of the community who have traveled or who are experts in certain fields can share their experiences with children in the classroom or assembly period, or individually in after-school clubs.

In a group, gifted children can learn to co-operate with others. They should not always be allowed to lead. While recognizing and appreciating excellence, the teacher should not glorify the achievements of the gifted at the expense of other pupils. With older elementary children, the group process is an especially dynamic force. They are carried along by a common experience—saluting the flag, singing a favorite song, doing a folk dance together. They are motivated to work hard on their respective parts of a jointly planned project. They catch ideas and enthusiasm from friends; as a result of responsibilities assigned to them by the group, they often reveal previously undiscovered abilities.

These desirable results are usually not attained if either the school's atmosphere or the child's attitude is highly competitive. Then the child tends to become angry, depressed, jealous, or resentful when he cannot be first. He needs to learn that one cannot always be tops, and that there is much satisfaction in the learning experience itself.

3 Special Projects

Gifted children continually show interest in special topics and projects. They should be free to work on projects of their own choice when they have finished their required work. The alert teacher shares the child's interest and tries to make way for it in the daily activities of the classroom. In thinking back over their school days, gifted children often mention projects of this sort as high lights in their educational experience. The following are only a few examples of intensive studies and creative activities carried on by gifted children either independently or in a group:

Making a map of the trees on the school grounds and a booklet describing them.

Making reports to the class on some special topic—dinosaurs, road-building, care of pets, space travel.

Preparing special programs for the class, for assembly periods, or for parent groups. These may involve creative writing, art, music, dancing, handwork, and research in the interests of authenticity.

Performing school and community services such as preparing publicity for a Red Cross drive, painting a mural for the school corridor, making a study of local history or of regional conservation, finding ways to sell surplus farm products.

Editing, printing, or contributing to a class or school newspaper or magazine; preparing a column for the local newspaper on sports or other school events; publishing original short stories and poems written by the class.

Amplifying certain classroom experiences, as, for example, making an intensive study of certain personalities in history; setting up original experiments in science; getting detailed information on the nursing profession for a health class.

One third-grade teacher provided special opportunities for a very bright but frightened little boy who was keenly interested in science. She was concerned about his all-round development as well as about his special interest.

When John brought in special science equipment, the teacher got the science instructor to help John demonstrate it to the class. She also obtained the co-operation of the fifth-grade teacher; John went to her class to help her pupils when they were studying certain topics in science.

The librarian helped John find scientific books that he could read, and permitted him to come to the library when the regular classroom frightened or bored him.

The teacher spent many hours gaining information so that she could answer John's questions. She also helped him to learn to play games, and encouraged the other children to turn to John for help.

In her personal relation with him, she made him feel that she was his trusted friend. One day he said, "If you sit by me, I think I won't be afraid any more." One day the class as a whole had a discussion about things they were afraid of. Thus John had a chance to bring his fears out in the open, and to discover that he was not the only frightened person in the world.

General Principles

The teacher should be guided by the following principles in making provision for gifted children:

They should be encouraged to suggest projects, recreational and creative as well as educational, and should be given initiative to explore their interests.

They should have a chance to do things for others.

They should be helped to acquire higher-level skills in the language arts and in arithmetic.

They should seldom be allowed to engage in superficial discussion of topics that are beyond their knowledge and experience.

They should learn to apply themselves to difficult tasks, and not give up when they do not get results as soon as they expected. They should be encouraged to participate sometimes in activities in which they do not excel.

Until a child wants to know, he cannot be taught. There are two basic appeals: self-realization and service to humanity. Children are intrinsically motivated; they enjoy intellectual activity just as much as physical activity. There's nothing that they hate more than doing nothing. "Joy of doing is one aspect of self-realization."

When we speak about "accepting a child as he is" this does not mean that we are to give him the impression that "anything goes." A child may accept himself as he is, but still wish to overcome some of his faults. He accepts them in the sense of facing them without undue discouragement or loss of self-esteem.

GUIDANCE OF THE SCHOOL CHILD

One very bright eleven-year-old boy expressed a rather common attitude toward guidance by adults—as he understood it:

"No one has ever really helped me. I like to be alone and to correct my own mistakes. I also like to study by myself."

This point of view may have sprung from a variety of sources: a strong drive to be independent, a hostility toward adults, experiences of ineffectual guidance, or a misconception of guidance.

In the elementary school most guidance is indirect; it is guidance in the children's ongoing activities. The children are hardly aware of it. The teacher guides as he teaches. He gains understanding of individual children while teaching them. It is his role to present to the child experiences that seem suitable, note the child's response, and infer what is going on in the child's mind. A big order! And only imperfectly carried out, of course. But many gifted children are first identified by teachers. With special training, teachers can identify most of the gifted children in their classes; without such preparation, they may identify only about 40 per cent.

A teacher with the guidance point of view described her extraordinarily sensitive work with children as follows:

"I have been teaching the elementary grades for five years, and have found teaching little children not only the most satisfying occupation one can have, but the most amusing as well.

"During the first year of my teaching, the problems of my youngsters became my problems. . . .

"As I gained experience in teaching, I consistently spent more of the school day giving the youngsters individual help, and far less time giving mass explanations with book and blackboard.

"To satisfy my sincere desire to understand my pupils, I began to visit their homes, informally chatting with the parents about all kinds of things. I could sense tensions from economic conditions and, most of all, from what the parent expected of the child. In my most trying cases, I found parental expectations far above the ability of the child.

"As I found out more about each child, I began to keep records, in order to remember all the details on each one. My record book consisted of several pages of dated observations for each child in my class and notes on the home visits. I jotted down his health report in one corner, important facts about the family in the other, and noted his level of reading.

"I could tell if my teaching was getting across by the responsiveness of the children. . . .

"I know that I, personally, cannot learn unless the desire comes from within me. So I tried to teach positively and to make each child feel important—that he had a particular contribution to make to the class. And so I praised every effort which I knew was *their* best.

"At the end of the year, parents came to me telling me of the remarkable changes in their children. What those parents did not see was the remarkable change in *them*, too. They were happier with their children because the children had apparently got along well at school for the first time. Some of them were just beginning to see what a wonderful thing a child is—and how much understanding and love he needs to grow."

And this teacher ended her description with the statement: "I did not know then that this was *guidance*."

This is the kind of sensitive, continuous developmental guidance that all parents would be pleased to have for their gifted children. This teacher did not single out any child for special attention, but met the needs of all in the ongoing activities of her class.

Some technical case studies, reported by Crowder and Gallagher [7] give a more detailed description of the complex interaction of the child's personality, his home conditions, and the adjustments made in the school.

The goal of guidance is to foster ever-increasing self-understanding on the part of the child—understanding of what he can do well, what he might learn to do, what his limitations are, and the kind of person he is becoming. With this understanding, the child comes to take more and more responsibility for what he is, what he does, and what he becomes.

In many school systems there is a special guidance co-ordinator or director of guidance; sometimes there is a counselor in the large elementary school. His or her duties are (1) to help teachers understand their pupils and guide them as they teach, (2) to confer with the principal, other administrators, and various committees about ways of making school conditions more conducive to child development, (3) to have interviews with pupils and parents, and (4) to meet with groups of parents, speak at community meetings, and make contact with guidance agencies outside the school.

You may request an interview with the guidance worker to talk over any aspect of your child's development. The skillful guidance worker, by promoting mutual understanding between child and parents, may help them to reconcile any discrepancies between the parents' hopes and the pupil's own goals and potentialities.

Guidance workers should provide both teachers and parents with information about children of exceptional ability, and bring to their attention the opportunities that are available to such children. Guidance workers may outline special programs, or make plans for special classes or clubs. However, the responsibility for decisions and choices rests upon the parents, and upon the children themselves as they grow increasingly capable of self-appraisal and self-direction.

Questions and Answers

1. *When is a child ready to enter the first grade?*

Misinterpretation of "readiness" has led some parents to overprotect their children. If the mother is anxious and uncertain about the child's entrance to school, she may convey these feelings to the child. Even though leaving home may be difficult for a young child, he will grow through overcoming obstacles. Usually, gifted children are eager to go to school. Reluctance to go may arise not so much from a fear of school, as from a too intense and confusing attachment to home and mother.

A child's readiness for school, as Anton Brenner [8] pointed out, is not a matter of chronological age or physical size; of ability to count or read and write his name; or even of verbal facility, intelligence, or sociability—though all these traits are important. His readiness for school involves his total development in terms of the forces in his present and future environment—family, neighborhood, church, teacher, classmates, and the school atmosphere. He has certain needs that must be satisfied before learning can take place.

If a child seems physically, socially, emotionally, and intellectually ready for first grade at an age earlier than that specified by the board of education, it may be possible to enroll him in kindergarten; if he soon demonstrates his ability to profit by more formal instruction, it may then be possible to promote him to the first grade.

2. *What preparatory experiences lead happily to the child's first day in school?*

The following suggestions were made by Robert W. Eaves in the *N.E.A. Journal* for April, 1959:

The child should:

Be read to from the very early years.

Have his own library of familiar picture and storybooks.

Do regular chores such as watering plants, taking care of pets, feeding the chickens, helping at mealtime.

Learn to use the toilet properly, wash his hands, tie his shoes, manage buttons, zippers, and overshoes.

Be accustomed to talk with his parents at mealtime.

Be told truthfully about school, about some of its difficulties as well as its pleasures.

Play and share with other children.

Be able to state his own name, address, and telephone number.

Learn the route to school and be familiar with safety rules.

Have what he needs the first day—including such things as a smock for painting and other articles requested by the school.

Go to bed early the night before so that he gets about twelve hours sleep and does not have to hurry through breakfast or be late to school.

Come to school the first day with some of his friends rather than with his mother.[9]

3. *How much of a child's homework is the parents' business? Should they encourage, nag, enforce, or mind their own business?*

It is the parents' business to be interested and to care, but not to nag; to give the child as much privacy and quiet as possible; to encourage him to work hard on his special interests; to see that he does not avoid everything that is difficult or initially uninteresting to him. Homework can be a bond between parent and child, instead of a battleground.

4. *"My seven-year-old child doesn't seem to take to reading. What can I do about it?"*

A most attractive booklet written by Henry Bissex and printed for the Essie Olive Abeel Private School, Inc., 293 Lookout Avenue, Hackensack, New Jersey, gives the following concise and precise answer to this question:

"1. Read yourself.

2. Read to him.

3. Have him read to you. . . . .

1. By seeing you read he will learn that reading is natural and satisfying to others . . . and that reading is important . . . not just a medicine for children. When was the last time you brought a load of books home from the library?

2. By hearing you read he will learn the form of his language and he will learn the excitement of having words tell him what happened next. Do you read to your child only to put him to sleep at night?

3. By reading to you he will practice the flow of language that your reading first revealed. Then he will be on his own with the best companions of all time." [10]

5. *"What can I do to further my child's reading interests?"*

From the earliest years parents should read aloud to children. This is an intimate contact, a shared experience, that is not obtainable through television or radio.

As the child comes to be "on his own in reading," the parents may make available a balanced collection of books, in the hope that the child will pick them up and read. The parents can call attention to new titles, and read especially exciting, amusing, or otherwise appealing episodes or chapters to arouse the child's desire to continue. At mealtime, they can give the child opportunity to share his reading experiences with the family group. If the child wants to communicate a reading experience by means of drawing or dramatization, the parents can encourage these creative responses to literature. They may also help the child to relate books to films, television and radio programs, and children's theater productions.

6. *How can a parent control a rebellious, obstreperous gifted child?*

Gifted children must learn to face up to their responsibilities. It is better to punish a child justly than to neglect him. Some bright children may interpret extreme permissiveness as indifference.

The parent who releases some of his tension by spanking a child may be easier to live with than one who keeps all his annoyance bottled up. Children have to learn that an adult's patience can reach the breaking point. Some children would rather be spanked than have their parents nagging at them all the time.

When a child steadfastly refuses to listen to reason and comply with the wishes of the group, spanking is the last resort. In a home where everyone has rights as well as responsibilities, corporal punishment will seldom be necessary. "But when it is, parents need not feel guilty."

However, a word should be said here about the emotionally disturbed child. Corporal punishment may intensify his problem and complicate it beyond all hope of solution.

7. *In a small mining community, there is the son of a miner whose chronological age is nine but who appears mentally to be somewhat above sixteen years. Special educational facilities for gifted children are unheard of in this area and we are completely at a loss as to how to plan the future education of this gifted child. What plans could be made commensurate with the boy's potentiality?*

Variations of this problem have been presented by many parents. Here are several possibilities:

It might be possible to interest his present teacher in making provision for one or more gifted children in her class. This chapter would give the interested teacher suggestions for providing experiences for this boy without making him feel conspicuous among the other children.

Another possibility that has been carried out in other communities is to select the most gifted children from several schools and organize a class for them in the most centrally located schools with a special teacher. Whether this were feasible or not would depend on the number of children and the distances involved.

Another recent development is to employ on the county- or district-wide basis a supervisor who is particularly qualified to work with gifted children. This person would go from school to school helping teachers to identify gifted children in their classes and giving them materials and suggestions that could be used in the regular classroom. This would benefit not only the gifted child; the other children in the class would profit from the special reports the gifted children gave on significant topics, the plays or songs they write, and so forth.

As to a special boarding school, the tuition would be high. Most of the good independent schools do have children whose IQ's range considerably above the average. This would be a more congenial intellectual environment, but it might present special problems of social adjustment for this particular gifted child.

Scholarships are offered in some good private schools.

Practice schools in some universities usually have many gifted children in their classes, and there is not the tuition problem in these schools that there is in the private school. It might be that the boy could board with a private family and attend a nearby university practice school where they charge little or no tuition.

FIVE

The Gifted Adolescent

BETWEEN infancy and adolescence individual differences increase. It is therefore especially difficult to describe "the typical adolescent." The following glimpses of several adolescents will highlight their differences; the next section will call attention to some of the traits that gifted adolescents are likely to have in common.

GLIMPSES OF GIFTED ADOLESCENTS

The first case exemplifies the moderately gifted adolescent.

A Well-Adjusted Gifted Child

Sally is attractive in personal appearance, comes from a comfortable home, and displays an extensive vocabulary. On high-school personality rating sheets her teachers rated her high in industry, seriousness of purpose, initiative, influence, concern for others, responsibility, and emotional stability. Her social studies teachers added this note: "Excellent in every way"; the algebra teacher commented, "Outstanding in all phases." The dean of girls of her junior high school made this comment: "Does excellent work, is well liked and happy, so presents few problems." The speech teacher noted that Sally was "most expressive in choral speaking and reading poetry. She should be encouraged along these lines." Another teacher called attention to the fact that Sally "has high personal standards and is sympathetic and generous to others." Like many other gifted children, Sally has always appealed strongly to her teachers.

At the time when she was beginning the third grade, it was proposed that she be skipped to the fourth; however, it was decided to keep her where she was because she seemed very happy and had many outside activities.

In the health class in the tenth grade Sally was a superior discussion leader; she did not monopolize the class, but listened with interest to the other students.

She thinks more deeply than the average child in her grade, organizes her thoughts well, and has a fine command of sentence structure, diction, and vocabulary. She makes mature comments and cites examples to illustrate her points. In giving a book report she explained a difficult book so well that all the class were interested.

Apparently Sally is making the best use of her ability and has made a special effort to establish friendly relations with her classmates. Mental ability snowballs; it adds to itself as the individual makes the most of his or her environment.

A Creative Thinker

In contrast to this gifted girl who is so energetic and quick and busy in so many ways, Bert seems somewhat dreamy. However, when he gets into action, he is a compelling speaker and forceful writer. He exemplifies the type of person who seems to absorb knowledge effortlessly. His writings reveal considerable depth of thought, plus an ability to relate what he has learned to practical living. For example, he reported on a book by Harold Lamb in a "broad context" assignment in English. His report described the formation of Genghis Khan's empire, and likened it to present-day Soviet Russia. He presented this report as an adjunct to the study of world history. It was his contention that world history as taught is not world history at all but the history of European peoples. Therefore, to get a well-rounded picture one needs to pay more attention to Asian developments such as the empire which was the subject of his report. Bert's report, which was more than a book review, was superbly organized and interestingly presented.

This is an example of what a truly gifted child can do when he has access to stimulating material. Gifted students like Bert are happiest when they are being creative, and when they can make known the results of their creativity.

"Science Is My Hobby"

Ted, who is almost twelve years old, is two years younger than the other members of his class. His IQ is 143. His sandy hair is usually uncombed and he ordinarily wears khaki trousers and a flannel shirt. He moves quickly, almost impulsively. When the psychologist told him, along with two other gifted youngsters, that she would like to take some tests, all three in unison said, "Tests? Hurray!" In the course of an animated discussion after one test, the examiner remarked that she guessed they all enjoyed math tests. Ted replied, "Sure, you can enjoy anything."

Ted's science teacher made the following comments about this gifted boy:

"I have Ted working on special projects. He does the regular work, too, but spends about ten days on what takes other children four to five weeks. I use him as a resource person in his science class. He's just way ahead of everybody. For instance, I was giving the class a test the other day. Of course, Ted had finished all that work a month ago, but I couldn't let him go over and work on his project because that would make too much noise. So I thought, 'I'll keep him busy.' I gave him a physics book and asked him to find out how far a body would fall in one-tenth of a second. Ten minutes later he came up with the answer and it was right. I know fellows in college who couldn't do that. I tell you that kid's terrific—he even likes gym! [The science teacher apparently took a dim view of gym.]

"He's constructing an apparatus to be entered in the state-wide Science Fair. I just suggested the problem and he took it from there. Of course his father, who's an expert in electronics, helped him work out the practical parts, but the idea was Ted's."

His English and social studies teacher says he does his work, but never volunteers in class. "His handwriting is terrible and his papers are sloppy. He reads well, but I can't get him to read anything but science. Of course, he reads the assignments in my class, but that does not use up all the time he should give to reading for English." [The English teacher apparently takes a dim view of nonconformists and also of students who do not spend what she considers a full measure of their preparation time on English.]

The physical education teacher commented: "I was worried when they skipped him a grade, and wondered how the other fellows would react to him. I was prepared for the worst, but they all accepted him and seemed to want to help him. He's sort of big and clumsy, but he's not afraid of getting hurt. He's right there on the mats, tumbling with the rest of them."

Ted's preoccupation with science probably springs from a combination of sources: the current interest in science and science projects, his identification with his science teacher and with his father who is a scientist, and his own special ability in this field. Since his interest seems to be genuinely absorbing, and since he does complete the minimum requirements in his other subjects, the science teacher is wise to encourage his wholehearted efforts. It is good for a youngster to have the experience of devoting himself unstintingly to a purpose in which he is, at the moment at least, keenly interested.

Unfulfilled Promise

Two highly gifted individuals were described by Miriam Pritchard:[1]

> Both came from homes that were low in the economic scale. One was a broken home, and the other a home in which there was a great deal of parental disharmony. In the elementary school, the teachers recognized that both of these children had serious problems of adjustment and tried to help them. But by the time the child from the broken home was fifteen, he had come into conflict with the law. One completed high school; the other did not. Both are married; both express dissatisfaction with their vocations and are looking for a chance to "get rich quick." Their superior potential ability, combined with a grudge against society, makes them a threat to society.

These two youths have little in common with most of the gifted children reported in Terman's study; for more than thirty years the vast majority have used their intellectual ability in socially useful ways.

CHARACTERISTICS OF GIFTED ADOLESCENTS

In our country we are too much concerned about the immaturity of our adolescents. In an article entitled, "Manifestations of Maturity in Adolescents," the author said:

> "Being so concerned with their faults and lapses into childish behavior, we forget that a large number of teen-agers are more intelligent, more capable of making and carrying out plans, and more emotionally mature than some of their parents and teachers."[2]

Let us see what the adolescent has to build on. As an infant he should have acquired a basic sense of trust in himself, in other people, and in life itself. As a preschool child he should have attained a nice balance between independence and essential dependency. During his elementary-school years he should have achieved a certain amount of socialization without loss of individuality. His main task during adolescence, as Erikson has pointed out, is to attain a sense of personal identity—to be able to answer the question, "Who are you?" He should also begin to take more responsibility for what he becomes.

He has a right to be different. As one gifted adolescent said, "We are different and why not accept it." Another youngster said:

"You want to maintain your own individuality, but at the same time you don't want to be too different from others. I think a person can find ways to be a part of the group and still be unique in his own way."

Another adolescent expressed her desire to achieve individuality in these words:

"I do not want to be just one of the bunch. I want to stand out, not be like everybody else. It's as if I wanted to be the center of attraction, but I just want to be different."[3]

Gifted adolescents usually face the adolescent tasks of growing up a little earlier than the average teenager. This applies especially to the areas of religion and philosophy of life. Friendships formed during late adolescence often last a lifetime; boy-girl relations established in the teens frequently lead to marriage. Educational plans made during these years channel the course of future educational and vocational development. To establish themselves successfully among persons of their age group, teenagers need to feel that they are not too closely tied to their families.

Physical Development

Gifted children in general mature earlier than the average. Terman found that 100 per cent of the fourteen-year-old boys included in his study had matured (were postpubescent); 48 per cent of the thirteen-year-old girls had reached their first menstruation. Both boys and girls showed advanced physical development and superior health, as they had done from their earliest years.

This does not mean that gifted adolescents are necessarily free from worry about physical appearance. Some think that they are too short or too tall, too fat or too thin. Some are worried about acne and oily hair. Even a disheveled appearance, when such an appearance is in vogue, requires attention if one is to get just the right effect.

The way an adolescent views himself is more important than the way he looks to us. His self-image is not necessarily the one he sees in the mirror; it is a complex entity built from the responses and expectations of people who are important to him. Parents sometimes overdo their efforts to prevent a teenager from becoming vain or over-conscious of his physical appearance; they sometimes forget that he needs sincere compliments and genuine approval.

School Achievement and Reading

Though Terman found that his gifted group were superior in school achievement, many gifted adolescents show an apparent lack of motivation that worries their parents.

This is a complicated problem that can be traced back to child-rearing practices in the first years of life and to later home influences. According to Nicholas Hobbs, bright, high-achieving adolescents, as a group, come from homes that are culturally more stimulating than the homes of bright, low-achieving adolescents. In the homes of the high achievers there is more sharing of ideas, more family group activity, and more definite planning for the development of members of the family.

The adolescent's motivation for high achievement is also affected by the values and goals that are being insidiously set for American youth by advertisers, movie stars, and television and radio programs. When the adolescent is besieged on all sides by appeals to the pleasure motive, and is urged to accept the easy way of effortless entertainment, is it any wonder that he should slacken his effort to reach high standards of achievement? The remarkable thing is that so many gifted adolescents *are* interested in scholarship and *do* want to use their imagination and intelligence to the full, despite the tenor of the times.

However, many parents attribute low achievement entirely to the school's failure to challenge the gifted child. We are not denying that the school must bear some share of the blame. Some teachers and administrators have been too much concerned with making things easy for students.

All roads should not be made smooth for the gifted, nor all rough places plain. Many gifted adults worked their way through college, developed habits of thrift and hard work, and learned to do what they did not feel like doing. In the case of many of our academically talented young people who do not go to college, or who do not graduate, poverty is not the limiting factor. These young people have simply not learned to enjoy learning; school has not brought them keen satisfaction. But "eagerness to overcome difficulties and readiness to work hard," as Garry Myers has said, are learned at home as well as at school.

With older children, the ability to think critically may be fairly generalized; they may have acquired the habit of considering all sorts of problems and issues in a thoughtful way. But skill in applying methods of logical inquiry and reasoning is more specific; it depends upon possession of knowledge about the particular field.

The reading interests of adolescents are affected by their adolescent problems or developmental tasks. In their eagerness to gain status in the peer group, they turn to books to find out how to be popular and what is "the thing to do" in social situations. Their interest in the opposite sex leads them to books on how to make oneself more attractive and how to handle boy-girl relations. Most of all, they want books about teenagers like themselves that deal with family relations, friendship, love and marriage, and problems of vocational choice. They want stories that are true to life and that express genuine emotion. In their own words, they have expressed preferences for:

"True stories about young people and the world we live in."
"Articles on how to develop your personality."
"Books that deal with your own problems."
"Something that's always moving and adventurous."
"Books in which the people are real and things that happen to them can really happen."

Adolescents have suggested the following titles for books they would like to read:

"Teenagers of Today and Tomorrow."
"Teenage Troubles."
"Now I Am Seventeen."
"From Pigtails to Pincurls."
"On Your Own."
"Beyond Tomorrow."

Older adolescents want books that help to clarify the meaning of "life, liberty and the pursuit of happiness."

As to style, they prefer one that is simple, free, and easy—"written in words that everyone can understand. A person can hardly enjoy something he doesn't understand." (Of course, gifted adolescents can take fairly difficult words in their stride.) They add these further notes about style:

"Vivid narrative—you feel you were right there with the character and living his life."

Brevity appeals to them—other things being equal: "The author should not go all around Robin Hood's barn to put across a point."

"He should tell a story in a straightforward manner; present the idea and let you judge for yourself."

The gifted share the general desire for "plenty of humor; plenty of action."

They are also capable of understanding a deeper interpretation of literature—looking beneath the surface action to the symbolism it implies.

Books may also have value for personality and character development. Paul Witty[4] suggested certain books that may help to build a worthy self-ideal. He mentioned stories such as Marguerite De Angeli's *Door in the Wall,* a story of a seventeenth-century boy, son of a nobleman, who overcame an affliction; Eleanor Estes' *The Hundred Dresses,* which shows how one girl achieved status in her group; and *Amos Fortune, Free Man,* the story of a boy's triumph over misfortune and his concern for the unfortunate. More recently published are such books as Althea Gibson's *I Wanted To Be Somebody,* which emphasizes the importance of individual effort, and makes a strong case for the recognition of individual worth regardless of race, creed, or home background.

Gifted children and young people are often clearly aware of the personal values of reading—for enjoyment, for building vocabulary, for broadening interests, for gaining information, and most important of all, for understanding themselves and other persons. As one high-school boy said:

"In reading *Silas Marner*, you get an idea of what the life of a miser is like and how he feels. In reading Dickens, you gain understanding of how a poor person lived in his times. From other books you learn what is involved in making a decision, and how to handle certain kinds of situa-ations. You make applications to yourself: 'Am I doing this with *my* life? How can *I* make myself a better person?'"

This active, thoughtful approach is quite different from mere "day-dreaming with a book." As Donald Durrell said, "Reading should be a way to enrich living, not simply a way to escape and endure living."

Summer reading is especially important for teenagers whose volun-tary reading during the school year has been crowded out by other activities and academic requirements. Some reluctant readers—and there are a few among the gifted—will pick up a book that happens to be lying around. You can see to it that some of the books you bring home suit the youngster's interest, reading ability, and needs.

Other adolescents welcome your personal recommendations of books you think they should read. More and more children and young people are joining book clubs and building up their own libraries. They sometimes say it is easier to buy a paperback at the corner store, where some paperbacks of high quality are sold, than to go to the library. Others frequent the library, which for some city youngsters is a cool oasis among hot, crowded streets and apartments. If summer reading is required by the school, youngsters may express some resistance; however, they may admit to being interested once they get started on their reading program.

Relations with Peers

Although gifted youngsters generally mature earlier than the average, they show wide individual differences in this respect. Girls mature earlier than boys. Some girls become interested in boys several years earlier than others. The late-maturing girl has special problems of boy-girl relations. One of these youngsters described her feelings at a boy-girl party:

"After lunch, we started dancing and everything went perfect until the hostess (whom I don't admire much) announced that we were going to play kissing games. I had never played them and I didn't want to start now. But instead of being a party pooper and sitting out I played post office, but my number wasn't called.

"After that they played a necking game. This one I sat out.

"Thank goodness, right after that it was time to go home.

"The next morning my parents asked me how the party was. It was my father whom I told about the games because I felt, since he was a man, he would know more about boys than my mother. He explained all about boys and girls of my age and why it was better to wait until I was older to start getting interested in boys. I agreed with him and, although I *like* boys to a certain extent, I feel it's better to wait until I am older before I get really interested."

Friends are very important to teenagers. They become alarmed at the prospect of losing friends, or of not making friends in the first place. When an adolescent has a problem, a real chum is often more helpful to him than his parents can be. One thirteen-year-old girl described this situation:

"I'm shy. People don't think I am because I act happy and am talkative. But really underneath I'm scared to death that I'll say something wrong and no one will like me.

"I went to Nancy, a friend, for help. Nancy was shy, too, so I felt she could help me more than anyone else. We talked it over and decided that I should get into activities with others and that she would help me to be more at ease.

"Things are working out pretty good, but Nancy told me some of the girls don't ask me places because they think I'm too cute and might steal their boy friends."

Another girl said, "When I have a real problem I cannot talk it over with my mother or father. But I can talk it over with my girl friend or her mother."

Some gifted teenagers have difficulty in establishng good relations with their classmates. A small group of gifted youngsters gave the following sound suggestions on this matter; parents might pass these on to their children:

"The way to be modest is to remember there is always someone who knows a great deal more than you do."

"You don't expect the other kids to like you if you go around bragging that you got 90 in math, while someone else only got 65. Instead you can show your relative ignorance in another subject. I'm sure everybody is not an expert in everything."

"The best way to make friends is to help other people feel good about themselves. You can play up their virtues or whatever they know most about. You can let them have the best assignment and take the toughest for yourself."

"It's a good idea to befriend and associate with those who resent your ability and achievement. I know a boy who some time ago didn't like me at all at first, but then I started talking to him and we got to be very good friends. Some people who consider you a 'brain' don't really know the other side of you until you give them a chance to be friendly."

"Often you make friends through your interests and hobbies."

"Sometimes you can help other students in their studies. It's not just getting their homework done that's important to them; it's having a friend."

Sometimes the parents of a gifted youngster make it hard for him to get along with his age group. One teenager said:

"Sometimes you are modest and show appreciation of the others in your group, but your parents go around bragging about you. Everything the parent says may be true, but you still feel very embarrassed. It's a real problem."

3 *Initiative and Responsibility*

When asked, "Does a person have any responsibility for his gifts?" bright youngsters will usually agree that he has. One high-school boy put it this way:

"I think the gifted child's first debt is to himself. He should know himself and who he is. I definitely feel that he does have responsibility for not letting his ability go to waste, and for making use of it. I guess everyone owes a debt to society no matter how 'ungifted' he may be. If you're gifted, you should realize this quicker and do something about it. Some who have ability are not aware of it. If they discover themselves and get a little push, they'll take a step forward."

Emotional Development

It surprises us when we find out that a gifted youngster feels inferior. Yet inferiority is a common feeling among the gifted. The great majority of the students in one of our best colleges expressed feelings of inferiority; their performance fell short—or they feared it would fall short—of their level of aspiration and their parents' expectations.

Inferiority feelings may arise from a very strong reluctance to assert oneself or to take a prominent place. They may be occasioned by comparing one's own achievement with that of the great persons whose biographies he has read. One may give undue weight to some physical handicap, or to inability to work with his hands or to participate in certain sports as well as others. Sometimes a gifted child believes he has only average ability, and never exerts himself to do well in school.

The adolescent's emotional development depends a great deal on his previous experiences. Adolescence is a good time for making desirable changes in personality patterns; its very instability represents an opportunity to sort out childish ways of feeling and behaving.

Search for Spiritual Values

During his adolescent years, the young person's idealism may find outlets in church activities and in making vocational choices. Moral issues may concern him intensely.[5]

Gifted children tend to develop a philosophy of life earlier than the average. They need help in seeing themselves as they are and the world as it is. In this world, they should face the fact that there is no life without some frustration and pain. They cannot avoid pain and disappointment. But they can learn to be aware of their moments of happiness as well as their moments of pain. In their anonymous compositions many adolescents reveal a deep religious feeling. "I think of God," one said, "as my very best friend." Another mentioned the value of Bible reading and added, "The Bible has helped to stabilize my thoughts—" a very important counterbalance to adolescent periods of moodiness.

The search for identity is well illustrated by the effort of one gifted boy to describe the kind of person he thinks he is, the kind of person others think he is, and the kind of person he would like to be. His IQ on one test was 145; on another test, taken four years later, he scored higher than 93 per cent of persons his age. His achievement test scores were two or more years above the grade in which he was placed. He has been on the school honor roll each term, and was cited for outstanding leadership and co-operation. He participates actively in his church. He is very sensitive to poetry, and to literature in general. He is trying to reach philosophical conclusions of his own.

In response to the question "What kind of person do you think you are?" he stated:

"I think I am the kind of person which everybody could like, however I am very selective about who I choose to be a friend.

"I am a person who dislikes anybody who pretends to be something that they are not, somebody who tries to be cute, immature, or overly mature.

"I'm lazy; I'd rather have anybody else do my work, and I can usually persuade somebody to do it.

"Most of the time I don't believe in God, however sometimes (when I'm in trouble) I do.

"I'm honest and can be trusted to keep a secret unless I don't believe in holding the secret that I have been told.

"I dislike egotists and try to avoid them as tactfully as I can.

"I wouldn't want to hurt *anyone* by what I say, so I manage to say very little until I know a lot about who I am talking to; this keeps everybody happy.

"I hate the very word 'hate' and don't believe in its existence. I don't see how anyone could hate anything.

"I like people who don't know what they are talking about because I can correct them. I think that there are very few people who actually think over what they are about to say in normal conversation.

"I dislike people who try to disprove God. I don't think that people have the right to put any questions like that in anyone else's mind.

"I dislike people who are dishonest or reveal what they have been entrusted to keep.

"I dislike people who will say or promise something and fail to follow up their promise."

His reply to the question "What kind of person do others think you are?" was as follows:

"As far as I know nobody knows about me because I dislike to talk about myself. Other people must think that I have potential because in school, in the Boy Scouts, and in church I have risen to leadership positions. Many people think that I work hard—probably because I did once. "People think that I'm honest and trust me with all sorts of secrets."

And in response to the question "What kind of person would you like to be?" he said:

"I'd like to stay just the way I am except for a few details. "I would like to have a belief in God. "I would like to enjoy working rather than watching."

It is significant that his dislikes predominate in his concept of himself. Despite his dislike of "hate," he seems to have a good deal of hostility toward people who do not measure up to his ideals and values. Perhaps this attitude is necessary in order to clear the way for building a positive philosophy of life.

CONDITIONS CONDUCIVE TO THE BEST DEVELOPMENT OF GIFTED ADOLESCENTS

Home, school, community, national, and world conditions all contribute to the development of children and young people. Adolescents need parents who understand and will listen, who will reinforce desirable behavior and set firm limits against behavior that might be harmful. They need a fairly well-balanced daily schedule that provides opportunities to follow up their special interests and hobbies intensively. In school, they need stimulating small-group work on projects, and opportunities to carry on independent work in the regular classroom, in the library, or in the laboratory. Special provision may also be made for exceptionally able students by means of extraclass activities that supplement the regular classes and give added opportunities for leadership. To develop altruism and social-mindedness, young people need to participate in school and com-

munity service projects, and in church organizations and other wholesome youth groups.

School Conditions

In written compositions, interviews, and panel discussions, gifted
high-school students have clearly and emphatically described school
conditions that they consider favorable or unfavorable. Here is a
summary of their advice to teachers:

Don't waste our time in school (1) by spending class time fussing
about discipline problems instead of applying problem-solving methods
to improve conduct; (2) by offering us dull books to read or asking us to
write on topics that have no meaning, use, or purpose for us; (3) by
giving us busy work to do instead of challenging assignments; or (4) by
reviewing and repeating facts we already know and drilling us on skills
we already possess.

Don't single us out and hold us up as examples, or give the class the
impression that we are "teacher's pets"; this makes us unpopular with our
classmates. Rejection by them may make us withdraw more into books
and prevent us from getting the social experience we need. Or it may drive
us to do only mediocre work, in order to avoid being different.

Don't let us drift into the habit of loafing through our classes.

Instead, give us opportunities (1) to take additional subjects in which
we are interested, (2) to engage in creative work such as the writing of
plays and the giving of marionette shows, (3) to learn to speak before
an audience, (4) to take part in discussions that move forward toward
their goal, (5) to apply principles and theories to life problems, (6) to
match wits with other gifted persons in special advanced subject classes
or discussion groups, (7) to learn the most efficient reading and study
methods, (8) to study one thing intensively. (These students frequently
mentioned projects that they had carried out; many said that they enjoyed
most the things on which they had worked the hardest. They also enjoy
having free use of the library; they expressed a wish for more library
sessions as a part of the regular school day.)

Give us bright, interested teachers for bright, interested students—
teachers who know their subject, allow time for discussion, use diversified
methods of teaching, and have a flexible plan with occasional surprises.

Some parents are disturbed when their child comes home from
high school and tells them that he is not taking as many separate

subjects as they did. He may be covering several related subjects in one class, staying with one teacher for two or sometimes three periods. This kind of program—called the *broad-fields curriculum,* or sometimes the *core curriculum*—relates one subject closely to another, and thus prevents duplication and repetition. Every student is encouraged to read widely and purposefully and to present his findings effectively to the group. It is obvious that the teacher must have adequate knowledge of all the fields with which he deals, and must stimulate each student to do intensive work on the topics and problems; otherwise there is danger of superficiality and overemphasis on social skills to the detriment of intellectual achievement. When taught skillfully, this type of program is especially effective with gifted students.

2. *Home Conditions*

Your attitude toward your teenager and your expectations of him have a great deal to do with the way he thinks and acts. Suspicion corrodes the parent-child relationship. So does thinking of adolescents as "crazy mixed-up kids" or as "potential juvenile delinquents."

The role of the parent is to facilitate positive growth. This often involves making rules and regulations and enforcing standards of behavior. Gifted children can understand this; they realize that discipline is an expression of the parents' concern and affection, rather than an indication of annoyance or the desire to dominate. Like George in Thornton Wilder's play *Our Town,* they are glad to have a "person who's fond of you, too—at least enough to be interested in your character. . . ."[6]

The reasons why some teenagers do not more often confide in their parents are clearly expressed by a thirteen-year-old girl:

"Many teenagers often carry their problems alone without seeking advice from parents or teachers. This may be due to the fact that a teenager feels his parents and teachers do not really understand his or her problems and their advice would be completely useless. Another factor may be fear that disciplinary actions might be taken against them. Then too parents often offer help when it is not wanted. As a result the student feels that the teachers and parents are intruding upon his privacy.

"If parents and teachers really made an increased effort to understand the youth of today they would build up an atmosphere where a boy or girl felt he could really receive good advice. There would be less tension between the adult and the child."

A boy wrote rather wistfully, "When I have a problem, I would like to go to my father, but I am afraid he will not understand me."

Other youngsters attributed their parents' lack of helpfulness to the fact that they had busy lives:

"My parents work and consequently are both tired when they get home. They would like to relax when I need help on my homework."

In case teachers fail to do so, parents can provide challenging reading experiences for bright students such as those described by Phyllis Bland of Evanston Township High School.[7] In their conversations with their youngsters, they can convey their own fascination with words, and can leave within easy reach books on interesting word origins such as Wilfred Funk's *Word Origins* and Margaret S. Arnet's *Picturesque Word Origins* and *More About Words*. They can point out to their youngsters examples of the way language continually changes—by the generalization of trade names such as "Frigidaire"; by the shortening of well-known words such as "polio" and "H-bomb"; and so on. In return, they might receive some instruction in teenage slang!

Then, too, the conversation might occasionally focus (which incidentally is a word taken directly from the Latin word meaning "fireplace") on the deeper interpretation of certain words and figures of speech as you find them used in advertising or in books. Your high-school-age child might become interested in reading Catherine Mintier's *Words and What They Do to You*, Stuart Chase's *The Tyranny of Words*, or Thomas Cleveland's *Language Power for Youth*. Together you might explore the multiple meanings of certain words such as "capital": a form of letter, a center of government, something well done, money that can be invested, *et al.*

At home, as well as in school, a certain book may serve as a springboard for the discussion of life's deepest problems, about which the gifted adolescent may be as much concerned as you are. In discussing with your child a book you both have read, you can informally help to raise the level of his interpretation. Sometimes you may call his attention to an inaccuracy in his interpretation of the author's thought. Except in highly imaginative poetry, which invites varied interpretation, the reader should first understand what the author intended to say—what he is trying to communicate; then he may express his own opinions of the thought or the style.

Sometimes you may search together for the exact meaning of a word or phrase as used at a particular time and place and by a certain person in a given mood. It is fun, too, to analyze metaphors and other figures of speech—what the point of similarity is, and why the author used the metaphor. Gifted adolescents are also interested in the symbolism behind words, as, for example, the use of frost as a symbol of death in Edith Thomas' "Frost Tonight."

Discussion of characters and their development can be most rewarding. You may notice together the clues to character that are scattered through the story or poem. Physical appearance often suggests personality traits, and characters reveal themselves through actions, anecdotes, and dialogue. Such a discussion of fictional characters is more rewarding and often more interesting than the gossip about real people that is such a large part of many conversations.

Your purpose, of course, is defeated if these discussions degenerate into drudgery or even show an obvious attempt to teach. They should have a light touch. You should also bear constantly in mind that the same book may be read on different levels of appreciation: for relaxation and entertainment; for personal development through better understanding of people and the ways they solve life problems; for insight into literature as an art. The more technical aspects of style and function would normally be left to school instruction. However, conversation at home about books and characters often stimulates a youngster to acquire deeper insights and sharper interpretive skills.

In other subjects, too, parents may supplement school instruction in informal or casual ways. For example, if a youngster is struggling with a problem in social studies, the parent may raise such questions as these:

What sort of information do you need to study this problem?
Where can you get this information?
How can you skim to locate the information you need?
What is a good way to take notes?

How can you organize facts and opinions that have a bearing on the problem?

Gifted children are not necessarily free from reading problems. Most of them can profit by instruction in reading. They learn quickly, and readily adapt suggestions to their own needs.

Sometimes their reading difficulty stems from school conditions—a teacher who has aroused antagonism, an unsuitable program of studies, an excessive amount of unimaginative homework. For example, an attractive fourteen-year-old daughter of a man who was very able and prominent in public affairs was becoming nervous and unhappy about her schoolwork. Even though she usually stayed up until almost midnight, she could not complete her assignments. An analysis of her reading and study methods showed that there were many places where her efficiency could be increased. For example, for her book reviews she selected big, thick volumes and felt that she had to read every word. She was encouraged to consider the nature and purpose of book reviews, to appraise the nature of a book and determine the purpose for which she was reading it, and to evolve a reading technique that combined judicious skimming with intensive reading. Thus she was able to complete her outside reading in much less time. As her reading and study efficiency increased, she became more confident of her ability to do high-school work, and her worry diminished.

The gifted mother of a fifteen-year-old girl who had continual difficulty with reading showed unusual psychological insight in her ways of handling this problem:

"I have learned more about the nature of reading. I have come to realize its enormous complexities, and so perhaps to be more intelligent about what I expect from (1) my child and (2) her school.

"Using the developmental approach, I know better what to expect of her at this stage, and have some clues as to how to help her develop those abilities, and overcome some difficulties:

"I know that she needs materials on her *reading level*. I have tried to ascertain that level from listening to her read graded materials, observing her written work and spelling, and trying to synthesize my informal appraisal with what I know of her scores on standardized reading tests.

"I have supplied supplementary books and magazines on this level. (I have no control over the textbooks used in school, of course.) I also try to provide for *progression* by having available materials of high interest to her, a little more difficult than the easy material.

"It has been suggested that the *content* of materials might be incompatible with a child's self-concept, and so become a block to learning—not that it was dull, or hard, or unrelated to experience, but threatening. I'd like more information, if there is any, on this.

"Of great importance is the parents' attitude. Having learned that pressuring is not a help, but a hindrance, I am endeavoring *not* to pressure, but to try to understand my own feelings about her reading, and not to project my ambitions—or anxieties—on to her.

"I am trying also to broaden her experiences in every way possible—even movies and television are encouraged, and they *have* engendered reading interest—specifically, in *Johnny Tremaine* and *Oklahoma.*

"I read as many of her books as I can so that I can discuss *her* reading with her. I also discuss *mine* with her, as much as possible, and she is more interested, often, than I think she will be. We often discuss the newspaper and its content, too, and I point out to her articles in magazines which we think may interest her. She often goes from those to others we haven't pointed out. So her interests are broadening.

"Another helpful suggestion I obtained from my reading was to recognize that the child's 'don't-care' attitude is often a cover-up for a 'do-care-very-much' attitude, and to allow her this apparent attitude. I can now do this, whereas that attitude used to annoy me to death!

"I have improved my own study skills, and some of these I have been able to share with her. For example, I have learned to take notes more efficiently, and have explained to her how to do this on a limited scale. (The most important rule, of course, being don't do it as you go along, but go back later after you've read it and *know* what is important, also make them precise and brief.)

"I have introduced her to the SQ 3R method—not by name, but by procedure—survey, raise questions, read, review, recite—and although neither of us uses it as thoroughly as we should, we *do* use it, and it is enormously helpful.

"I have learned a great deal about how to read a book and have handed on as much of that as she is ready for. Perhaps best of all, I can offer her *clues* on how to read better and more easily in content areas: on difficult subjects, to read something simple and nontechnical first, then move on to the tougher material; to find and know *key words,* and to use different reading methods for different purposes. She is being taught these things at school, but they are not always clearly explained, and it is a great help to be able to show her how to *skim*, to use headings, picture clues, suggest various headings under which information on a subject may be found. I can help her with word analysis, especially with dividing words into syllables.

"And I am ever grateful for having learned that 'phonics' is not the end-all in learning to analyze words. (I had the feeling it was.)

"I do not have objective measures of her mental ability, but from observing her written work and her comprehension of material she reads and has read to her, I am sure she is able. Her school achievement tests indicate this also. However, I would like to get a measure of this ability, preferably with a non-reading IQ test, so that I would have an idea of her potential—and be better able to evaluate when she was reading up to capacity, and when she wasn't.

"Another insight I have gained concerns resistance. A certain amount of resistance is *normal* and is a healthy indication of a child's endeavors to maintain his integrity as a person, or to manage some degree of independence. When resistance is a factor in reading disability you must therefore as parent *or* teacher respect it. That is, you cannot overcome it by drills, exercises, or exhortations, but only by changing the child's attitude. Help him to see, by accepting him and letting him know you feel he is worth while, that this resistance is not necessary for integrity and independence. Somebody pointed out that every child has a specific attitude toward reading—for, against, or indifferent. If he is 'indifferent' you may be able to interest him by knowing his interests and offering something related to them, or to some specific need he has to read for a particular project, such as making something or following directions.

"This all boils down to the truism that all readers need to be motivated by interest and need; and they should be taught with methods and procedures closely related to those needs and interests. This is especially true for the retarded, and for them also the need to set goals, see concrete evidence of progress is particularly strong.

"On this point I want to say that an appreciation of the complexity of the problem has also led me to a real appreciation of *any* evidence of progress in my child and in myself. I used to say a polite "Oh, isn't that nice" when she made some small headway, like figuring out a word, or getting two more spelling words right. Now I know how hard these small successes may be, and I really appreciate the effort. Children, of course, can tell."

Many of the psychological insights shown by this mother in dealing with a reading problem could be profitably applied to other aspects of an adolescent's development.

If parents overemphasize getting along with people and being popular, the youngster may become too willing to conform to undesirable group pressure. It may be the most co-operative member of the gang who takes the gang's dare to steal or destroy property. The cagey delinquent urges the most agreeable of his companions to do the things that are most likely to get someone into trouble.

Supervision is necessary, of course, but it should be used in moderation. Adolescents are at a period when they want to be on their own, to get ahead on their own steam. Chauffeuring them and escorting them everywhere deprives them of their opportunities to do things for themselves. They want to contribute to adult life and participate in it. They want to "belong." What use, they think, is all this training for adult life if they cannot participate in it when they feel ready? However, many bright adolescents are relatively backward in emotional and social development; they may not be ready for the more sophisticated experiences that they desire.

In some communities gifted adolescents are caught in a whirlpool of irresponsible behavior. Accidents happen. Tragedies occur. All the beauty, vivacity, and brilliance of a young life may be snuffed out as a result of a single wild party. When a tragedy of this kind occurs in a community it has a sobering effect. People try to do something about it. Sometimes they work out a code of conduct. Such a code may also be developed as a preventive measure; it would include regulations such as the following:

Parties only on weekends.

Closing hours for parties: 9:30-10:30 for twelve- and thirteen-year-olds; 12:30 to 1:00 A.M. for high-school seniors.

Youngsters are to return home promptly after a school party—not go to another party.

No alcoholic beverages are to be available.

Outsiders are not to be admitted.

Disruptive behavior is to be dealt with firmly.

Supervision of home parties is required.

Young people are likely to live up to a code if they have had a share in making it. With their parents and teachers they should participate in thorough and frank discussions of each point. Agreements should be reached by parents, teachers, and youngsters working together. A great deal also depends on the attitude of the natural leaders and popular members of the adolescent group. This is where your socially gifted youngster wields important leadership; he can help to win acceptance for sound values and standards.

During adolescence, youngsters need parents who will stand by them through thick and thin.

"There is nothing more comforting to a worried and confused adolescent," one fourteen-year-old girl wrote, "than parents whom they feel they can go to freely and get aid on a problem good or bad—aid from parents who will understand. Truly the children I feel genuine pity for . . . are those who don't feel that they can confide in their parents."[3]

When children in the same family differ in ability, parents need to be particularly sensitive to the relationships among them. The less able child is often jealous of the bright child. It is very hard for him to handle this feeling. He may try to cope with the situation in various ways: He may be openly aggressive—may fight and quarrel with his brighter brother. He may be covertly aggressive, lying in wait to hurt him on the sly, sometimes in subtle ways as did the elder brother in Eugene O'Neill's powerful play, *Long Day's Journey into Night*. He may lose his own identity and initiative in a vain effort to be like his brother. Or he may feel it is hopeless to try to compete, and refuse to attempt anything in which the more able child excels.

The role of the parents is to accept differences in their children. This does not mean saying to the less able child, as one parent did, "These marks are good for you, Jerry, but we're not satisfied when John gets only average marks because he is capable of doing better." Imagine how this remark made Jerry feel! It was a blunt accusation of inferiority. This parent should have avoided comparing the two boys' marks, and should have discussed their report cards with them individually. By accentuating the positive, the parent can give recognition to the special abilities in each child. Both the able and the less able need to learn to acquire the socially approved virtues of tolerance, considerateness, and healthy self-regard untinged by either subservience or arrogance.

GUIDANCE OF GIFTED ADOLESCENTS

The guidance that gifted children want from their parents is described in the next chapter. The guidance you can expect from school counselors will be summarized here.

Counselors and teacher-counselors can first of all identify the high-school students who are gifted. They can then schedule an interview with the child and his parents. In this interview, they consider together such questions as these:

What kind of person is this student, and what kind of person can he become?

Are his educational plans appropriate?

Does he need financial assistance in getting the kind of education he should have? "Many young people," one boy said, "realize too late that they have ability. Consequently, they didn't buckle down to studying. They didn't realize until the last year of high school the importance of good marks, and then it's too late to win a scholarship."

What are his tentative vocational plans?

Does he feel a special responsibility to use his gifts?

Does he need help with any personal or social problems—for example, appreciating the good qualities of others and establishing friendly relations with all sorts of people?

As a basis for understanding your child, the counselor will have at hand the cumulative record of his development during his school years, together with his ratings on whatever standardized tests have been given. He should also have the recorded observations of the teachers in each school that the child has attended. In the interview, you and your child can verify, modify, or supplement this information. Together, you can try to see what all this information means with reference to the child's present program, both in school and outside of school, and for his future plans.

You may also expect the school counselor to confer with the teachers about your gifted child, and to suggest special provisions that they can make in their classrooms.

When your child is beginning to make plans for college—and this planning should start in the first year of high school, not in the senior year—the school counselor should furnish information about various colleges, about procedures of application, and about scholarships, if there is financial need. There should also be opportunity for the student to learn something about the world of work, to explore his vocational abilities and interests, to engage in tryout work experiences, and to plan ways of getting the preparation he needs to go ahead in an appropriate vocational field.

The counselor should know about new techniques for making special provisions for gifted adolescents; he may suggest that·administrators or curriculum committees adopt some of these. He should keep up to date with such developments as the following:

The high-school science program developed at Forest Hills, New York, High School by Paul F. Brandwein, in which after a year of general science able students can elect an honors program that includes science and mathematics each semester.

Early admission to college, sans high-school diploma—an educational experiment undertaken by the Fund for the Advancement of Education.

The School and College Study of Admission with Advanced Standing— a plan that allows superior high-school students to begin their work in college with advanced credit and thus complete the regular college course in three years.

The Portland, Oregon, study, with its emphasis on identification and the enrichment of the regular school program.

The Scholarship Camp for Gifted Boys in Lake Bluff, Illinois, which provides a home for dependent or neglected boys of exceptional intelligence and gives them a chance to develop their abilities.

Special high schools of music and art for those who are talented along these lines.

The choice of a vocation is often especially difficult for gifted children; there is such a wide range of vocations in which they could be successful. The following statement by a thirteen-year-old boy is quite characteristic:

"I am a boy who doesn't know what he wants to be when he grows up. I have thought about becoming an astronomer or a criminologist. Last year when I went traveling I met a professor of criminology. After talking to him I became very interested in criminology.

"But ever since I was about four years old I've been interested in astronomy. I have a reflecting telescope, a junior planetarium, and many pictures and newspaper clippings."

Boys are likely to begin thinking fairly early about what they are going to do; girls are more apt to be concerned with the kind of person they want to be. One thirteen-year-old girl wrote a typical statement:

"I would like to be a popular person. By popular I mean the type of person everyone likes and likes to be with. I would also like to be a generous person—not a 'stingy old maid.' I would like to lead a normal, healthy life, full of fun and enjoyment."

Personal contacts and tryout experiences play a large part in vocational choice. One boy wanted to be a surveyor because a popular camp director taught the Scouts

"to survey with a 'sextant,' you know those little telescopes that surveyors use. He taught us how to find a point and take a degree reading, how to pace and tape off the distance, and make a map. Ever since then I've wanted to be a surveyor when I grow up."

A girl of thirteen had become increasingly interested in art through her participation in an art club:

"In the fifth grade they formed an art club in school for children exceptionally talented in art. I was not one of the three or four children selected, but that did not bother me. A week later my teacher asked me if I liked art, and of course I answered yes. Before I knew it I was in the art club. I became very enthusiastic about art. I made decorations for the halls, posters for sales, and scenery for plays. This went on in both fifth and sixth grades. In fact, I was in the art room more than any place else. By this time I was positive I wanted to teach art when I grew up. My mother said that teaching art is a very limited field, also you don't meet many people other than your fellow teachers. But when I told her there was nothing else I really wanted to be, she said that although she thought there were many other occupations that might offer better opportunities, it was my future and I should do what seemed best after considering other possibilities."

So important a decision as choice of vocation should not be made on an inadequate or bizarre basis. Gifted young people should consider very systematically the various factors involved: their abilities and interests, the preparation required, the nature of the work, probable openings, opportunities for advancement, job satisfactions, and social usefulness. A vocation is a way of life, not just a way of making a living. It is an expression of the person's concept of himself.

No test or series of tests taken at any one time will give your child the final answer to the question, "What should my vocation be?" Tests may be helpful in answering certain questions such as, "Do I have the required level of ability?" and "Are my interests similar to those of people who have succeeded in this vocation?" However, the child will learn more by his own appraisals of the kind of person he wants to be, the interests he has developed, the values that are important to him, and the satisfactions or dissatisfactions he has found in his studies, his recreation, and his work experiences.

In this rapidly changing world the gifted child must have an appropriate educational program in order to be able, when the time comes, to specialize—to make a specific vocational choice. Failure to obtain advanced academic and professional education will limit his level of accomplishment and result in failure to make the maximum use of his talents.

QUESTIONS AND ANSWERS

1. *What can a parent do to help his gifted child who hopes to—and ought to—go to college?*

The following are a few pointers given by Nancy C. Wimmer in *The National Parent-Teacher* for September, 1957:

1. Help your child to develop the basic reading, listening, speaking, and writing skills.
2. Help him to develop effective study habits.
3. Encourage him to engage in various extraclass and out-of-school activities.
4. Help him to see the importance of doing well in his studies in the elementary school, and certainly in the high school.
5. From the beginning of high school help him to choose the courses he will need for college admission.
6. Begin to lay plans now for financing your child's college education. The average yearly cost at a residential college has been estimated at $1,600. Community and public junior colleges cost much less. Any estimate varies with the rising cost of living and with individual differences in colleges.

2. *Why do some children, apparently talented in music, fail to fulfill the promise they have shown?*

If the child is required to practice nothing but technical exercises, practicing may become drudgery. This kills his enjoyment and stifles his imagination. Learning to play by ear is fun for the child. As with learning to talk, it helps him to become a better sight reader. If we start our music teaching with ear-training, rhythmic exercises, and so forth, the child understands their purpose and will acquire a liking for music. Then practicing will be no problem.

3. *What real service activities are open to adolescents and what is their value?*

To combat self-centered individualism, service activities for teenagers are most effective. Social agencies need their help. Adult workers often catch youth's enthusiasm from these volunteers. For example, a girl may assist an art teacher or physical education teacher in a recreation center. Other teenagers are recruited and trained to help in hospitals and pharmacies as members of the Junior Red Cross. Their jobs are varied and interesting, once they have been analyzed by the agency. This is not busy work; these young volunteers are needed.

Such volunteer work helps the gifted adolescent to realize his social responsibility. He also sometimes finds himself in the work. Certainly he learns about the needs of others, about community agencies, and something about different kinds of work. Volunteer service gives gifted adolescents an opportunity to try themselves out, to convince themselves of their own worthiness, and to achieve recognition.

4. *When bright students can learn so fast, why don't they?*

The reasons are many and complex, such as rebellion against a parent's unreasonable insistence on excellence or, at the other extreme, acceptance of their standards of mediocrity. Their school achievement depends a great deal on personal relations and on their attitude toward life. Many today have no heroes whose achievement has been in the realm of the intellect. They resent being urged to put forth more effort— "Get off my back" is their attitude. For outstanding achievement, they must respect themselves and the subject to be learned. The underachiever usually has a defective image of himself; he has little or no sense of his potentialities. He needs a vision of what he may become. His major motivation must come from within, from a clear picture of his most acceptable self.

5. *Are some adolescents "overachievers," that is, do they achieve more than would be expected of them from their test results?*

Yes, there are individuals like this—"Mamma, or Papa, winds them up." They are expected to spend all their time in studying. These youngsters usually show a great deal of tension and nervousness. The "overachievers," too, have a defective self-image. Some have the "wise guy" attitude; others are very intolerant and disparaging of fellow students.

6. *Do maladjusted parents make maladjusted children?*

Not necessarily. Some gifted children, especially as they grow older, are able to make allowances for their disturbed parents![7] As a matter of fact, everyone is more or less maladjusted. It is the way we handle our maladjustment that is important. Although we may not be able to change our deep-seated attitudes and basic person-alities, we often can modify our behavior sufficiently so that it will not have a detrimental effect on the child.

7. *Can popularity become a burden to a child?*

Parents who want their child "to be popular," according to Dr. Mary L. Northway of the University of Toronto's Institute of Child Study, may be increasing his anxiety, tension, and conflict. On the basis of her study, she has found that the extremely popular child suffers more from inner conflicts and anxieties than less popular chil-dren do. He is an energetic conformist and often carries the burdens of his classmates as well as his own.

These extremely popular children are helped by being placed in situations where they are "nonentities" and are liked for themselves, not because of the prestige of being popular.

SIX

Problems of Gifted Children

WITH respect to the problems of gifted children, Terman made the following summary statement:

"Gifted children do not fall into a single pattern but into an infinite variety of patterns. One can find within the group individual examples of almost every type of personality defect, social maladjustment, behavior problem, and physical frailty; the only difference is that among gifted children the incidence of these deviations is, in varying degrees, lower than in the general population."[1]

We should remember that many young people have to deal with "problem parents and grandparents" and with "problem teachers." And they do it fairly well.

(1) UNDERACHIEVEMENT

Gifted children have one problem that receives more attention than any other. And strangely enough, that is underachievement. Although most of them pass their subjects, many fall below their optimum achievement. They may show their lack of interest in school by daydreaming, getting into mischief, or defying authority.

The gifted child is normally eager to learn. However, we often allow this potential to slip through our fingers. We allow the child to become bored at the outset of his school career. Maybe his books are dull or too easy for him. Perhaps the instruction is ineffective. The classwork may have no meaning, use, or purpose for him. Or he may feel that the teacher does not like him; if so, he begins to dislike the teacher and to resist learning. Home relationships accompany him to school. If his thoughts of home are disturbing, he cannot put his

mind on learning to read or do arithmetic. Often the little child does
not understand that the teacher cannot listen to him or let him talk
as much as his mother does; she has to share her time with the other
children. These are only a few of the conditions that make a child
psychologically unable to take advantage of instruction, even, in
some cases, of effective instruction.

Many parents are aware of the frustration a child feels when his
schoolwork bores him or seems futile to him. As one gifted child said,
"You can't imagine how *horrible* it is to sit in a classroom for a whole
year and not learn a single thing."

One parent described her son's experience as follows:

"Stanley entered kindergarten when he was four. He hated it. He didn't
like dancing like butterflies and dead leaves, he said. He particularly disliked pasting. He has always been a great talker and the teacher complained constantly of this. When I felt concerned over his attitude, the
teacher told me he would have to learn to conform to the group or he
would have serious trouble later. This went on until a month before school
was out. He seemed so unhappy, even though he no longer protested, that
I sent him to visit his grandmother. She listens to him, talks to him and
loves him very much.

"Before he entered school the next year I questioned his age. He would
not be six until January. He was given several tests and I was assured that
he was quite ready for first grade.

"In first grade he showed signs of becoming an avid reader, and this
interest has continued. He read constantly at home and was in the top
reading group. Spanish instruction was given and he topped his class in
that. In the middle of the year we had to move to another community.

"In the new school we ran into trouble. He would not do all the arithmetic drills that were required, and began to complain of being sick at
schooltime. The teacher was new at teaching and solved the problem by
putting him back in the kindergarten for days at a time. She also spanked
him—but to no avail. He barely passed the grade. His papers were
marked 'poor' or 'very poor.' However, the standardized test at the end
of the year showed achievement as high as sixth grade in some subjects;
the lowest score was second grade.

"Stanley had always been a well-adjusted and self-confident little boy,
but he was somewhat shaken by his experiences that year. There were
times when he was upset, but it was not apparent to the average teacher.

In fact, we were told he was too self-controlled and we should do something about it.

"During his second year we moved again and in this school he had a teacher who seemed to understand him and recognize his abilities. He had a rich school year with this teacher. He was slow, but thorough and accurate, and she was patient and encouraging. He simply blossomed under her teaching.

"Unfortunately, he had to change schools again in the third grade and once more in the fourth grade. His marks this past year are only average. Even his reading test scores are low, because of his slowness. Yet he reads from the encyclopedia with ease and uses it freely. He is interested in history and geography to the point where he bores most of his friends. He knows a great deal about photographs and spends hours reading magazines on the subject. He works by himself a lot, and when he gets with other boys he seems like another person—silly and noisy and trying to do things their way. He has never been very good at sports, and his writing is poor.

"I see in Stanley, now nine years old, a real and consistent desire to learn, an inquiring mind, an excellent memory, originality, confidence, and unusual ability. At present he is a dawdler, but I know with the proper challenge this would cease. The potential is there and I can do no less than try my utmost to help him.

"The other three children of our family are doing their best. They are all very different in personalities, abilities, and in every way. I have tried to be as objective as possible in thinking over this problem. Stanley could never be nagged or scolded into any achievement. A task has to challenge his mind and then he will go to great lengths, and he has great persistence."

Certainly Stanley has had more than his share of moving from place to place and of unfortunate school experiences. If we were to consider what might have been, we should suggest the following:

It would have been well to postpone Stanley's entrance into kindergarten, and to give him more preparation for it so that he would have had a better idea of what to expect.

If parent-teacher conferences had been held at the beginning of each school year and at intervals thereafter, the parent would have had the chance to give the teacher helpful information about the child.

The parent might have enlisted the aid of other mothers in providing books, educational games, art materials, and other equipment that would provide suitable experiences for the able learners in the class.

A parent-assistant might have been of help to the new inexperienced teacher, to relieve her of some of the routine, and work individually with children like Stanley who were not adjusting to the classroom methods.

By discussing certain of his school experiences, or play-acting them with him, Stanley's mother might have helped him to accept the situation instead of rebelling against it. A conference composed of mother, teacher, and child might have helped each one to reach a better understanding of the problems of the others.

In the third and fourth grades the parent might have suggested that Stanley be given special assignments, such as making interesting reports on topics that the class needed to know more about. He might also have been made a member of small, congenial committees working on special projects.

His older brother might have helped him acquire skill in some of the sports popular with the other boys in his grade; skill in sports would have helped him make the friends he needed, and would have enabled him to feel like a real boy.

Every effort should be made in the next grades to see that Stanley has plenty of challenging work and instruction, and a minimum of drill. When they are asked to do work that is much too easy for them, gifted children become bored and frustrated. Consequently, they do not put forth effort. They work in a desultory way and do not develop good habits of study and of thinking.

When the child is faced with unsatisfactory school conditions, the parents can contribute to his informal education outside of school. When a child shows a worthwhile interest that is really absorbing, it is often wise to let him follow it as intensely as he wants to.

By enriching the home environment, in ways that have already been suggested, the parents may supplement the meager offerings of the school. In a conference with the teacher, they may suggest experiences that she can easily provide for the bright children in her regular classes. By so doing they will benefit other children as well as their own. It is very important that parents spend some time each day in listening to the child and discussing topics of interest with him.

In answer to the question, "Why do some bright students fail in one or more subjects?" panels of gifted children give reasons that fall into three categories: those relating to the child himself, those relating to the home environment, and those relating to school conditions.

Poor previous preparation. Students who fail may have missed some basic instruction because of illness, absence, or other causes.

Too much pressure or too little encouragement at home.

Habits of idleness. If their intellectual ability is not challenged, able students become inattentive and fall into the habit of wasting time.

Poor study and reading methods. Since they learn easily, gifted pupils do not have to acquire more efficient methods of study in order to meet minimum requirements. Later, when confronted with tasks commensurate with their intelligence, they may lack the necessary reading and study skills. This may upset them seriously. They may begin to lose confidence in their ability, or to think of themselves as "dumb" or stupid; in extreme cases, they may give up trying.

Overconfidence. Having "got by" easily in other subjects, they may underestimate the difficulty of a new subject; they may not get down to work on it until it is too late.

Absorbing interest in another field, or in some extra class or social activity, may lead them to neglect a given subject.

Lack of interest in the subject.

Rebellion at having to do what they consider "*busy work*." Some teachers require homework of this kind, and fail students who do not hand it in.

Not enough time to study. Home duties, remunerative work, or other outside activities may interfere.

Poor teaching. Gifted students need good personal relationships with stimulating teachers who know their subject, relate it to young people's lives, maintain order, lighten the lessons with humor, and take a personal interest in each student.

Wrong choice of subjects. If the student has selected an inappropriate program, he will lack motivation to succeed in it. If his program is too heavy, he may become discouraged.

Low group morale. If academic achievement is disparaged, a gifted student may do poor work just to be accepted by the group.

Low standards of scholarship. If scholarship is not truly respected in the school, if teachers and parents do not seem to value it, or if the teachers expect too little of gifted students, able learners may become indifferent or lazy.

Home worries. If home problems and family conflicts usurp the student's attention, he cannot put forth the effort required by a stiff high school course.

Attitude toward learning. Family relationships as well as school conditions may affect the child's attitude toward learning.

If there is too great a discrepancy between the self-concept and the ideal self, the child may feel the frustration of never reaching his goal. If, on the other hand, his goals are set too low, he may feel he is failing to fulfill his potentialities. Jean Walker MacFarlane made the following keen analysis of this problem:

> Among other factors, "too high and unrealistic aspiration levels by proud and pushing parents for intellectual achievement in their children, deflating teachers, and the presence of an older and more competent brother or sister often make children uncertain of their abilities and lead to the strain of competitive intellectual driving or to inhibited and unfree use of abilities, or to defensive lack of effort or misbehavior in class so that others wouldn't detect this misperceived 'dumbness.' "[2]

☺ GETTING APPROPRIATE EDUCATION

The Right School for the Bright Child

Many problems would be prevented if all gifted children could have schools such as that proposed in the following letter:

> "We have a six-and-one-half-year-old daughter whose IQ is 165 and whose present school set-up is not suited to her. Could you tell me the names and locations of any schools in the United States that really provide for gifted children? We want a school where children are encouraged to use their own originality and do not have cause to feel scared when mistakes are made, one that has the minimum of strictly rote learning, one that inspires children to work together and help one another in a happy environment, one that inspires children to learn for the sheer desire to know with little or no emphasis on grades, competition, failures and rewards, one that presents material suited to a gifted child and yet does

not demand adult standards of behavior for children. We want a day school that is co-educational and whose fees (all included) are under $500 for a school term. Is there such a school? We plan to move to the location where the best school is. Also it is important that there be a suitable junior and senior high school in the same locality, so frequent moving will not be necessary."

This parent has admirably described the ideal school for a gifted child. Probably the laboratory or practice schools connected with teachers' colleges or university schools of education, which usually offer a limited number of scholarships, are most likely to provide such an education.

For example, the laboratory schools of the University of Chicago help children to learn to solve problems appropriate to their maturity and ability. The children acquire the facts and the tools necessary for present and future problem-solving. They have many opportunities for creative work—music, sculpture, painting, and handcrafts. Homemaking and shopwork are also a part of the curriculum. Basic consideration is given to health and physical education. Gardening takes them out of doors; it is also an aid in the teaching of science. Instead of pushing and prodding, the school helps the children to set reasonable individual standards of achievement, work toward these goals, and periodically evaluate their progress. There is a continuity of educational experience from preschool through the tenth grade, which leads into the four-year college program.

Similar programs are offered by other practice and laboratory schools, as well as by certain private and public schools, some of which are located in the residential suburbs of large cities. The best plan for the parents would be to select the geographical location they prefer and spend several days visiting the schools so that they can judge their suitability themselves.

Public or Private School?

Both public and private schools can be either good or poor. The public school has the advantage of proximity—an advantage to both the child and the parent. School friends may become neighborhood friends. Parents can see just what is going on. The public school saves the parents money that may be used for the child's higher education. There is evidence that the selected youngsters from public schools who get into first-class colleges do better academically, as a group, than those from private schools.

Private schools in general enroll a larger proportion of gifted children. Since the average IQ in many private day and boarding schools is between 120 and 130, your gifted child would probably have the advantage of equally bright associates. Private-school classes are smaller and there is greater opportunity for close relationships with teachers. The academic standards of private schools are generally high; most of the students are preparing for college. The pros and cons of public and private schools are admirably presented in two chapters of Cutts and Moseley's book, *Bright Children*.[3]

Your decision as to which kind of school to choose for your gifted child would depend on a number of factors. First you would consider what kind of school your child seems to need. Many parents, for example, want their children to have the religious instruction in church-supported schools. Then you would consider the quality of the local public school, the background and level of ability of the children who attend it, and what special provisions it makes for gifted children. Many personal factors would also enter in: the child's relationships with other members of the family, his established friendships, and the economic status of the family.

If you decide to send your child to a private school you may consult a comprehensive, up-to-date directory such as Porter Sargent's *Handbook of Private Schools*.[4] This handbook analyzes most of the private schools in the United States with respect to location, character, enrollment, and cost. After you have selected several that seem promising the next step is to write for their catalogues. If possible, visit them to see for yourself what kind of education they are offering, and whether they would be appropriate for your particular child.

The most popular private schools receive applications for admission many years in advance of entrance; some parents apply as soon as the child is born. Many admissions committees meet in the fall to make their decisions about next fall's admissions; the new students are enrolled by January. This means there is little chance of getting a student enrolled this fall if one waits until spring or summer before applying. However, some good private schools still have openings during the spring and summer.

You should be especially careful in considering the advisability of sending a girl away to secondary school. A good home and local community offer valuable contacts and experiences that she might miss if she went away to boarding school. They also may offer her more chance to associate with the opposite sex. Of course, circumstances such as illness in the family, a broken home, an undesirable neighborhood, or poor local schools may make it desirable or even necessary to place a girl in a private school.

Choice of High-School Course and College

The student's general academic capacity should be at least tentatively determined by the eighth grade. The important thing then is for the student to select a high-school course that will meet college entrance requirements. Whether he eventually goes to college or not, the bright student should not be deprived of a college education, or delayed in getting it, simply because he has taken the wrong high-school course.

If he will need financial assistance to go to college, he should begin early in the high-school years to explore the possibilities of obtaining a scholarship. If he does not recognize the importance of his high-school record, he may do mediocre work when he could be doing superior work.

In times of overenrollment, college admission depends to a large extent on the applicant's score on the College Entrance Board examination. A boy or girl with a score of less than 500 is often rejected; scores of 600 to 750 are preferred. (The highest possible score is 800).

Choice of a college depends on a number of factors, similar to those mentioned in connection with choosing a private school. Choosing a college is like choosing a suit—it should fit the individual. For example, some girls are likely to do better at a small co-educational college than at one of the Ivy League women's colleges. For some boys a college in a rural community may be better than a university in a large city. Several books that give sound suggestions on choosing a college are listed in the bibliography at the end of this book. Most useful is the compilation of information about colleges and universities issued by the American Council on Education, Washington, D.C., which is brought up to date every few years.

 GUARDING AGAINST ONE-SIDED DEVELOPMENT

There are two points of view on this problem. Some parents feel that their gifted child should be well rounded—that he should be helped to develop socially, physically, and emotionally as well as intellectually. Others believe he should specialize along the lines of his absorbing interest. Two factors should be considered—the child's age, and the degree of his giftedness. It is unwise to specialize too young. Sound health and wholesome social relations are a good foundation for almost all kinds of later achievement. The child will have plenty of time later on to specialize and concentrate on the field of his choice. However, in the case of genius, all rules may be laid aside; the genius should be free to follow his special bent. But the large majority of the children whom we call gifted are not geniuses; they need a broad program that gradually becomes more specialized.

 CHOOSING A SUITABLE VOCATION

The vocational field is very wide for gifted adolescents; they have a bewildering number of vocations to choose from. The problem is intensified if there is disagreement in the family as to what Junior should become. One bright boy said his father wanted him to go into business with him, his mother wanted him to become a lawyer like her brother, and he wanted to go into the field of social work. The only way to resolve conflicts such as these is by means of a thorough developmental study and a joint conference of parents, student, and counselor. A few vocational interest and aptitude tests will not predict success in a specific vocation. The developmental study would include information on the individual's interests and abilities as they have evolved during school years: which subjects he liked best; which he made the highest marks in; the results of standardized tests; the hobbies to which he has devoted time and effort; the way he prefers to spend his leisure time; jobs he has held and his satisfaction or dissatisfaction with them. It would include his values—what things are most important to him—and also the history of his vocational choices from his early fantasies about being a cowboy or spaceman to his more realistic consideration of the world of work.

Youngsters who are free to choose any vocation should make a systematic study of their interests, abilities, achievements, work experiences, resources, and values. The handbook *You: Today and Tomorrow*[5] has been used successfully in vocational-guidance groups. It could be used individually by a gifted student.

If a young person has built up over the years a realistic, accurate view of himself, this self-concept will largely determine his choice of vocation. His choice is guided by the kind of person he wants to be. Each choice he makes predetermines to some extent his future possibilities.

 PROBLEMS OF SOCIAL RELATIONS

"The Other Kids Don't Like Me"

The highly gifted child generally finds social adjustment more difficult than academic achievement. He must especially guard against boasting. Any form of conceit may arouse jealousy and antagonism in some of his friends and classmates. It may lead them to ostracize him or call him a "brain," a "square," an "egghead," or whatever derogatory designation is current. A twelve-year-old boy in the ninth grade described an experience of this kind:

"We had a math test and I came out with the best mark. When we returned to our homeroom, the teacher asked us how the test went. I blurted out, 'I did the best.' I didn't really mean to say it, and I never completely lived it down. But I learned not to speak out that way before I thought."

Unfortunately superior schoolwork is one cause for a child's incurring the enmity of his classmates. This problem is illustrated by the following case:

"Claire has always been in good health and [according to her mother] had learned to read before she entered school. She has also been studying music since she was five years old. Because of her superior achievement the school system skipped her from the first to the third grade. She has always been well adjusted to the other children and liked immensely by her teachers. She wrote a play when she was in the fifth grade, with a part in it for every student in the class. She is particularly interested and does well in dramatics. She has always been an enthusiastic student and her grades have been consistently excellent. Her fifth-grade teacher sent home a note on her report card telling us how pleased she was to have Claire in her class and that she found it 'interesting to observe Claire's enjoyment of living.'

"When Claire was ready to enter sixth grade, we moved from one part of the town to another, which necessitated a transfer from one school to another. Here the children, most of whom had come up together from kindergarten, did not accept her when they discovered that she presented competition. They made things difficult for her, with the result that she was unhappy all through the sixth grade. I feel that her teacher was partly at fault in failing to recognize the situation and attempting to remedy it. In the sixth grade she won the first prize in a city-wide vocabulary contest.

"Now Claire is in the seventh grade in junior high school. Her home-room teacher, who is also her science teacher, told me that she has an IQ of 170, the highest IQ in the school. He also said that all her other teachers are delighted to have her in their classes and feel that she makes a definite contribution of benefit to the other students. Recognizing the other children's attitude toward her, he does not call on her as often as she is ready to answer. He appointed her librarian for the class and she gives up a study-hall period to work in the school library.

"Her English teacher, who has her for two periods a day, one for grammar or spelling and one for literature, told me that in all her years of teaching, she has never had a student like Claire.

"All this sounds fine, except that now her classmates won't accept her—some of them call her 'the brain' and 'Einstein'—and they don't say it in a complimentary manner! She has no friends, is not invited to parties, and feels hurt and miserable.

"She has outside interests, is in the Glee Club, is active in the Girl Scouts, studies music, swims and dives, skates, rides a bicycle, and likes outdoor play. Of course, she reads a great deal.

"My husband and I are worried about her not being accepted by children of her own age. Perhaps we have failed in some way, but we don't know where we went off the track. We fear that this nonacceptance may result in maladjustment, which could warp future development.

"Her schoolwork does not tax her at all. In a reading test taken recently, she tested above the eleventh grade. Our greatest concern is for her happiness and well-being. We have a son who is eight years old, a normal child. Claire vents her unhappiness and frustrations on him, which results in disharmony at home.

"Would you recommend getting help from a child-guidance clinic?"

This mother has described a situation in which very bright children often find themselves. Children like Claire often appeal strongly to teachers, who may unwittingly create the impression that such a child is "teacher's pet."

It was a good thing for Claire to write a play in which all the children could take part. It would have been desirable for her to engage in other projects that made use of her creative ability and at the same time brought her in contact with other children in a helpful way. Claire's teachers apparently tried, for the most part, to avoid arousing jealousy among the other children; they seem to have done what they could to set the stage for her helpful participation in the group

But apparently there were other factors causing antagonism. It may have been something in Claire's personality—a basic self-centeredness that showed through the veneer of politeness that she had probably acquired; an imperfectly concealed contempt for her classmates' relative stupidity in many situations; a playing-up to the teachers that was obvious to the other pupils.

Or the basic cause may have lain in a pervasive anti-intellectual attitude in the school and community; this kind of atmosphere cannot be dispelled even by a gifted child with great good will. Sometimes, too, school cliques become so firmly established that it is difficult for even a socially acceptable new student to break in.

Whatever the exact factors may be, it would be helpful to Claire if she could understand them. A skillful school counselor or a psychologist at a guidance clinic might help her to understand herself and the situation a little better. If she could bring the matter out in the open, she would be better able to handle it, either by changing her own behavior, or by changing her attitude toward things that cannot be changed at present.

There are a number of questions that might be asked about this case: Did the parents, who were *very* unwisely told the child's IQ, become too much impressed with her intellectual ability, and subject her to subtle persuasions to achieve in too many fields? Did the

child become infected by this inflated ambition, push herself forward
in the new school situation, thus intensifying competition and
resentment?

In the case of boys, being good in sports may overcome the stigma
of being bright! Children admire those who are competent in games
and resourceful in group projects. In some games mental alertness
is more important than size and strength. Achievements along this
line can help to win social acceptance for boys who also make high
scholastic records.

"The Ins and the Outs"

A closely related problem is caused by the restless moving from
place to place that is becoming so common these days. Although
gifted children usually adjust to a change of residence more easily
than the average, they too feel the wrench of losing their friends and
classmates, and being uprooted from their familiar surroundings.
Many of today's children would not know what the poet meant when
he sang, "How dear to my heart are the scenes of my childhood";
their childhood recollections resemble a blurred panorama—no
place is to them a beloved spot.

When a change in residence is necessary, Dorothy Barclay says,
the parents can try to make it an adventure, and help the children to
make the most of their opportunity to see new places and meet new
people. To do this, they should tell the children about the move well
in advance; the children should help pack and take an active part in
the process of moving. They should be allowed to take their cherished
possessions with them, even though some precious items do not fit into
the new home. Getting settled should not be all work; it can be an
occasion for picnics, camping out, and exploring the neighborhood.

The gifted child's energy, imagination, and wide interests can help
him to make new friends, if he is sympathetic to the plans and interests
of others. Of course, he can suggest ideas of his own, but deferentially
at first. A blend of natural independence and cheerful co-operation
will win him acceptance in a new group. He should not become impatient if acceptance turns out to be a rather slow process. It takes
time for a newcomer to be accepted. The child who meets friendly
overtures half way but does not push himself forward or seem

"pathetically pleased by attention" is likely to be sought by others in time.[6]

The child who has interests of his own does not need "friends at any price." If he is quite happily occupied, the newcomer can afford to take time to choose the friends most congenial to him. The same qualities of personality that attracted friends in his old home will eventually win new friends. This truth is illustrated by the story of a traveler who asked an old-timer, "What kind of folks live here?" "What kind of folks were there where you came from?" the old-timer asked. "Oh," said the traveler, "they were kind, helpful, friendly people." "Well," said the old-timer, "I reckon you'll find the same kind of folks here."

Social Fears

Social fears loom large with many adolescents. They fear not being chosen and not knowing "the thing to do" in social situations. Sometimes these fears are imaginary; sometimes they are well founded in fact.

If a child is not accepted socially, he may seek solace in solitary pursuits. He turns to books and hobbies for his satisfactions, because this is a world that he can manage. Occasionally parents and teachers encourage an exclusive interest in books and studies because they do not recognize it as an escape from other important tasks of adolescent development.

"Problem Friends"

Friends may sometimes *be* a problem. Gifted children generally gravitate toward older friends. This sometimes causes problems such as those described by a thirteen-year-old girl in the seventh grade:

"The children in my class seemed childish, so I began to go with more mature friends. This is where my problem started. These friends introduced me to boys—which I liked. I had no trouble with the boys, but I started to have trouble with my girl friends. I'm kinda cute and the boys preferred me to them.

"Then my parents resented me seeing boys and getting phone calls all the time and having the boys over. That's when I went for help.

"The person whom I feel is the easiest to speak to is my seventeen-year-old brother. He understands me. He advised me not to see the boys for a while. So I did as he said—to a compromise point. I mean I didn't take them out of my life altogether. So now everything's working out fine even with the kids in my class."

6 EMOTIONAL PROBLEMS

Adolescents have a right to be somewhat temperamental. It is no easy matter to adjust calmly to new feelings, new situations, new problems, and new demands. A fourteen-year-old boy in the ninth grade told how a friend helped him in his temperamental moments:

"When I got excited or angry, my friend used to calm me down. Then after it had blown over, he would talk to me as an equal and discuss my problems with me. Confidentially, I think he had had the same problems as I have and could naturally better understand mine. I've become more mature in those situations and I'm not petty any more."

Parents could give similar help.

Frequency of Emotional Disturbance

Some gifted children are emotionally disturbed. They are difficult to identify because we lack criteria as to what constitutes an emotionally disturbed child. The more actively a child reaches out to his environment, the more conflict he is likely to have. However, we should not try to eliminate insecurity from the child's life; we should spend more effort, as he grows older, in helping him to cope with it.

Delinquency also occurs among gifted children though not so frequently as in the general population. It is sometimes difficult to distinguish symptoms of potential delinquency from the normal rebelliousness that most children go through. It has been found that upper-class children are more likely to turn their hostility inward against themselves and thus become neurotic, while lower-class children are more likely to act it out and thus become delinquent.

Resiliency of Gifted Children

Although gifted children tend to be more sensitive and to respond more intensely than the average child to emotional stimulation of any kind, they also have a greater capacity for understanding and solving their problems. Perhaps they realize more clearly that a certain amount of frustration and tension is an unavoidable part of life. Terman found that although a small proportion of his gifted children succumbed to mental disorder, their superior intelligence helped them to overcome their difficulties. A study of gifted children who had been referred to child-guidance clinics confirmed the importance of harmonious family life, good family relationships, and consistent and reasonable treatment in the early years.

A psychologically healthy child can take some early fear-arousing experiences in his stride. His fears tend to subside in the normal course of events. However, if he is subjected to an experience of real severity, the fear initially aroused may be persistent and pervasive. More important, if a child learns hostile, aggressive, or unresponsive behavior in his early years, this pattern tends to be constantly reinforced as he grows older. This is because his behavior does not evoke affectionate responses from others; they react to his antagonistic behavior, and do not perceive that he is a child who needs an extra amount of affection and approval. Thus a circular response, described so well by Mary Follett many years ago, is set in motion: the child's initial feeling of fear or hostility is expressed in withdrawal or in overaggressive behavior. This behavior evokes punishment or withdrawal of affection on the part of adults or other children. And this unfriendly response, in turn, reinforces the child's fear and hostility. Though these defensive reactions may temporarily relieve his tension, in the long run they intensify his maladjustment.

To break this vicious circle, parents and others who have a close relationship with the emotionally disturbed child need to recognize the persistent fear that underlies his behavior. They should see that their natural tendency to reject or punish him will only reinforce his negative behavior. Their role is to try to respond to any positive behavior that he shows. They should feel genuine sympathy and affection; the frightened, anxious, sensitive child simply does not know how to obtain from others the attention, affection, and approval that he needs. This approach must be made gradually. It takes time. And it is hard not to be disappointed or even resentful when he does not respond at once.

Natural Therapeutic Agents

Many modern parents seem too ready to seek the help of a psychologist or psychiatrist in the case of children whose problems may be quite normal and transitory. To label a child as emotionally ill may have a more detrimental effect than to allow the difficulty to work itself out under the natural therapeutic influence of life—work, love, play, and religion.

Fortunately, most families and communities contain therapeutic personalities—people who understand children and young people and feel warmly toward them. The therapeutic personality maintains standards and limits which reinforce the child's inadequate inner controls. That is to say, it is not merely a sweet, indulgent personality. If a parent is able to handle his own maladjustments and to avoid standing in the way of the child's best development, this in itself will have a therapeutic influence, regardless of the parent's lack of psychological training and knowledge.

When professional help is needed, the parent usually turns first to the pediatrician or family physician who knows the child, the parents, and the family background better than any other professional person. If other expert assistance is needed, the physician will help the parent obtain it from a private psychologist or psychiatrist, or from a clinic, child-guidance center, or social-work agency. The American Association of Psychiatric Clinics for Children, 250 West Fifty-seventh Street, New York 19, publishes each year a list of qualified child psychiatric clinics throughout the United States and Canada.

⑦ DEVELOPING A SENSE OF RESPONSIBILITY

If the gifted child is to develop his gifts, he must have a sense of responsibility for the fortunate combination of heredity and early childhood experiences with which he has been favored. Without such a social incentive, the gifted youth tends to be content to settle down on a plateau of mediocrity. Sometimes fear is at the bottom of this kind of inertia—fear of changing a familiar pattern that has brought satisfaction in the past.

Adolescents often use parents and teachers as a sounding board. They may express a point of view that they think will shock the adult.

If the adult expresses no standards, no moral expectations, or ethical judgments, the young person may think that "silence gives consent"; he may interpret the adult's attitude as approval of what he has said.

It is the role of the adult to help the young person gain insight and perspective. Dr. Harry Emerson Fosdick told of a bright boy who came to him and said defiantly, "I don't believe in God." To this statement Dr. Fosdick replied, "Suppose you tell me about this God you don't believe in." This was a sound procedure: to find out first what was already in the boy's mind and then help him to gain new perceptions and new motivations.

It is important that the youngster express his convictions in action. If he has special competence in some field, he may help others to acquire knowledge and skill along the same line: for example, if he is good at tennis he may help others to learn to play well. If he is good in math, he may tutor a "weak sister" in the subject. Being gifted, he has more than the average obligation to help others.

GUIDANCE GIFTED CHILDREN AND ADOLESCENTS WANT

In describing persons who have helped them with their problems, gifted children frequently use such words as "understanding," "trusting," "easy to speak to." Their attitudes toward parental guidance cover a wide range—from rejection to appreciation.

Dissatisfaction with Adult Guidance
When children and adolescents reject adult guidance, it is largely because of previous experience with it. One bright fourteen-year-old expressed his dissatisfaction with parental guidance clearly and concisely:

"When I need help, my parents are liable to help too much, or not at all; neither of which is any good. And teachers usually are too impersonal or are not understanding."

Independence in Problem-Solving
The general attitude in our culture that one should solve his own

problems is reflected in the following composition by a gifted thirteen-year-old girl in the ninth grade:

"Frankly, I can't recall an incident when someone gave me just the help I wanted. There very well may have been such an incident; I recall none. When I have problems, I solve them by myself or else they go unsolved. My parents have tried, I realize, to help me but I have difficulty explaining myself clearly and fully. Up until this year, I have confided only in a very few close friends about my problems; they experience similar ones and can discuss the matter openly. Not meaning to brag, I do think that I have learned to solve my own problems, and I resent attempts by older people to pry into my personal thoughts. This year, however, I have gained a closer friendship with leaders and members of our church group. With this group I am gradually growing able to discuss myself."

A thirteen-year-old boy in the same grade described a combination of independence and reliance on parents:

"From my parents I would like help on a few personal matters and also on school problems. Most things, however, I prefer to puzzle out for myself. I can use guidance from my parents in some instances but in others I prefer to make my own decisions. One kind of 'help' I don't want is punishment that is not deserved—punishment given without full understanding of the situation."

Multiple Sources of Help

"Who do I go to when I have a problem? I think it depends on the problem itself. When I have a problem concerning school, such as a change in program, and so forth, I usually discuss it with my teacher or guidance counselor and then with my mother.

"If the problem is a personal one, such as how to stop a boy friend from calling too late, how to break away from a girl friend you don't think is doing you any good, and so forth, I always go to my mother. She knows me better than anyone else and can best help me. At times I tell my friends the usual girl-type problems but I don't trust them with large personal problems. I know they talk to someone about it because I do it myself.

"I would like to see a guidance department devoted to helping the student. It should have enough teachers in it to really help in a large school."

Guidance from Friends and Older Brothers and Sisters

Some teenagers turn to friends of their own age for guidance because, as one girl said, "they are on my level and able to understand my problems better than an adult."

Older brothers or sisters are sometimes mentioned as sources of help:

"Usually when I am faced with a problem I turn to my twenty-four-year-old sister. My problems are mainly about dating and school. I expect honest and truthful opinions that are for my benefit. My sister was my age not so long ago and I always get useful and honest opinions from her. I like to discuss my problems and not be forced into a solution. I don't have many problems in school, only what subjects to take. I also go to my mother with some of my problems, but my sister is more patient and has more time to spare on my problems.

"I don't go to the school counselors with my problems."

Guidance from Church Associations

Some adolescents mention receiving help with their problems from religious leaders, as did this thirteen-year-old girl in the ninth grade:

"My lesser problems are presented to my mother while my larger problems are usually presented to various persons at the church I attend. I really haven't had many problems, but have had a tremendous number of questions which I wanted answered on life, school, my vocation, passions. My mother has helped me immensely in my schoolwork. She keeps me working when the going is rough. At various retreats in our church for young people of high-school age, I have learned what I must do in life and why, and how to cope with many problems myself."

Appreciation of Parental Guidance

Some youngsters make a practice of going to their parents for guidance. As a fourteen-year-old girl said:

"They know me and understand me even more than I understand myself. They guide me back into a normal path of emotion when I become frustrated. For example, one morning, when I was upset over pressing homework assignments, my mother calmed me down and launched me into the homework. My father has given me many suggestions with much understanding."

Another girl of the same age said:

"The kind of help I would like to get would be about school, home life, and social life. From the teacher I would like help on how to improve my grades. From my guidance counselor I would like to receive advice as to which vocation is best suited for me. To my parents I would bring all my other problems—mostly social and personal."

Another bright youngster expressed similar appreciation of her mother's guidance:

"The person to whom I can always go with a problem is my mother. I feel I am very fortunate in this respect, since many of my friends cannot do so.

"My mother will always sit down and discuss a problem with me, no matter how busy she is (perhaps this is because she comes from such a large family and her mother never got around to all the kids)."

Other boys and girls of this age have similar points of view. They mention that their parents help them with homework and help them set time limits on watching television, dating, and going to the movies.

Adolescents are concerned about the nature and quality of the help they receive. One youngster said:

"Too many times the answers I get are too complicated and in adult language. When I get a complicated answer, I either give up or try to think of a new approach. Too often the new approach doesn't pop up. Help should give the answers you want, but it should also lead to thinking."

Another youngster said his parents gave him the right help most of the time because he took care to ask only such questions as they would know about.

After describing the help she had obtained from teachers as mostly comprised of pep talks, a fourteen-year-old girl in the ninth grade had this to say about parents:

"As for my parents, they always give me the help I need. They are always willing to talk over some little problem I have. Parents should be our closest friends, but maybe there are certain things we don't want to tell. They are always available and waiting. The help I think all teenagers should receive from their parents is discipline, advice, and comfort."

Another ninth-grader of the same age summed up the help she would like to receive from parents and teachers in two words: "understanding" and "faith."

Gifted children can "talk out" and thus clarify their problems. A friendly talk about points of difference often uncovers common ground for agreement, whereas a wall of silence may widen the distance between parent and child. It is very important to keep the lines of communication open.

Questions and Answers

1. *How can a parent tell whether his child's problems are serious?*
There is no pat answer to this question. The more understanding you get by observing other children of the same age as well as your own, studying and reading about child development, and asking questions of teachers who know children well or of parents who have been successful in bringing up their children, the greater your ability to ascertain what the child's behavior means to him. If you can determine this, you will be in a better position to distinguish between potentially serious problems and normal "phases" of growth.

2. *How can a child weather a broken home?*
It is hard on a child, though not necessarily disastrous, to be shuttled back and forth from one parent to another and from one school to another. It helps if there is some one person who maintains a constant warm relation with the child. This may be one of the parents or some other person who is close to the child. If there are two children, they may lend support to each other. Difficulties are intensified if one of the parents shows jealousy or hostility toward the other, or if they maintain conflicting standards and values. Under such circumstances it is very important for the child to talk things out with a person who understands the child's point of view and knows how to talk with children.

3. *Does an adopted child in the family present special problems?*
When a couple who have children of their own adopt a child, it does indeed make a difference in family relationships. If the adopted child turns out to be less bright than the parents had hoped, or than

their own children, a situation arises that may intensify his feeling of inferiority. Many appealing babies adopted during the first two years of life fall below the expectations of their adoptive parents. Such a child is likely to be sensitive to his status as an adopted child and may have difficulty in accepting the fact that his natural parents gave him up. He may believe it was because something was wrong with him. Children adopted at adolescence or preadolescence may carry the scars of an earlier period of severe family turmoil.

A child like this comes to his new parents with a past, with memories, with feelings that must be recognized and accepted. There are sure to be ups and downs in his many-sided development. It takes time and understanding, warmth, and patience to restore his sense of trust. To persons who can supply these qualities to an unwanted, lonely child, the unfolding of his potentialities is a source of the deepest satisfaction.[7]

4. *Can a gifted child read too much?*

Few parents seem to be worried about this. Probably today's world is "so full of a number of things"—besides reading—that children seldom read excessively.

However, an occasional child may use reading as an escape from some of the responsibilities and disappointments of life. One extremely bright girl felt that she was socially ostracized in the fourth, fifth, and sixth grades. This was due not only to the fact that she was different from other children in dress and manner, but also to the circumstance that she was indifferent to their feelings and wishes. She found in reading an escape from a social world with which she was not able to cope.

Gifted children can become too bookish. Like all children, they should have opportunities to develop physically, socially, and emotionally. They enjoy, as much as other children, games and sports that have social benefits as well as health values. Some academically-minded parents and teachers go too far in encouraging a child to read at the expense of other aspects of his development.

5. *Do gifted children who go to special schools attain a higher level of achievement than children who go to ordinary schools?*

Conflicting results have been obtained from experiments on this question. Dr. William E. Blatz of Canada reported "no appreciable difference in the level of achievement of children with IQ's of 140 or over who went to a special school." We also found that three classes, grouped according to their ability, showed little or no difference in achievement after they had returned to the regular school. Other experiments in this country have reported better results from putting bright children together in special classes. The differences in these results may be due partly to differences in teacher personality and quality of instruction.

6. *How should tests be used in the guidance of gifted children?*

During school years tests are useful in measuring academic aptitude and achievement. They supplement day-by-day observation of a child's performance. A series of test scores obtained over a number of years gives a developmental picture and helps to avoid faulty appraisal.

Tests are only one element in prediction of future success in school and in life. They do not measure the intangibles that determine achievement—aspiration, purpose, determination, courage, vitality, and other qualities of character.

No important decision should be based on the results of a single test. Any test results should be used in conjunction with all the other information available about the individual.

Terman answered this question with reference to tests of "general intelligence" given as early as six to ten years. He said these tests "tell a great deal about the ability to achieve either presently or 30 years hence. Such tests do not, however, enable us to predict what direction the achievement will take, and least of all do they tell us what personality factors or what accidents of fortune will affect the fruition of exceptional ability." [8]

7. *If a child is to be accelerated one or two years during his school career, when is the best time for such acceleration?*

The best time, like the decision to accelerate, depends on a number of factors in the home, the school, and the child. He should probably not be accelerated before he has acquired the tools of learning— reading, writing, and basic arithmetic. Between the second and fourth grades, some gifted children will be ready to move ahead.

A good plan seems to be to complete the first three grades in two years and the three junior high school grades in two years. Some children who develop rapidly in high school may profit by advanced placement programs which enable them to save one year of college.

8. *Do parents really want their child to be set apart as "gifted" or "extra smart"? Doesn't it create a caste system in the school?*

What would be your answer to these questions? Probably we would find three points of view represented among parents:

(1) Parents who are eager and insistent on having their child put in the special group. These parents present problems to principals when they insist that their child who actually is not up to the standard required for the class be admitted.

(2) Parents who would be glad to have their child take advantage of any appropriate opportunity to develop his potential. They feel that provision for the gifted is as important as meeting the needs of the handicapped or the average student.

(3) Parents who, for one reason or another, refuse to believe that their child is exceptional and want him to be "just a normal child."

The second group, we hope, are in the majority.

9. *If a child is potentially gifted but "lazy," should he still be put into the gifted group?*

Yes, in the hope that he will be challenged to do better. These are the youngsters who are the special responsibility of the school. However, if "lazy" means unable to work up to his capacity because of emotional disturbance, physical or social causes, then he should first be referred to a counselor. Having ascertained the possible causes of his lack of effort, the student and counselor can then decide whether the special class for able students is appropriate for him.

SEVEN

Your Responsibility for the Best Development of all Children

IT IS often the parent who first becomes concerned about the education of gifted children. He sees the need for additional educational opportunities for his child, and for other children as well. As a member of the board of education, a citizens' study group, a parent-teacher association, a service club, or some other community group, the parent may focus attention on the importance of an educational program that will develop the potentialities of all the children in the community. He can contribute most by working with teachers, principals, and the school superintendent. He can also enlist community support for constructive steps. He can seek the help of other individual citizens who may be able to provide additional ideas, stimulus, or service.

TYPES OF PROGRAM

Realizing that no group should be educated at the expense of another group, parents will give careful consideration to each proposal for the education of gifted children. To acquaint parents with various possibilities, we will briefly review each of the principal methods of making provision for the gifted.

Meeting Gifted Children's Needs in Regular Classes

Various ways of doing this have already been described in earlier chapters. To be successful, this plan requires a wide range of instructional material, a flexible curriculum, and a teacher who has both interest and skill in individualizing instruction. Let us be realistic: this combination of conditions does not exist in many schools. However, more and more teachers are providing special opportunities for the gifted within their regular classes. They are forming study groups, attending workshops and conferences, and taking courses that will increase their understanding of the needs of the individual pupils in their classes.

Real enrichment implies additional experiences calculated to foster the development of each child; it does not mean merely more of the same classwork. The Portland, Oregon, program is a fine example of this type. Under this plan, even the pupils whose program had not been enriched began to do better work after a few months; apparently they were stimulated by the more intellectual atmosphere of the school as a whole. Moreover, some students who had had severe behavior problems became good citizens when they had challenging work that was within their capacity. When they had something worth while to occupy their minds, they no longer thought up annoying things to do.

In such a program the principal is a key person. He creates conditions that facilitate effective education of the gifted. He encourages teachers by showing approval of their efforts. He involves them in co-operative planning for better education not only of the gifted, but of all the children. In choosing new teachers, he selects those who are qualified by personality as well as by training, and tries to give them the kind of assignment in which they will get the most satisfaction.

His advisory committee of lay people helps him to establish sound public relations. In some schools the principal seeks the co-operation of the parents of gifted children; he may arrange for conferences between parents and members of the staff. It is also the responsibility of the principal to see that the teachers have access to other kinds of in-service education that they feel the need of—study groups, case conferences, or workshops on the education of the gifted.

Forming Clubs and Interest Groups

Various school clubs and outside-of-school groups supplement the students' schoolwork as well as affording fun and companionship. There are nation-wide organizations such as the 4-H Clubs, Scouts, Campfire Girls, Girls' Clubs, and others; local interest groups in music, painting, and acting; outdoor groups that sponsor camping trips; associations that conduct playground activities; groups that discuss selected radio and television programs; and church schools. One of the problems is to avoid overscheduling the gifted child.

There are so many things he can do and wants to do; "the world is so full of a number of things" . . . he often runs himself ragged and has no time to be alone.

Scheduling a Special Period for the Gifted

Special provision may take the form of a library-discussion period once a week; a foreign-language class beginning in the third or fourth grade in which children gain facility in speaking the language; or a period a day in which the able learners in the class study certain topics intensively, as in the Colfax Plan in Pittsburgh. Such special periods may be arranged with the co-operation of the librarian, a member of the community who has a special talent, or a teacher employed specifically for the education of the gifted. When the children go back to their regular classes, they easily make up the work they have missed.

In rural communities, children may be brought together to a central school for a special seminar once a week. This kind of program was developed by Glyn Morris of Lewis County, New York.[1]

Extending the School Day

Under this plan a thirty-minute period is added to the school day for the benefit of gifted children who want additional instruction in a foreign language, music, or some other subject. It would seem better to fit such special classes into the regular school day, since these children often have school time that they do not use to the best advantage. Moreover, many parents would not accept a proposal that involved a longer school day.

Setting Up "Honors Groups" or Special Advanced Sections in Each Subject

This plan has been in operation for some time in many large high schools. Honors groups in English provide for intensive study of literature or creative writing. Advanced mathematics courses include calculus; science workshops permit advanced study or extra work on projects. An advanced course in a foreign language aims to increase efficiency in both oral and written expression.

Grouping All Students into Slow-Moving, Regular, and Fast-Moving Sections

In the fast-moving sections gifted students who have passed the fifth grade may complete two years in one, or three years in two; this plan has an advantage over grade-skipping in that the student not only covers all the content of each grade, but does a better quality of work.

In the ungraded primary school, pupils move along with their classmates for three years with no formal promotion at the end of each year. The accent is on individual progress and growth. The teachers take the children as far as they can go in the three years. The exceptionally mature and fast-learning child can take advantage of new experiences, and may complete the three years in two if he has the social and physical maturity to match his intellectual superiority. Similar special-progress plans have been introduced in junior high schools.

Half-Day Programs for the Gifted

In a few elementary schools the gifted children are brought together for half the day for classroom instruction; the other half-day they work with the other pupils in clubs, music, art, and physical education. An example of this type of program is the well-known "Major Work Classes" of Cleveland, Ohio. Children who have a minimum IQ of 125 on an individual test administered by a psychologist are invited to join a "Major Work Class," if their maturity, social development, emotional stability, and health are also satisfactory. In these classes they do advanced work in every area of learning appropriate to their age. They also carry at least one additional subject. In the elementary school, they all study a foreign language under a special teacher. In high school they carry one or more additional major subjects. Both children and parents are pleased with this program, which has been in operation for more than thirty-five years

At the Lloyd School, one of the Chicago public schools, there is a special primary class comprising able learners from the first grade through the third. In the morning these pupils attend their regular grade classes and meet their academic requirements. In the afternoon from one to three o'clock these bright children come to a special class which offers them more challenge. They plan and carry out special projects, delving more deeply into each topic than they would be able to do in the ordinary class.

The same form of organization is continued in grades four through six. They choose a topic and study it in depth, combining trips and other firsthand experiences with intensive reading and activities that enable them to communicate the knowledge they have gained.

Special Schools for the Gifted

A few large cities have special schools for the gifted. New York City has the Hunter College Elementary School and the special high schools of science and arts. Other special schools include the "Opportunity Classes" in Allentown, Pennsylvania; the Lee Junior High School of Baltimore, Maryland; Walnut Hills Junior-Senior High School of Cincinnati, Ohio; and the Boston Latin School in Boston, Massachusetts. Many private schools have a preponderence of gifted children; their average IQ is often between 120 and 130. The effectiveness of these schools, like that of other schools, depends largely on the goals and values of the teachers and administrators.

Special schools are obliged to be somewhat exclusive. Many children who apply for admission cannot be accepted. Those who are rejected often experience intense frustration, a sense of defeat, or a feeling that the decision was unfair.

Neighborhood schools have some genuine advantages. They usually enroll at least a small group of more or less gifted children, who can be helped to stimulate one another. And the parents are likely to make co-operative efforts to improve the neighborhood school.

Provision Through Programing

Various methods of acceleration enable the gifted child to gain a year or more, and thus to finish secondary school and college at an earlier date:

Early admission to primary school.

Being moved ahead a year somewhere between kindergarten and grade three.

Completing two years in one, or three years in two.

Taking courses in high school that will give college credit.

Leaving high school at the end of the second year to enter college. Acceleration imposes social and emotional strains on some children. The decision as to whether to accelerate a particular child should be carefully considered by the parents, teachers, administrators, and the child himself.

Programing may also be a means to enrichment. A gifted child is often able to carry an extra subject easily—an advanced course in mathematics, in history, in English; a practical course in handcraft, home economics, or typing; or a class in art, music, physical education or drama.

Under the advanced placement program college-level subjects may be taken by gifted high-school students who show (1) a past record of excellence in the subject (2) a high IQ, (3) a record of emotional stability and maturity. The student decides whether he wishes to take one or more of these courses; parental permission is necessary.

APPRAISAL OF PROCEDURES

You will hear objections raised to any method of grouping gifted children according to ability. If gifted children associate only with other gifted children, it is charged, they become snobbish, conceited, and incapable of understanding or making friends with children of different abilities and backgrounds. Although this is sometimes true in individual cases, studies have failed, in general, to support the contention. To be sure, individual intellectual development is sometimes overemphasized in a special class, and certain children become too self-centered. But this tendency can be corrected by adequate attention to the social development of each child. It is more usual for bright children to give, often, generous recognition to one another's talents and frequently to have feelings of inferiority. They sometimes compare themselves with the heroes and heroines in the biographies they have read and despair of ever reaching similar heights.

In this regard, the parents sometimes present more problems than the children. When a special class is formed, some parents try to push their children into it, whether they are qualified or not. For example, the following case, cited by a teacher:

"When we set up a special 'Arts Level' English class based on high reading achievement plus teacher recommendation, there was a hue and cry from every parent to have his child in such a group. Largely owing to parental pressure, we now have some youngsters with average ability painfully plodding along in a valiant effort to keep up with the very superior group."

It is not clear how the average children are affected when the gifted are drawn off into special classes. We must remember that there is a range of ability in all groups—in the gifted groups and in the groups from which they have been withdrawn. The average students may miss somewhat the stimulation that would have been supplied by the more able and more creative students; but this lack may be counterbalanced by the fact that the average students now have more opportunities for leadership within their own group.

Most of the objections to special classes for the gifted can be removed by combining regular classes and special classes in a balanced program.

The educational program for the gifted should fit the school situation; there is no one best program for all schools. The program for each school should be developed co-operatively by staff, students, and parents. It should usually include a combination of:

1. Enrichment—special opportunities for the child to broaden and deepen his understanding in every way.
2. Acceleration of one or two years if the child is physically and socially, as well as intellectually, mature; decision to accelerate should be made on an individual basis.
3. Grouping for advanced work in certain subjects. Some schools are now employing a special teacher who divides her time between teaching these special groups and helping the other teachers make better provisions for the gifted in regular classes.

Any of the methods of providing for gifted children that have been described in the previous paragraphs might prove helpful in your community. You might suggest a P-TA meeting on the topic: "What Special Provision for Exceptional Children Is Made in Our Schools?" If you have evidence that your child is gifted, talk with the school counselor or psychologist; if no specialists are employed, consult the principal or teacher.

If the only provision for the gifted is in the regular classes, then you might tactfully suggest some special projects which your child would like to carry out, or assist the teacher in other ways as suggested in the next section.

PARENT-TEACHER COLLABORATION

Parents and teachers need each other's help. They are natural allies in the process of bringing up a gifted child. Their common goal is to do what is best for the child. Both teachers and parents usually prefer a frank, realistic approach to matters they can do something about.

Parents' Approach to Teachers

Parents need not be afraid to express their points of view. To be sure, the teacher has usually had more education in child psychology and methods of teaching than most parents have had. But parents have a more intimate knowledge of their own children, which should be shared with the teacher. And you would be surprised to know how often teachers are afraid of parents!

A positive approach pays. Teachers are people; they need recognition, approval, and acceptance, just as everyone else does. They often feel frustrated and discouraged; they appreciate parents who understand. A word of sincere appreciation may be a good way for the parent to begin a parent-teacher conference. This appreciation will be genuine if you will put yourself for a moment in the teacher's place—confronted every day with thirty or more little rugged individualists, whom she is expected to bring up right.

Any serious criticism or complaints about the teacher or the school can be presented constructively. Criticism is hard for the teacher (or anyone else!) to take unless it is offered as a way of achieving goals that the teacher, too, holds to be important. If a parent feels inexplicably hostile toward a teacher, it may be because of his or her own unhappy early experience with a teacher, or with someone whom the teacher resembles. Emotions have a way of recurring in situations in which they are not appropriate. If the parent recognizes this possibility, he may be able to take a more friendly attitude toward a teacher who impresses him unfavorably at first.

Parent-Teacher Conferences

A parent-teacher conference is a two-way communication. The parents gain understanding of what the teacher is trying to do and of ways in which they can supplement her work. It is often a relief to parents to be able to talk frankly with someone about their child. Somehow a problem does not seem quite so serious when it is brought out in the open in an atmosphere of calm acceptance. As you try to explain a situation to another person it often becomes clearer to you. In discussing a child, the parents may begin to perceive him in a new light. As a consequence of this changed perception, they behave differently toward him. Changes in the parents' behavior often evoke a more favorable response from the child.

Ideally, instead of asking the teacher to tell them what to do, parents should try to think things out themselves with whatever help the teacher can give. Parents are more likely to carry out plans they have made themselves than ready-made advice given by the teacher.

Parents may expect teachers to reach out for information that may help them understand the children in their classes; their questions are not to be regarded as symptoms of idle or mischievous curiosity. Teachers do not want to be told about deeply personal matters that have little or no bearing on the child's behavior. Parents should also guard against the natural tendency to talk exclusively about problems and to overlook signs of wholesome growth.

What, then, should parents tell teachers in their conferences? It is usually best to keep the conversation centered on the child's school performance, and on any home conditions that might help the teacher understand the child's behavior in school. How the child feels about school; any health problems such as poor hearing or vision that need special consideration in school; how the child spends his free time; what his home responsibilities are and how well he fulfills them; his special interests and hobbies; how he gets along with other children in the home or in the neighborhood—information of this kind is helpful to teachers.

From the teacher, the parents may get information about the child's ability and about whether he is working up to ability so far as the school can recognize it. The parents should not expect the teacher to tell them the child's IQ because this figure is so often misunderstood and misinterpreted, but they can legitimately ask whether the child may be expected to meet grade standards or achieve better than the average child of his age. They will be content to know that their child is in the upper fourth or upper 10 per cent on intelligence and achievement tests.

Since the child's behavior at home is often different from his behavior in school, the parent might well ask what special interests and abilities he shows in class, whether he takes initiative and fulfills responsibilities that he has accepted, how well he gets along with his classmates, and what difficulties he may be having. Thus informed, the parent is in a better position to be helpful at home.

Perhaps the most common complaint made by parents of gifted children is that the schoolwork is not sufficiently challenging. The teacher may counter with the accusation that the parent is exerting undue pressure on the child. This conflict can be resolved by accurate information about the child's ability and the educational experiences he needs.

Parents' Assistance to Teachers

Parents who have leisure time can assist teachers in many ways. They can serve as sources of information on specialized topics, assist in the teaching of any arts and crafts in which they are proficient, obtain needed materials and equipment for projects in which the pupils are engaged. An experiment now being conducted by Paul Diederich[2] presents evidence that lay persons can effectively assist English teachers with the correction of students' compositions. All these activities and many others benefit all the children.

Parents can also assist in providing reading material. Ideally each class should have a library, each school should have a library, and the public library should co-operate closely with the school. Raising money for books for the gifted, as well as for retarded readers, is a project that often appeals to P-TA's and to other social and civic clubs in the community.

Parents' Night

Most schools have a "parents' night" or "open school week" when parents are invited to visit the school. On such an occasion you may expect to establish an informal, friendly relation with your child's teacher, to become acquainted with some aspects of his school life, and to learn about the parent-teacher conferences—when they will take place and how they will be conducted. You will also learn how pupil progress is reported. For older pupils perhaps the best method is to supplement the report card with frequent self-appraisals by the pupil, occasional notes from the teacher commending exceptional performance, and one or two conferences per year in which pupil, parent, and teacher sit down together.

PARENTS' CO-OPERATION WITH HOMEWORK

Homework is more or less a family affair. Although gifted children are likely to prefer to study independently, they quite frequently involve their parents in some phase of the task. Thus homework is a primary source of impressions for the parents about what the school is teaching and how well their child is learning. Homework should be a bond between home and school, not a bone of contention. Most parents approve of homework, even in the elementary school.

Some schools give five- or ten-minute homework assignments in grades one through four; by grades five and six the time is up to thirty minutes per night. Children who become accustomed to having some homework in the upper grades of elementary school are in a better position to make the transition to junior high school, where more extensive homework assignments are given.

Other elementary schools give homework only on an individual basis—to children who have been absent, who are having difficulty in a subject, or who have become so much interested in a project that they want to continue work on it at home. If homework is required of all children, it should be personalized to meet individual needs. It should help the gifted child to develop initiative, self-direction, and independent thinking; it should be sufficiently worth while to reward his perseverance.

Even though a gifted child who is in the lower grades of elementary school does not come home with definite assignments, he will often find school-related things to do, if the schoolwork has been challenging to him. Home study enriches school instruction and builds independent reading habits.

It is the parents' responsibility to provide the conditions under which the child does his best work. It is desirable that he have a change of activity right after school—preferably happy outdoor play. Watching television is not the best thing he can do at this point; it does not furnish much activity for either mind or muscles. Two of the best times for the child to do his homework are just before and just after supper. If the evening meal is late, so that the father can join the family (or for other reasons) the child may have a snack right after school and do his homework before supper. It is a good idea to ascertain the time at which the child does his best work, and encourage him to do it regularly at that time.

The best place to do homework is a room that is remote from disturbance and interruptions. Good light, without glare, should come from behind and above. The chair should encourage good posture, and the table or desk should have ample room to spread out papers and books. Some youngsters, however, study better under the watchful but unobtrusive eye of a parent.

Youngsters have described the conditions under which they study best (see *The Adolescent Views Himself*, pp. 485-521).[3] Most frequently they mention the need for privacy and freedom from interruption. Television and radio distract some bright children more than others. Personal relations are most important; some youngsters feel that their parents take no interest in their schoolwork, and that no one is really interested in them. On the other hand, as one girl said, "If your family pushes you too hard, it's not good. I find it very difficult to study under pressure." Other children are lackadaisical about homework because they have no goal or purpose.

Although you do not want the child to depend on you, it is often helpful, if you are on hand, to answer some of his questions or encourage him to find the answers. For example, if he asks what "amiable" means, you can help him find it in the dictionary. If he is curious about the location of South Africa, you can show him how to find it in the atlas. If he asks who Pasteur was, you can show him how to use a one-volume encyclopedia.

One father described his modest participation in his gifted child's homework as follows:

"Actually I haven't spent much time on Christine's lessons. She does them almost always by herself, and has got straight A's for years. Near the beginning of the fifth grade she brought home much more work than she had been used to having, and sometimes asked me to check her work. I always did, but she knew that she had to do the work herself, and then, if there were questions, I'd help. For example, suppose she was doing some simple rate-time-distance problems such as, 'If it's 500 miles to New York, and you go 50 miles an hour, how long would it take you to get there?' If she said, 'Twenty hours,' I'd ask her how long it *actually* took *us* to go there—twelve hours. In this way I tried to interest her in answering according to what is reasonable."

If the school gives no homework or offers little stimulation to the bright child, parents can provide many kinds of enriching experiences at home: creative use of clay, colored paper, paint, wood, and other materials; experiments in science; excursions and visits; reading road maps or figuring mileage on trips; keeping a record of the weather; writing stories, plays, and letters. In fact, the bright child will suggest projects himself for which you need only supply the material and sources of information.

PARENT CHILD-STUDY AND SERVICE GROUPS

Parents help themselves through child-study groups. An advisory committee is formed, time and place of meeting are suggested. Newspaper and radio announcements invite all parents, or letters are sent to parents who, the committee thinks, will work well together in a group. The members of the group feel their way in the first session. Each sees that his ideas are respected and accepted for consideration. Soon all begin to speak freely, stimulated by the frank approach of several natural leaders. One leader is chosen to guide but not dominate the discussion.

There are two main types of parent groups: the child-study group, and the group concerned with a particular problem. The child-study group, as admirably developed by Daniel Prescott, focuses on understanding an individual child. The parent presents information about the child; the group offers possible interpretations, makes rec-

ommendations for further observation and study, or suggests ways
of handling the situation.

In one community, parent groups were formed in conjunction with
the counseling of the children. These weekly groups were called "discussion groups in self-understanding." Their purpose was to help the
adults reach a better understanding of the problems of children. One
of the difficulties encountered in conducting them was the stigma at-
tached to having a problem, or a child with a problem.

A parent in Utah described a group that was studying a particular
problem:

> "I am a member of a study group, sponsored by the local branch of
> the American Association of University Women, which is currently in-
> vestigating the problems of identifying and educating gifted children—
> what is being done here, what could be done here, and what is being
> done elsewhere."

Another parent, as chairman of the education committee of the local
Woman's Club, wrote that she "would like to bring the problem of
better education for the gifted to the attention of my group in some
constructive way."

Groups of this type may make it their objective to become
acquainted with local cultural resources for gifted children—library
facilities, opportunities in art, music, drama, dance, crafts, and so on.
They may organize co-operative nursery schools or supervise weekend activities for elementary- or high-school children.

Through various kinds of organizations, parents can help their
own children, and others as well, to develop their potentialities more
fully, and thereby become happier and more socially useful
individuals.

IS SPECIAL PROVISION FOR GIFTED
CHILDREN UNDEMOCRATIC?

There is no essential conflict between "the pursuit of excellence"
and the democratic ideal of equality. The essence of democracy is
that each individual have the opportunity to develop his potentialities. This means that each child and young person should receive an

education that is suited to his needs and capacities. Democracy requires diversity rather than uniformity. Valuable individual differences need to be cultivated.

Few people object to making special provisions for the athlete, or for the handicapped child. Gifted children may become handicapped if appropriate provision is not made for them. The ideal, of course, as Anne Hoppock[4] maintains, is to "lift the level of the educational program for all, including the most able."

This ideal implies recognition of the social worth and value of all kinds of useful endeavor. No occupation should be considered high or low; the only question is whether it is suited to the individual and of service to society. The development of individual potentialities should always be "in a context of values."

The aim of society is to develop a social individual—one who is also concerned with the welfare of others. This is an especially important emphasis for gifted children, who sometimes tend to be too self-centered.

Questions and Answers

1. *What conditions are favorable for fostering superior ability?*
Among the favorable conditions at home and at school are:

(1) An atmosphere of genuine interest in ideas, books, science, and art.

(2) A respect for all kinds of excellence—athletic, social, moral, and intellectual.

(3) Association with kindred minds—opportunities to work and play and discuss deeply with persons of similar ability.

(4) Instruction that makes achievement on a higher level possible.

(5) Encouragement and recognition of real progress and achievement.

(6) Time and facilities to pursue special interests. Home and school supplement each other in providing these favorable conditions. Sometimes the home makes up for deficiencies in the school and sometimes the school offers opportunities not available in the home.

2. *In talking with a principal or superintendent about provisions for gifted children, or in taking part in a parent group that serves in an advisory capacity to the administrator, what sound points of view may the parent contribute to the discussion?* [6]

The following points of view would be sound for a parent to emphasize:

(1) A variety of flexible grouping, programing, and promotion practices that permits all children to progress through school in accordance with their own rate of development is recommended. This means that a gifted child may spend part of his school day in a regular class and part in a special group with pupils of similar ability. In both types of class he will have opportunity to go more deeply and widely into the subjects. He will be accelerated, if an individual study shows him to be physically and socially as well as intellectually able to progress more rapidly than the average.

(2) To ensure enrichment for the gifted and success for the less able a wide variety of materials of instruction must be provided—not only books and magazines but art and science equipment to stimulate creativity and experimentation.

(3) Special provision for the gifted is not undemocratic; it is the responsibility of a democracy to help every individual develop his best potentialities.

3. *How can a parent evaluate a school's provision for the gifted?*

Although certain objective factors such as number of pupils per teacher, salary scale of teachers, and specialized services are, in general, related to the quality of education in a school, the real test lies in the influence of the school on the individual pupils. Does the gifted child have opportunities (1) to acquire the tools of learning; (2) to go more deeply into a subject than the average child; (3) to range more widely in his intellectual, social, and artistic experiences; (4) to do tasks that are slightly beyond what he has already accomplished—tasks that will "stretch" his abilities; (5) to follow a special interest intensively, without being distracted; (6) to use his school time to good advantage, not have periods of time wasted in drills he does not need, unnecessary explanations and reviews, or listening to the teacher scolding the class as a whole; and (7) to use his initiative and originality and take responsibility? Any program—whether in regular classes, special classes, or special schools for gifted children—that provides these experiences for the gifted child may be considered a good program. In the opinion of the writer these opportunities will be best provided in a school where all teachers recognize and provide for individual differences in their regular classes, and special classes for the gifted are offered in certain fields.

4. *Isn't it better to have a better program for all the children, instead of costly special programs for the gifted? If the gifted are now neglected, doesn't it follow that the whole school program is deficient? Isn't a special section for the gifted apt to stir up bitter controversy in the P-TA's?*

These are pertinent questions. It seems desirable to move in the direction of providing for the gifted in regular classes, in science clubs and other extracurricular activities, and in honors classes in certain subjects. In high school, all students must have skillful guidance if they are to take advantage of the educational and recreational opportunities that are available in the school and in the community. A better program for all children will benefit the gifted in many ways.

5. *What are some current trends in the education of the gifted?*
Recent developments include:
(1) A broader definition of "giftedness."
(2) Earlier identification of gifted children.
(3) Limited acceleration based on study of the individual child and the given situation.
(4) Placing gifted children in regular heterogeneous classes for part of the day, and in special classes for the rest of the time.
(5) Better provision for gifted children in regular classes.
(6) More emphasis on the social responsibilities of the gifted.
(7) Formation of voluntary discussion and study groups on matters related to giftedness; some of these groups are for teachers, some for parents, and some for both.

6. *How can we provide for a relatively small number of gifted children in a school where the mental ability level is low?*
After the gifted children have been identified, various provisions may be made for them:

(1) They can be grouped together in a core class covering several grade levels.

(2) They can be given opportunities to be in advanced classes in certain subjects. Correspondence courses may be used when the number is too small to form a class.

(3) They can be given special library time and privileges.

(4) Students from different schools may take excursions together or have a seminar one afternoon a week in a centrally located school.

(5) They can engage in work on school publications and other extraclass activities.

(6) They can use community resources such as museums, membership on community council or youth council, church activities, youth groups.

(7) Alert teachers can provide challenging work in their regular classes.

7. *Are average children being neglected?*
Probably not, for teachers tend to gear their instruction to the average ability of their classes. And the teacher who is skillful in individualizing instruction will provide experiences suited to high, low, and average ability.

8. *What, briefly, are the essentials of good education of the gifted?* [8]
Four essentials are:

(1) Early identification.

(2) Gradual development of the student's insight into his abilities.

(3) Finding, making available, and encouraging him to use the kinds of experiences that will develop his abilities.

(4) Developing the desire and will on his part to use his talents in a socially constructive way.

Evidence of Concern About the Education of the Gifted

WE SHOULD be encouraged by the many signs of interest in the education of the gifted. "Everybody's doing it"—at least everybody's talking about doing something about it. It is time, as an old Kentucky farmer said, that "our doings catch up with our knowings."

Parents are concerned. They ask mathematics and science teachers whether their child is truly gifted, before deciding whether or not to continue in these fields where he will meet keen competition. Parents discuss their children's ability with the child's teacher or counselor. Conversation about the gifted is frequently heard from people not connected with school.

Communities are also concerned. In every field there is a shortage of gifted people. This shortage is not caused by lack of potential ability. Much talent is undiscovered and undeveloped. Scientists and businessmen are offering scholarships to stimulate youth to get the education suited to them. They are trying to stimulate gifted children's interest in science through the *National Science Fair* and similar programs.

There are also continuing education programs for adults with special talents—museums, art groups, and music societies that sponsor groups of talented young people, and other separate but not centrally co-ordinated opportunities. A Community Talent Search project begun in New York to identify and provide special cultural and educational opportunities for gifted children among low socioeconomic groups is spreading to other cities.

Although several communities in the United States, such as Portland, Oregon, have remarkable programs for the recognition and development of talent, largely within the public school system, no community, Robert J. Havighurst asserted, "seems to have made a systematic effort to discover and develop a variety of talents."*

Schools and school systems here and there are holding workshops for voluntary groups of teachers and administrators who want to make better provision for gifted pupils. A few school systems have hired special consultants to work with teachers and sometimes to teach classes of gifted children. A number of large school systems, such as those of Baltimore and Long Beach, California, have published bulletins on different aspects, for example, "Reading for the Superior Student," "The Counselor's Role in Identifying and Guiding the Superior Pupil," "What Vocational Education Offers for the Superior Pupil."

Some attention has been given to the selection of teachers and their qualifications for teaching the gifted. The U.S. Office of Education Bulletin on teachers for the gifted illustrates this interest.

Curriculum committees have made changes to benefit the gifted student. For example, in one high school there have been established workshops in science, special language classes, and numerous clubs and activities to encourage the gifted, a new creative writing group, and the appointment of a speech and drama teacher to develop that department.

Guidance workers are being alerted to their responsibility for the gifted.

Extensive studies are being made to determine the reasons why the gifted underachiever is failing to realize his potentialities.

On the state level, Wisconsin has appointed a subcommittee of the Curriculum Guiding Committee of the State Department of Public Instruction to consider provisions for gifted children. Parents and persons representing community groups, as well as teachers and administrators, meet with this committee to state principles and raise and answer questions about the education of gifted children. California's legislature recently enacted a Gifted Child Law, with an initial appropriation of $40,000. In New York State a special supervisor was appointed by the Department of Education to head up the task of encouraging schools in the state to identify the gifted and to set up means of providing for their needs.

* Robert J. Havighurst, et al. A Community Youth Developmental Program. Chicago: The University of Chicago Press, 1952, p. 17.

On a national level, the United States government has appropriated large sums of money for training institutes to prepare counselors more adequately for their responsibility of guiding gifted students. Money has also been appropriated for scholarships and loans to enable the academically talented to go to college.

Numerous articles, reports, and books on the gifted have been written during recent years. Newspapers with sections devoted daily and weekly to education, as well as professional magazines, have frequently considered the education of the gifted, as have also radio and television programs. Such papers as the *New York Times* and *Herald-Tribune,* the Associated Press, the *National Parent-Teacher* magazine, the *N.E.A. Journal,* and many others feature articles on the gifted.

At most of the conventions of educational organizations there is at least one meeting on the gifted, usually very well attended.

Experiments on ways of developing the abilities of the gifted more fully have been undertaken privately and financed by foundations.

Selected Books and Pamphlets of Interest to Parents of Gifted Children *

Abraham, Willard. *Common Sense About Gifted Children.* New York: Harper & Brothers, 1958. 266 pp. A readable, well-documented book about gifted children and what to do about them.

American Association for Gifted Children. *Guideposts for Parents, Gifted Children, Teachers and Administrators.* New York: Bureau of Publications, Teachers College, Columbia University, 1958. Four leaflets, four pages each, of concise suggestions for helping parents, teachers, administrators, and the gifted children themselves, provide conditions conducive to their best development.

————. American Association for Gifted Children. *Creativity of Gifted and Talented Children.* New York: Bureau of Publications, Teachers College, Columbia University, 1959. 51 pp. Three addresses by Paul Witty, James B. Conant, and Ruth Strang with special emphasis on developing the creative powers of gifted children; also included are statements made by gifted children concerning the qualities in teachers which appeal to them.

Barclay, Dorothy. *Understanding the City Child.* New York: Franklin Watts, Inc., 1959. 288 pp. $4.95.

————. Weekly articles in the *New York Times Magazine.* These articles are delightful, informative, up-to-the-minute, psychologically sound, and make instantaneous connections with parents' needs and interests.

Brumbaugh, Florence N., and Bernard Rosheo. *Your Gifted Child.* New York: Henry Holt and Company, Inc., 1959. 182 pp. Valuable for its concrete practical suggestions, and enlivened by a wealth of ancedotes about gifted children.

Canadian Mental Health Association. *How To Know Your Child.* 1790 Broadway, New York 19: Human Relations Aids, 1954. Unpaged. A

---

* These titles are, for the most part, in addition to the references given in connection with each chapter.

small pamphlet, simple, sound, and sensible in its point of view; appealing and helpful to parents.

Conant, James B. *Finding and Educating the Academically Talented Student in the Secondary School.* Washington 6, D.C.: National Education Association, 1958. 15 pp. A concise description of the roles of the student, the teacher, the counselor, the administrator, and the community in the secondary-school program for academically talented students.

Cutts, Norma E., and Nicholas Moseley. *Bright Children.* New York: G. P. Putnam's Sons, 1953. 238 pp. The first book written specifically for parents of bright children, with special emphasis on their school education and mental health.

DeHaan, Robert F., and Robert J. Havighurst. *Educating Gifted Children.* Chicago 37: The University of Chicago Press, 1957. 276 pp. A comprehensive, critical, and up-to-date treatment of school and community programs for the identification and development of gifted children.

Frank, Mary, and Lawrence K. Frank. *How To Help Your Child in School.* A Signet Key Book. 501 Madison Avenue, New York 22: The New American Library of World Literature, 1950. 288 pp. Definite answers to parents' real questions about nursery school and elementary school, as well as discussion of problems that may arise at each stage of development.

French, Joseph L. *Educating the Gifted.* New York: Henry Holt and Company, Inc., 1959. 555 pp. A carefully selected book of readings, indirectly giving parents background in research, programs, and evaluated procedures in the education of the gifted.

Grant, Eva H. (Editor). *Guiding Children as They Grow.* 700 North Rush Street, Chicago 11, Illinois: National Congress of Parents and Teachers, 1959. 256 pp. A paperback edition containing articles by outstanding authors on aspects of preschool, school, and adolescent development, which every parent needs to understand.

Havighurst, Robert J., *et al. A Survey of the Education of the Gifted Children.* Supplementary Educational Monograph No. 83. Chicago, University of Chicago Press, 1955. 114 pp.

Henry, Nelson B. (Editor). *Education for the Gifted.* The Fifty-seventh Yearbook of the National Society for the Study of Education, Part II. Chicago 37: The University of Chicago Press, 1958. 420 pp. Social, psychological, and educational aspects of the education of the gifted, presented with perspective and a balanced point of view as well as with considerable concreteness.

Johnson, Eric W. *How To Live Through Junior High School.* Philadelphia: J. B. Lippincott Company, 1959. 278 pp. A wise and practical treatment, from the standpoint of parents, of education during the generally neglected pre- and early-adolescent period.

Oswalt, Edna R. *The Role of the Parent in the Education and Training of the Mentally Superior Child.* (Bulletin V. 45 No. 6) Rev. ed. Kent, Ohio: Kent State University, 1957. 47 pp. A booklet of practical, "what-to-do" types of suggestions summarizing the committee work of parents and teachers.

Strang, Ruth. *The Adolescent Views Himself: A Psychology of Adolescence.* New York: McGraw-Hill Book Company, 1957. 581 pp. Through adolescents' comments and descriptions, many written by gifted adolescents, the uniqueness of each individual as he perceives himself is emphasized.

————. "The Psychology of Gifted Children," in *Psychology of Exceptional Children* (William M. Cruickshank, Editor). Englewood Cliffs, New Jersey: Prentice-Hall, 1955. Pp. 475-519. A more technical consideration of "giftedness" as a product of the interaction of native ability and life experiences.

Terman, Lewis. *Mental and Physical Traits of a Thousand Gifted Children.* Stanford, California: Stanford University Press, 1925. 648 pp.

————. and Barbara S. Burks. *The Promise of Youth.* Stanford, California: Stanford University Press, 1930. 508 pp.

————. and Melita Oden. *The Gifted Child Grows Up.* Stanford, California: Stanford University Press, 1947. 448 pp.

————. *The Gifted Child at Mid-Life.* Stanford, California: Stanford University Press, 1959. 187 pp.

Witty, Paul. *Helping the Gifted Child.* Chicago, Illinois: Science Research Associates, 1953. 48 pp. A booklet giving to parents and teachers high lights of our knowledge of gifted children and their education.

Witty, Paul (Editor). *The Gifted Child.* Boston: D. C. Heath and Company, 1951. 338 pp. A basic book developed by the American Association for Gifted Children with chapters by authorities on essential aspects of the gifted, their nature and nurture.

APPENDIX C
Children's Book Clubs

CHILDREN's book clubs have skyrocketed in popularity. By now probably more than two million children in the United States are subscribers. Most clubs mail books directly to the children's homes. Children get a thrill from receiving their own books through the mail. The selection of books is good and the club ensures that the child receives new books at regular intervals. Since the gifteds' reading interests tend to follow children's interest in general but a year or two in advance, you might subscribe for books in the chronological age group slightly above your child's age. The names, addresses, and some other pertinent information about these book clubs are given below:

For four or five age groups:
Picture books, 6–9; Intermediate, 9 to 12; older girls, 12 to 16; and older boys, 12–16.
CATHOLIC CHILDREN'S BOOK CLUB, 260 Summit Avenue, St. Paul 2, Minnesota. Books are sent monthly or every other month, September through June. Books with a Catholic theme or background, with emphasis on character building and good family relations predominate. $20 for younger ages; $21.50 for older age groups, for 10 months
JUNIOR LITERARY GUILD, Garden City, New York. Books are sent monthly, fiction and nonfiction of high literary quality, varied and interesting. $1.75 per month.

For elementary school years, ages 7 to 12
ARROW BOOK CLUB, 33 West 42nd Street, New York 36, New York. Books sent five times during school year; paper-bound editions, but with larger page size and type than adult paper-bound books, fiction and nonfiction. Books delivered only to the schools. 25 to 35¢ each.

PARENTS' MAGAZINE BOOK CLUB FOR CHILDREN, Bergenfield, New Jersey. Fiction and nonfiction books of good quality are sent monthly. $1.47 per month plus 18¢ postage.

WEEKLY READER CHILDREN'S BOOK CLUB, Education Center, Columbus 16, Ohio. Five books per year, fiction and nonfiction of high literary quality. $6.00 per year.

YOUNG PEOPLE'S BOOK CLUB, Sears, Roebuck and Company, Box 6570A, Chicago, Illinois. Books sent monthly, story biographies and stories of significant events of the "We were there" type. $1.69 per month plus 16¢ postage.

For upper elementary and high school

YOUNG READERS OF AMERICA, 345 Hudson Street, New York 14. Ages 9 to 14. Books are sent monthly—nonfiction accounts of personalities and events in the United States and in other parts of the world and nonfiction science and nature books. $1.75 each plus postage.

TEEN-AGE BOOK CLUB, 33 West 42nd Street, New York 36, New York. Books are sent eight times during the school-year—paper-bound fiction and nonfiction, juvenile and adult books popular with teenagers. Sent only through the schools. 25 or 35¢ each.

Books for the Gifted Child *

Picture Books, Easy Reading, and "Read-To" Books for the Preschool and First Grade

Ardizoone, Edward. *Little Tim and the Brave Sea Captain.* New York: Oxford University Press, 1955. unp. A distinctive picture book about life at sea. A five-year-old boy is the hero.

Bemelmans, Ludwig. *Madeline.* New York: Simon & Schuster, Inc., 1939. unp. The rollicking text and humorous pictures relate how a little girl in a Paris boarding school had a gay time in spite of an appendectomy.

Beskow, Else. *Pelle's New Suit.* New York: Harper & Brothers, n.d. unp. Tells how a little Swedish boy earned his new suit by raking hay, bringing in wood, feeding pigs, going on errands, etc. The process in the making of the suit is followed from the shearing of the lamb.

Bishop, Claire Huchet. *Five Chinese Brothers.* New York: Coward-McCann, Inc., 1938. unp. Popular retelling of an old Chinese tale. An amusing account of five brothers who because of their remarkable powers saved themselves from catastrophe.

Brooke, L. Leslie. *Johnny Crow's Garden.* New York: Frederick Warne & Co. Inc., 1930. unp. Johnny Crow is the perfect, polite host to the friends in his garden. Told in perfect nonsense rhymes.

Brown, Marcia. *Stone Soup.* New York: Charles Scribner's Sons, 1947. unp. An old folk-tale picture book of the wily soldiers who befooled the peasants and got a good meal. Bright red double-page pictures.

Brown, Margaret Wise—Any of her many books are delightful to read to preschool children.

Buff, Conrad and Mary. *Dash and Dart.* New York: The Viking Press, Inc., 1942. 73 pp. Gives the first year of the life of two little fawns. The simple rhythmic sentences and exquisite illustrations make this a rare selection for the beginning science and nature concept.

---

* Bibliography prepared by Louise James, District Librarian, Palm Springs Unified Schools, Palm Springs, California.

Burton, Virginia Lee. *The Little House.* Boston: Houghton Mifflin Company, 1942. 40 pp. A little house in the country is gradually surrounded as a city springs up about it. Eventually the great-grandchildren of the builders put it on wheels and move it into the country where it is happy again. An original and charming picture book.

Chaucer, Geoffrey. *Chanticleer and the Fox;* retold by Barbara Cooney. New York: Thomas Y. Crowell Company, 1958. 36 pp. A well-told version of Chaucer's "Nun's Priest's Tale" with rich colorful and detailed drawings. The vigor and humor of Chaucer's version is retained, and the book is excellent for reading aloud.

Clark, Margery (pseud.). *Poppy Seed Cakes.* New York: Doubleday & Company, Inc., 1924. unp. The gay pictures of a small Russian girl and boy and their good aunt who brought to the new country a bag full of presents resemble picture books of Czechoslovakia and Russia.

Dalgliesh, Alice. *Bears on Hemlock Mountain.* New York: Charles Scribner's Sons, 1952. unp. A Pennsylvania folktale is the basis of this story about a small boy sent over Hemlock Mountain—where there were bears—to borrow a large iron pot. Well designed and illustrated.

Daugherty, James Henry. *The Picnic.* New York: The Viking Press, Inc., 1958. 79 pp. A version of the fable of the mouse who rescued a lion who had helped him. A delightful and humorous book with plenty of action.

Ets, Marie Hall. *Play with Me.* New York: The Viking Press, Inc., 1955. 31 pp. A funny and excited little girl tries one sunny morning to catch creatures in the meadow and play with them. There is a happy ending when she learns to sit quietly and wait.

Flack, Marjorie. *The Story About Ping.* New York: The Viking Press, Inc., 1933. unp. The story of a little Chinese duck whose home was a houseboat. An artistic and irresistible picture book.

Gág, Wanda. *ABC Bunny.* New York: Coward-McCann, Inc., 1933. unp. An alphabet that tells in brief verse and attractive black-and-white pictures the story of a little rabbit's adventures. Has been set to music, and music is given.

————. *Millions of Cats.* New York: Coward-McCann, Inc., 1928. unp. An unusual picture book of folktale quality. The story tells how a little old man and woman wanted one cat and became owners of "millions and billions and trillions of cats."

Geisel, Theodor (Dr. Seuss, pseud.). *Cat in the Hat.* New York: Random

House, Inc., 1957. 61 pp. A nonsense story in verse designed for the beginning reader. The author uses only 223 words in the story, at least half of which should be familiar to first-grade pupils.

————. *The 500 Hats of Bartholomew Cubbins*. Eau Claire, Wisconsin: E. M. Hale & Company, 1945. unp. To Bartholomew's astonishment he finds that he is unable to take off his hat to the king because as he snatches off one hat another and another appears. Amusing black-and-white illustrations.

Geismer, Barbara Peck. *Very Young Verses*. Boston: Houghton Mifflin Company, 1945. 210 pp. A collection of poems about animals, seasons, the weather, and humorous subjects that can be enjoyed and remembered by children.

Gramatky, Hardy. *Little Toot*. New York: G. P. Putnam's Sons, 1939. unp. An entertaining story of a saucy little tugboat too pleased with himself to do any work until he is caught in a storm and proves himself a hero.

Holland, Marion. *A Big Ball of String*. New York: Random House, Inc., 1958. 64 pp. An engaging story for the beginning reader. It tells of a little boy who was refused the string from his mother's knitting wool and his father's fishing pole but was able to collect an enormous ball of string at the dump.

Hutchinson, Veronica Somerville. *Chimney Corner Stories*. New York: G. P. Putnam's Sons, 1925. 149 pp. Sixteen short familiar fairy tales which are favorites of small children. An excellent choice for the home library.

Iwatamsu, Jun. *Crow Boy*. New York: The Viking Press, Inc., 1955. unp. An attractively illustrated story of a sensitive and shy little Japanese schoolboy. Pictures and text are perfectly matched.

Leaf, Munro. *The Story of Ferdinand*. New York: The Viking Press, Inc., 1936. unp. A hilarious bit of fun in the account of a young Spanish bull's astonishing behavior.

McCloskey, Robert. *Make Way for Ducklings*. New York: The Viking Press, Inc., 1941. unp. An unusual and stunning picture book of Mr. and Mrs. Mallard and their eight ducklings who make their home on an island in Charles River and march through the streets of Boston.

Minarik, Else Homelund. *Little Bear*. New York: Harper & Brothers, 1957. 63 pp. An I-Can-Read story with easy text which concerns the adventures of a funny, lovable little bear, including an exciting trip to the moon.

Mother Goose. Marguerite de Angeli's *Book of Nursery and Mother Goose Rhymes*. New York: Doubleday & Company, Inc. 1954. 192 pp. A

234 HELPING YOUR GIFTED CHILD

comprehensive collection of rhymes mainly from Mother Goose with
old favorites as well as the less familiar. An excellent selection for
home use.

Petersham, Maud and Miska. *The Christ Child.* New York: Doubleday &
Company, Inc., 1931. unp. Recreates in full color and in a child-ap-
pealing manner the story of Jesus' childhood. The text is taken from
the Bible.

Potter, Beatrix. *Tale of Peter Rabbit.* New York: Grosset & Dunlap, Inc.,
1942. unp. A charming story of the famous rabbit family consisting of
Flopsy, Mopsy, Cotton-tail and Peter Rabbit himself who disobeys his
mother and goes into Mr. McGregor's garden.

Seignobosc, François. *Jeanne-Marie Counts Her Sheep.* New York: Charles
Scribner's Sons, 1951. unp. Designed to help the preschool child learn
his numbers, this is a gay, colorful, and delightful picture book about
a little French girl and her lambs.

Titus, Eve. *Anatole.* New York: Whittlesey House, 1956. 32 pp. An amusing and colorful book which tells the story of a little French mouse
and his work in a cheese factory.

Tresselt, Alvin. *White Snow, Bright Snow.* New York: Lothrop, Lee &
Shepard Co., Inc., 1947. 33 pp. Describes for children the magical
beauty of snowfall. Points out the effects of a snowfall on the work of
the farmer, postman, and policeman.

Ward, Lynd Kendall. *The Biggest Bear.* Boston: Houghton Mifflin Company, 1952. 84 pp. About Johnny and his pet bear that grew too big
and mischievous. Johnny has a problem when he takes the bear into
the woods only to have it return. An outstanding picture book.

Simple Reading and Other Books for the Second and Third Grades

Andersen, Hans Christian. *The Swineherd.* New York: Harcourt, Brace
and Company, Inc., 1958. 32 pp. The illustrations of Erik Blegvad
have enhanced this story of the swineherd whose gifts were rejected
by the princess.

Atwater, Richard and Florence. *Mr. Popper's Penguins.* Boston: Little,
Brown & Co., 1938. 139 pp. Mr. Popper is sent one penguin from the
South Pole, acquires another, and eventually there are twelve. Children are delighted with the rollicking humor as the penguins rule
the household and take the Popper family on a vaudeville tour.

d'Aulaire, Ingri and Edgar Parin. *George Washington.* New York: Doubleday & Company, Inc., 1936. unp. A large picture-story book which
depicts in five colors scenes in the life of George Washington. Text is
informative and interesting.

Browning, Robert. *The Pied Piper of Hamlin.* New York: Frederick Warne & Co., Inc., 1938, 48 pp. The poem as well as the illustrations of this book merit its selection as a part of the child's literary heritage. It relates how the piper, employed to rid the town of rats, pipes the town's children into a mountain.

Carroll, Lewis (pseud.). *Alice's Adventures in Wonderland* and *Through the Looking Glass.* New York: E. P. Dutton & Co., Inc. 1954. 246 pp. Illustrated by Sir John Tenniel, this is an attractive and well-told edition of the beloved child's classic which was first published in 1865.

Cavanah, Frances. *Our Country's Story.* Chicago: Rand McNally & Company, 1945. 71 pp. Designed to give children their first glimpse into American history. In the pictures and simple text Columbus, Washington, Daniel Boone, Lincoln, the Pilgrims, and western pioneers are introduced. Tells why we celebrate the Fourth of July and how the "Star Spangled Banner" came to be written.

Cleary, Beverly, *Buzus and Ramona.* New York: William Morrow and Company, Inc., 1955, 159 pp. Ramona, a strong-willed four-year-old, has many ideas for trying the patience of her big sister Buzus. It's an easily read book of rare humorous quality.

Clewes, Dorothy. *The Runaway.* New York: Coward-McCann, Inc., 1957. 63 pp. Penny did not want to leave her home in the city and move to the rural suburb. When her mother told her to run away—go out and play—Penny took her literally and went back to the city. An understanding picture of a child's reaction to a new situation.

Coates, Belle. *That Colt Fireplug.* New York: Charles Scribner's Sons, 1958. 56 pp. Tim and Beth pay five dollars for an old scion of a long line of fire horses; and, in spite of family financial difficulties, they are allowed to keep him after Fireplug proves his worth.

Coatsworth, Elizabeth. *Away Goes Sally.* New York: The Macmillan Company, 1934. 122 pp. A refreshingly different story of pioneer life in the 1800's. Tells about a charming little girl who moved from Massachusetts to Maine in a house drawn on runners by twelve oxen. Has short poems between chapters.

Dalgliesh, Alice. *Courage of Sarah Noble.* New York: Charles Scribner's Sons, 1954. 52 pp. The story of an eight-year-old pioneer girl who went alone with her father into the Connecticut wilderness in the 1700's.

————. *The Columbus Story.* New York: Charles Scribner's Sons, 1955. unp. Relates incidents in the life of Columbus that are of special interest to children. A good historical narrative for reading aloud.

De Angeli, Marguerite. *Door in the Wall.* New York: Doubleday & Company, Inc., 1949. 111 pp. A poignant story. Set in thirteenth-century England. Tells the dramatic story of Robin, the crippled son of a great lord, and how he overcame his disabilities and won knighthood.

Edmonds, Walter. *The Matchlock Gun.* New York: Dodd, Mead & Co., Inc., 1941. 50 pp. When Edward Alstyne leaves settlement to search for marauding Indians, the ten-year-old boy successfully fires the old Spanish gun brought to America by his grandfather and protects himself and his mother against attacking Indians.

Estes, Eleanor. *The Hundred Dresses.* New York: Harcourt, Brace and Company, 1944. 80 pp. When a little Polish girl, Wanda Petronski, enrolls in school the children are amused that she wears the same faded blue dress every day and tells them she has a hundred dresses. Later the children learn what Wanda means, and a good point in human relations is stressed.

Field, Rachael. *Poems of Childhood.* New York: Charles Scribner's Sons, n.d. 199 pp. Selected from *Love Songs of Childhood* and *With Trumpet and Drum,* these poems have universal appeal for young children.

Gannet, Ruth S. *My Father's Dragon.* New York: Random House, Inc., 1950. 86 pp. An original plot in which a small boy rescues a baby dragon by his ingenious appeals to the greedy and conceited animals of Wild Island.

Grimm, Jacob L. K. *Household Stories;* from the collection of the Brothers Grimm. New York: The Macmillan Company, 1954. 260 pp. Translated from the German by Lucy Crane, this collection has the basic familiar stories which should be a part of every child's literary experience.

Haywood, Carolyn. *"B" is for Betsy.* New York: Harcourt, Brace and Company, 1939. 159 pp. Simple narrative descriptions of a little American girl's first year at school and the ensuing vacation on her father's farm.

————. *Little Eddie.* New York: William Morrow and Company, Inc., 1947. 160 pp. The story of a seven-year-old boy who knows what he wants and goes about getting it by his own ingenuity. Good storytelling quality.

Holden, Averill Esther. *Cartier Sails the St. Lawrence.* New York: Harper & Brothers, 1956. 108 pp. Based largely on the biographer's own logbooks of his journey into the St. Lawrence. A well-told and vividly striking biography.

Hunt, Mabel Leigh. *Benjie's Hat.* Philadelphia: Frederick A. Stokes (now by J. B. Lippincott Company), 1938. 119 pp. A delightfully funny and lovable story of an eight-year-old Quaker boy and his trials with hats, old and new.

Jones, Elizabeth Orton. *Twig*. New York: The Macmillan Company, 1942. 152 pp. A modern fairy tale of genuine humor. Twig, who lives on the fourth floor of a house in a big city, wishes for a fairy to live in a tomato can, and along comes a little elf!

Lattimore, Eleanor Francis. *Little Pear*. New York: William Morrow and Company, Inc., 1946. 127 pp. The escapades of a mischievous little Chinese boy who craved adventure, eventually fell into the river, and was rescued by a man on a houseboat. A simple, charming, and natural story for the beginning reader.

Lawrence, Mildred. *Peachtree Island*. New York: Harcourt, Brace and Company, 224 pp. A nine-year-old orphan girl lives with each of three aunts and then moves to the home of her delightful Uncle Eben, who has a peach orchard. A wholesome family story.

Lawson, Robert. *Rabbit Hill*. New York: The Viking Press, Inc., 1944. 127 pp. A robust and humorous book about the animals on Rabbit Hill who learn "new folks" are coming to live in the vacant house.

Leaf, Monro. *Wee Gillis*. New York: The Viking Press, Inc., 1938. unp. Gillis is faced with a hard decision—to live in the Highlands and hunt deer with his father's relatives or to go to the Lowlands and raise cattle with his mother's people. He solves the problem his own way.

Lenski, Lois. *Strawberry Girl*. Philadelphia: J. B. Lippincott Company, 1945. 193 pp. A story of life among the Georgia Crackers and especially Birdie Boyer, a warm-hearted little girl whose industrious family makes a living by raising strawberries.

Liu, Beatrice. *Little Wu and the Watermelons*. Chicago: Follett Publishing Company, 1954. 96 pp. Set against a Chinese peasant background, the book tells how young Wu succeeded in growing and selling watermelons in order to buy an ornament for his mother. Reveals in simple terms the spirit of the Chinese people, their love for the land, and their family customs.

Lord, Beman. *The Trouble with Francis*. New York: H. Z. Walck, Inc., 1958. 55 pp. Francis seemed like a girl's name and not at all befitting to a baseball player. After many attempts and tactics, Francis was dubbed "Buckets" and his "troubles" were solved.

Love, Katherine Isabel. *Little Laughter*. New York: Thomas Y. Crowell Company, 1957. 114 pp. A refreshing and delightful collection of humorous poetry from the works of well-known children's poets. The entertaining poems were selected by a children's librarian.

MacGregor, Ellen. *Miss Pickwell Goes to Mars.* New York: McGraw-Hill Book Company, 1951. 128 pp. Miss Pickwell returned from a month's vacation to find not only that someone had been living in her house, but that a rocket ship was in her pasture. Introduces the child to science fiction.

Mason, Miriam Evangeline. *Caroline and Her Kettle Named Maud.* New York: The Macmillan Company, 1951. 134 pp. Caroline, a pioneer girl, wants a gun but is given a kettle which she names as the men name their guns. Later she proves what can be done with courage and kettles.

Milne, Alan Alexander. *When We Were Very Young.* New York: E. P. Dutton & Co., Inc., 1924. 100 pp. An excellent collection of poems on various subjects of special appeal to children. The poems have unexpected surprises in rhymes and rhythm, freshness and vigor, and dainty meter.

Milne, Alan Alexander. *Winnie-the-Pooh.* New York: E. P. Dutton & Co. Inc., 1926. 159 pp. Delightful nonsense about Christopher Robin and his Teddy bear. Told with unusual skill.

Read, Sir Herbert Edward. *This Way Delight.* New York: Pantheon Books, Inc., 1956. 155 pp. An attractive collection, most of which is from well-known poets. Includes a few poems by children and a few not generally thought of as having appeal to children.

Thurber, James. *Many Moons.* New York: Harcourt, Brace and Company, 1943. unp. The little Princess Lenore is ill and her father promises to grant her any wish. She asks for the moon and Court Jester is the only one wise enough to get it for her. An amusing fantasy and delightful pictures.

White, Elwyn Brooks. *Charlotte's Web.* New York: Harper & Brothers, 1952. 184 pp. A fascinating and charming story of a pig, Wilbur, and his friendship with Charlotte, the spider, who could talk and write. Children have taken the book to their hearts, and likely it will become a classic.

Books for the Fourth Grade

Alcott, Louisa M. *Little Women.* New York: E. P. Dutton & Co., Inc., 1951. 303 pp. The famous story of the four March sisters and their New England farm life. Gives excellent characterization in the portrayal of each "little woman."

Andersen, Hans Christian. *Fairy Tales.* Cleveland: The World Publishing Company, 1946. 318 pp. Illustrated by Jean O'Neil, this is an attractive volume with many black-and-white and some full-page pictures. The tales are well selected.

Clark, Ann Nolan. *Secret of the Andes.* New York: The Viking Press, Inc., 1952. 130 pp. Cuse, an Inca Indian boy, lives high in the Andes with an old Indian herder where he helps to guard the flock of llamas while he learns the traditions and lore of his people.

Commanger, Henry Steele. *The Great Declaration.* Indianapolis: Bobbs-Merrill Company, 1958. 112 pp. Describes the evolution of the Declaration of Independence and gives the background of the state of Colonial affairs.

Dejong, Mundert. *House of Sixty Fathers.* New York: Harper & Brothers, 1956. 189 pp. Tien Pas lived in China during the days of the Japanese invasion, was separated from his parents temporarily, and went to live with sixty American soldiers. A vivid and realistic story.

de la Mare, Walter. *Come Hither.* New York: Alfred A. Knopf, Inc., 1928. 823 pp. A choice collection of American and English poems. Includes nearly 500 selections, some of which are modern.

Dodge, Mary Mapes. *Hans Brinker; Or the Silver Skates.* New York: E. P. Dutton & Co., Inc., 1955. 295 pp. Though this book was first published in 1865, it still gives a picture of life in Holland that has fascination for boys and girls.

Enright, Elizabeth. *The Saturdays.* New York: Rinehart & Co., Inc., 1941. 175 pp. With the help of an understanding father and a housekeeper four motherless children work out a plan whereby they take turns on successive Saturdays spending their allowances. Treats children with sympathy and insight.

Estes, Eleanor. *The Moffats.* New York: Harcourt, Brace and Company, 1941. 290 pp. Life of the Moffat family, four children from five-and-a-half to fifteen and Mama. Told mostly from the interesting viewpoint of nine-year-old Janey, it is a story of warmth and humor.

Foster, Genevieve. *Andrew Jackson.* Chicago: Follett Publishing Company, 1954. 224 pp. Portrays Andrew Jackson as a boy, as a lawyer, planter, soldier, and statesman. The book is a strong character study.

Gray, Elizabeth Janet. *Adam of the Road.* New York: The Viking Press, Inc., 1942. 317 pp. A thirteenth-century historical tale of a minstrel and his son Adam and their wanderings through southeastern England. Adam is separated from his dog and from his father, but all are reunited.

Hale, Lucretia Peabody. *Peterkin Papers.* Boston: Houghton Mifflin Company, 1924. 219 pp. A humorous book in which the Peterkin family

try to achieve wisdom, get into strange difficulties, and are saved
by the common sense of the Lady from Philadelphia.

Henry, Marguerite. *Brighty of the Grand Canyon.* Chicago: Rand McNally
& Company, 1953. 222 pp. Account of a little wild burro in the Grand
Canyon of Arizona and the old prospector who befriended him.

Hosford, Dorothy. *Thunder of the Gods.* New York: Henry Holt and Company, Inc., 1952. 115 pp. An outstanding account of the "adventures
of the God Odin and his son Thor, of good Balder, of Loki and his
evil pranks and of war between the gods and the giants."

Hufford, Grace Thompson. *My Poetry Book.* Philadelphia: The John C.
Winston Company, 1956. 504 pp. An anthology of modern verse for
boys and girls. Contains well-selected English and American poems
on a variety of subjects.

Judson, Clara. *Thomas Jefferson, Champion of the People.* Chicago. Follett
Publishing Company, 1952. 224 pp. Presents Jefferson in an admirable
manner both at home and in the work for his country. Brings in his
philosophy of government, his ideals of freedom, and his faith in
mankind.

Kastner, Erich. *Emil and the Detectives.* New York: Doubleday & Company, Inc., 1930. 224 pp. Emil who is going by train to Berlin to visit
his grandmother, falls asleep and his money is stolen. His clever
scheme for catching the thief and solving the mystery make for satisfying adventure.

Lofting, Hugh. *Voyages of Dr. Doolittle.* Philadelphia: Frederick A. Stokes
(now by J. B. Lippincott Company), 1920. 180 pp. The inimitable
adventure of a kind-hearted old doctor who loved animals and understood their language. Delightfully humorous.

Lorenzini, Carlo. *Adventures of Pinocchio.* New York: The Macmillan
Company, 1951. 206 pp. An Italian classic in which Geppetto finds a
piece of wood and carves it into an unforgettable marionette called
Pinocchio. A simple and practical moral underlies the theme.

McCloskey, Robert. *Homer Price.* New York: The Viking Press, Inc., 1943.
149 pp. Six rollicking short stories of Homer Price and his encounters
which include the amusing experience with the doughnut machine.

Norton, Mary. *The Borrowers.* New York: Harcourt, Brace and Company,
1953. 180 pp. A magical and charming story of the fascinating
and miniature inhabitants of the wall of a quiet old house who "borrow" skillfully the things they need.

O'Brien, John Sherman. *Silver Chief, Dog of the North.* Philadelphia: The
John C. Winston Company, 1933. 218 pp. A beautiful dog of the
Canadian wilderness is the hero of this story which will appeal to

both boys and girls. He is tamed and trained by a Mountie, and a strong friendship develops between the two.

Pyle, Howard. *Otto of the Silver Hand*. New York: Charles Scribner's Sons, 1928. 170 pp. A romantic tale of knighthood, robber barons, and feuds. Also of Otto's kidnaping and his adventures with the rough enemy soldiers.

Rounds, Glen. *Ol' Paul, the Mighty Logger*. New York: Holiday House, Inc., 1949. 173 pp. A tall tale of the incredible exploits and inventions of Paul Bunyan.

Seredy, Kate. *The Good Master*. New York: The Viking Press, Inc., 1935. 210 pp. A lively young girl from Budapest goes to live on her uncle's farm. Portrays authentically the customs of the people of the Hungarian plains.

Spyri, Johanna. *Heidi*. New York: E. P. Dutton & Co., Inc., 1950. 320 pp. Heidi, a little orphan, goes to live with her grandfather in the Swiss Alps in this story which has such popular appeal to young hearts.

Thomas, Henry. *Thomas Alva Edison*. New York: G. P. Putnam's Sons, 1958. 128 pp. An excellent biography which describes the vigorous and forceful personality of the scientist.

Wilder, Laura Ingalls. *Little House in the Big Woods*. New York: Harper & Brothers, 1953. 371 pp. Laura and Mary live with their parents at the edge of the Big Woods of Wisconsin, miles from neighbors and a settlement. Incidents in their daily lives are of interest to both boys and girls.

Books for the Fifth and Sixth Grades

Busoni, Rafaello. *The Man Who Was Don Quixote*. New York: Prentice-Hall, Inc., 1958. 209 pp. "A vivid and absorbing biography of Cervantes" in which the sixteenth-century author is brought vividly alive. The experiences of his masterpiece are found in his own life.

Clemens, Samuel L. (Mark Twain, pseud.) *Adventures of Tom Sawyer*. New York: E. P. Dutton & Co. Inc., 1955. 247 pp. The famous classic of boy life on the Mississippi is based on authentic reminiscences by the author; combines romance, realism and humor.

Colum, Padraic. *Adventures of Odysseus and the Tale of Troy*. New York: The Macmillan Company, 1918. 254 pp. An enthralling romance which will carry the child's imagination to long-ago Greece. Illustrations and text are true to the spirit of the Trojan War.

————. *Golden Fleece and the Heroes Who Lived Before Achilles*. New

York: The Macmillan Company, 1921. 289 pp. An excellent book on classical mythology. Contains: "Voyage to Calchis," "Return to Greece," and "Heroes of the Quest."

Defoe, Daniel. *Robinson Crusoe.* New York: E. P. Dutton & Co., Inc., 1954. 245 pp. A fascinating account of a shipwrecked mariner and his life alone for twenty-eight years on an island off the east coast of South America. Has remained a favorite adventure book for several generations.

Du Bois, William Pène. *Twenty-One Balloons.* New York: The Viking Press, Inc., 1947. 179 pp. The exciting and fabulous adventures of Professor Sherman who retires for a year's vacation in a balloon and lands on a volcanic island of the Pacific.

Eaton, Jeanette. *That Lively Man, Ben Franklin.* New York: William Morrow and Company, Inc., 1948. 253 pp. Portrays Franklin as a man of integrity. Tells how he worked for good relations with France and the result his work had on America's history.

Forbes, Esther. *Johnny Tremain.* Boston: Houghton Mifflin Company, 1943. 256 pp. The story of a young Boston apprentice and his role in the Boston Tea Party. An authentic background of Revolutionary times and outstanding characterization.

Foster, Genevieve. *Abraham Lincoln's World.* New York: Charles Scribner's Sons, 1944. Pictures world events during the lifetime of Lincoln and gives a background which helps in understanding world events today.

Frost, Robert. *Road Not Taken.* New York: Henry Holt and Company, Inc., 1951. 282 pp. A good collection of Frost's poetry. Has an introductory biography and a running commentary.

Gipson, Frederick Benjamin. *Old Yeller.* New York: Harper & Brothers, 1956. 158 pp. A skillful tale of a boy's love for a dog and vivid description of a pioneer boyhood.

Holbrook, Stewart Hall. *America's Ethan Allen.* Boston: Houghton Mifflin Company, 1949. 95 pp. The life of the courageous leader of the Green Mountain Boys. Lynd Ward's illustrations are colorful and dramatic.

Irving, Washington. *Rip Van Winkle and the Legend of Sleepy Hollow.* New York: The Macmillan Company, 1951. 105 pp. Both the famous legends of the Hudson Valley in one charmingly illustrated volume.

James, Will. *Smoky, the Cowhorse.* New York: Charles Scribner's Sons, nd. 310 pp. The range and the corral, the round-up and the rodeo are seen through the eyes of a cow pony in this sympathetic and understanding modern classic.

Jewett, Eleanore Myers. *Hidden Treasure of Glaston.* New York: The Viking Press, Inc., 1946. 307 pp. Two spirited boys seek and find great treasures in an ancient abbey of medieval England which relate to the life and death of King Arthur.

Keith, Harold. *Rifles for Watie*. New York: Thomas Y. Crowell Company, 1957. 332 pp. An outstanding Civil War story in which Jefferson Davis Bussey, a young farm boy, joins the Union forces, becomes a scout, and serves temporarily with Stan Watie's Cherokee Rebels.

Kipling, Rudyard. *Captains Courageous*. New York: Doubleday & Company, Inc., 1957. 322 pp. The spoiled son of an American millionaire is washed overboard on the banks of Newfoundland, is picked up by a fishing schooner and forced to live with and share the life of the crew.

Krumgold, Joseph. *And Now Miguel*. New York: Thomas Y. Crowell Company, 1953. 245 pp. Miguel lives with his family on a sheep farm in Taos, New Mexico, and his secret yearning is to go with the men to the Sangre de Cristo Mountains.

Pyle, Howard. *Some Merry Adventures of Robin Hood*. New York: Charles Scribner's Sons, 1946. 250 pp. Stories of Robin Hood's adventures with the king's foresters in Sherwood Forest. The book adheres to the events of the old ballads and has a strong historical background.

Sandoz, Mari. *The Horse Catcher*. Philadelphia: Westminster Press, 1957. 192 pp. Elk, a peace-loving young Cheyenne, despite the disapproval of his family, dreams of capturing and taming beautiful wild horses instead of winning glories for himself as a warrior. Eventually he proves his skill as a horse catcher and also fulfills his responsibility to the tribe.

Speare, Elizabeth George. *Witch of Blackbird Pond*. Boston: Houghton Mifflin Company, 1959. 249 pp. Experiences of a spirited young girl who comes in 1687 from a carefree life in Barbados to a community of strict Puritan standards. She is involved in a witchcraft trial but is proved innocent in this unusual historical novel.

Sperry, Armstrong. *Call It Courage*. New York: The Macmillan Company, 1940. 95 pp. A tale of a Polynesian boy who was a disappointment to his father until he ran away on a boat and proved his courage.

Stevenson, Robert Louis. *Black Arrow*. New York: Dodd, Mead & Co., Inc., 1949. 328 pp. Richard III is a dominant character in this exciting and adventurous story of the Wars of the Roses in England.

Trease, Geoffrey. *Escape to King Alfred*. New York: Vanguard Press, Inc., 1958. 251 pp. The Viking leader Gunthrum plans to make a surprise attack on Alfred, King of Wessex, but his words are overheard by the two young English captives. The defeat of Gunthrum and the success of King Alfred result in a stirring and vivid tale of ninth-century England.

Tunis, John Roberts. *All-American.* New York: Harcourt, Brace and Company, 1942. 245 pp. This book is more than the usual sports story in that the theme of democratic tolerance is an integral part of the plot and characterization.

Ullman, James Ramsey. *Banner in the Sky.* Philadelphia: J. B. Lippincott Company, 1954. 252 pp. The adventurous experiences of young Rudi Matt who is determined to reach the top of the highest mountain in Switzerland—an attempted feat which took the life of his father. As details of the original climbing of the Matterhorn are interwoven, the story has authenticity, atmosphere, and excitement as well as a well-constructed plot.

Untermeyer, Louis. *Stars to Steer By.* New York: Harcourt, Brace and Company, 1941. 352 pp. One hundred fifty poems arranged under a variety of headings. An excellent collection with informal interpretations.

Van Loon, Hendrik W. *Story of Mankind.* New York: Liveright Publishing Corporation, 1951. 548 pp. A most readable account of universal history from prehistoric to modern times. Deals primarily with movements and ideas rather than events.

Verne, Jules. *Twenty Thousand Leagues Under the Sea.* New York: Dodd, Mead & Co., Inc., 1952. 407 pp. First published in 1870, this book is still a favorite with young people. It is the story of Captain Nemo's submarine masterpiece and the adventures it encounters.

White, Anne Terry. *Lost Worlds.* New York: Random House, Inc., 1941. 316 pp. Reveals the mystery and excitement behind archeological discoveries. Discusses famous archeologists and their contributions to history.

Worth, Kathryn. *They Love To Laugh.* New York: Doubleday & Company, Inc., 1942. 269 pp. The story centers around a southern Quaker family of the 1830's and of five fun-loving boys and how they taught a little orphan girl to laugh. The characters are warm-hearted and vividly portrayed, and reveal a sense of true values.

Wyss, Johann David. *Swiss Family Robinson.* New York: The Macmillan Company, 1948. 307 pp. A tale of a Swiss Family who were wrecked on a desert island. The improbability of the tale such as the episodes where the characters sail in tubs and ride ostrichs makes the story delightful to children.

Books for the Junior High

Adshead, Gladys L. *An Inheritance of Poetry.* Boston: Houghton Mifflin Company, 1948. 415 pp. A collection of poems, English and American, both famous and little known gathered from a variety of sources.

Aldrich, Bess Streeter. *A Lantern in Her Hand.* New York: Appleton-Century-Crofts, Inc., 1928. 306 pp. Abbie Deal migrates from her cabin home in Iowa to Nebraska where in bringing up her family she proves her courage as a pioneer mother—and eventually dies alone in her pioneer home after a long, full life.

Allen, T. D. *Doctor in Buckskin.* New York: Harper & Brothers, 1951. 277 pp. A fictional biography based upon the lives of Marcus Whitman and his wife, Narcissa, and their pioneer experiences as medical missionaries in Oregon before the advent of many white settlers. The book ends tragically when the Indians become suspicious of the doctor's medical powers and massacre the entire family.

Barrie, Sir James Matthew. *The Little Minister.* New York: Charles Scribner's Sons, 1921. 510 pp. A romantic novel of Scotland in which the Auld Licht minister falls in love with Lady Bobbie who pretends to be a gypsy.

Baumann, Hans. *The Barque of the Brothers.* New York: H. Z. Walck, Inc., 1958. 245 pp. This tale of the days of Henry the Navigator recounts two of the ventures of Portuguese sailors in the fifteenth century. A stirring historical adventure of intrigue and vivid background.

Beach, Edward Lattimer. *Run Silent, Run Deep.* New York: Henry Holt and Company, Inc., 1955. 364 pp. A narrative of submarine warfare during World War II, this exciting novel not only gives detailed description of submarine training, patrolling, and fighting, but relates a dramatic story of revenge on the enemy sub hunter in the Pacific.

Blackmore, Richard Doddridge. *Lorna Doone.* New York: E. P. Dutton & Co., Inc., 1956. 571 pp. The outlaw Doones, the maid brought up in their midst, and Plain John Ridd, with his Herculean power, are characters in this romantic love story of Exmoore and the North Devon coast of England during the late seventeenth and early eighteenth centuries.

Boyd, James. *Drums.* New York: Charles Scribner's Sons, 1928. 409 pp. James Fraser, a North Carolinian boy, is sent to England by his Tory father who desires to protect his son from Revolutionary influences. Through an encounter with John Paul Jones, however, James plays an active part in the war.

Bro, Marguerite. *Sarah.* New York: Doubleday & Company, Inc., 1949.

343 pp. Sarah, who wishes to become a great pianist, experiences both sorrow and happiness before she realizes her father's dying wish that she should perhaps become a great artist. For the more mature girls.

Brontë, Charlotte. *Jane Eyre.* New York: Coward-McCann, Inc., 1955. 508 pp. The autobiographical novel of an Englishwoman who rebelled against narrow social and religious conventions of her day. Her love for the ugly Rochester is described, and after a dramatic tragedy a mystery is cleared and they are united.

Brontë, Emily Jane. *Wuthering Heights.* New York: Coward-McCann, Inc., 1955. 353 pp. "A work of true genius," this novel about Catherine Crenshaw and Heathcliff is set against a background of the somber moorlands around Wuthering Heights. It is a tale of hatred and terror among the people of the Yorkshire moors.

Cather, Willa. *My Antonia.* Boston: Houghton Mifflin Company, 1918. 418 pp. A New York lawyer tells the story by reviewing his Nebraska boyhood days and his friendship with Antonia, a young Bohemian girl. An authentic picture of pioneering conditions and of America's assimilation of the immigrant.

————. *O Pioneers.* Boston: Houghton Mifflin Company, 1933. 308 pp. This novel of pioneer life in Nebraska was inspired by Walt Whitman's poem "Pioneers, O Pioneers." It is about Swedes, Bohemians, and Frenchmen and their difficulties in taming the prairie land. The land itself, "the Divide," almost becomes a character in the story and supplies the source of elemental conflicts essential to genuine tragedy.

Caudill, Rebecca. *Susan Cornish.* New York: The Viking Press, Inc., 1955. 286 pp. For teenagers interested in teaching as a career, this serious and purposeful novel of a young woman in a poverty-stricken Southern sharecropping region will be thought-provoking.

Daly, Maureen. *Seventeenth Summer.* New York: Dodd, Mead & Co., Inc., 1942. 255 pp. A teenage love story that is expertly written. The locale is typically American and reveals the expectant sense of a seventeen-year-old girl involved.

Douglas, Lloyd Cassel. *The Robe.* Boston: Houghton Mifflin Company, 1942. 695 pp. About the family of a Roman Senator whose son was in charge of the Crucifixion, received the Robe, and later met his death for refusing to renounce his Christianity.

Du Maurier, Daphne. *Rebecca.* New York: Doubleday & Company, Inc., 1938. 457 pp. The mystery of Rebecca who has been dead for eight months unfolds against the setting of a great English estate of which she was mistress.

Edmonds, Walter Dumaux. *Drums Along the Mohawk*. Boston: Little, Brown & Co., 1951. 592 pp. A story of the American Revolution's effects on the frontier Mohawk Valley from 1776-1784. It relates how the unaided farmers withstood both British and Iroquois attacks.

Eliot, George. *Silas Marner*. New York: E. P. Dutton & Co., Inc., 1958. 246 pp. An old weaver becomes a miser and withdraws into solitude. His gold is stolen and a little child reforms his character.

Ferber, Edna. *So Big*. New York: Doubleday & Company, Inc., 1924. 360 pp. A study of the character of a woman whose sense of duty led her through a hard life of truck-farming in a Dutch settlement near Chicago. The contrast of mother and her son makes the book an interesting and genuinely human story.

Forester, Cecil S. *Mr. Midshipman Hornblower*. Boston: Little, Brown & Co., 1946. 662 pp. The chronological account which tells how the future captain, commodore and lord rose from midshipman to lieutenant in the English Navy.

Freeman, Douglas Southall. *Lee of Virginia*. New York: Charles Scribner's Sons, 1958. 243 pp. Found among Freeman's papers after his death was this one-volume life of Lee designed for young adults in which Lee as a man as well as a military genius is portrayed.

Friedman, Benedict. *Mrs. Mike: the Story of Katherine Mary Flannigan*. New York: Coward-McCann, Inc., 1947. 312 pp. Katherine O'Fallon in 1907 at the age of sixteen marries Sergeant Mike Flannigan of the Mounties and lives a hard but a great life in the far North.

Guareschi, Giovanni. *The Little World of Don Camillo*. New York: Pellegrini & Cudahy, (now Farrar, Straus & Cudahy, Inc.,) 1950. 205 pp. In this story of a parish priest and his trials and tribulations in dealing with his wayward flock, delightful incidents occur when Don Camillo wins over his friendly enemy, the mayor, in a parable for more thoughtful readers.

Heyerdahl, Thor. *Aku-Aku*. Chicago: Rand McNally & Company, 1958. 384 pp. Another mysterious adventure of early exploration and settlement in the Pacific by the author of *Kon-Tiki*. This book involves a scientific expedition to Easter Island and the uncovering of some surprising facts.

Homer. *The Iliad*. New York: E. P. Dutton & Co., Inc., 1955. 370 pp. The epic of the fall of Troy after it was besieged by the Greeks for ten years.

————. *The Odyssey*. New York: E. P. Dutton & Co., Inc., 1953. 309 pp. A sequel to *The Iliad* which relates the ten years' adventures of Ulysses as he returns to his own kingdom from Troy.

Lord, Walter. *Day of Infamy.* New York: Henry Holt and Company, Inc., 1957. 243 pp. Traces the drama of the Pearl Harbor attack, the spies behind it, the military personnel involved, and reactions of the citizens.

Mitchell, Margaret. *Gone with the Wind.* New York: The Macmillan Company, 1939. 1037 pp. A vivid Civil War novel with happenings before, during, and after the period with scenes laid in Georgia. Characterization of Scarlett O'Hara is excellent.

Norway, Nevil Shute. *Far Country.* New York: William Morrow and Company, Inc., 1952. 343 pp. A postwar refugee from London goes to Australia to spend the summer, is captivated by the beauty and appeal of the country, and decides to marry and settle there.

Sandburg, Carl. *Complete Poems.* New York: Harcourt, Brace and Company, 1950. 676 pp. Collection of six volumes of the poet's works which include his best contributions.

Scott, Sir Walter. *Ivanhoe.* New York: E. P. Dutton & Co., Inc., 1955. 454 pp. A romantic novel of the time of Richard the Lionhearted. Describes the life of the vanished Saxons under the Norman conquerors, the state of the Jews, chivalry, etc., of the period.

Stone, Irving. *Love Is Eternal.* New York: Doubleday & Company, Inc., 1954. 468 pp. A novel about Mary Todd and Abraham Lincoln. Gives a sympathetic, realistic, and understanding portrayal of their love and marriage.

Van der Post, Laurens. *The Lost World of the Kalahari.* New York: William Morrow and Company, Inc., 1958. 279 pp. An outstanding book of South Sea adventure. Through the one-man search for an island paradise, the beauty and warmth of Polynesia is effectively portrayed.

Books for High School

Balchen, Bernt. *Come North with Me.* New York: E. P. Dutton & Co., Inc., 1958. 318 pp. The autobiography of an airman, a Norwegian boy who became a United States Colonel and knew all the great heroes of the air.

Bowles, Chester. *Ideas, People and Peace.* New York: Harper & Brothers 1958. 151 pp. A former U.S. Ambassador contends that U.S. influence and prestige abroad has decreased because political and economic truths have been sacrificed to military expediency. Views world problems in an outspoken, realistic, and lucid manner.

Buck, Pearl. S. *The Good Earth.* New York: Grosset & Dunlap, Inc., 1955. 313 pp. A realistic portrayal of the Chinese, their way of life, customs, and love of the land. Centers around the life of Wang Lung, a Chinese peasant.

Cervantes Saavedra, Miguel de. *Adventures of Don Quixote de la Mancha.* New York: E. P. Dutton & Co., Inc., 1953. 371 pp. A travesty of the ludicrous adventure of a knight-errant. Gives a true insight into the life and customs of sixteenth-century Spain.

Chase, Mary Ellen. *Mary Peters.* New York: The Macmillan Company, 1934. 337 pp. A philosophical story pervaded by the glory of sea and earth and dealing with a courageous family who survive social change in a Maine seacoast village. Reveals strength and beauty of character.

Collins, Wilkie. *The Moonstone* and *The Woman in White.* New York: Modern Library, Inc., 843 pp. First published in 1868, *The Moonstone* traces the theft and final restoration of a moonstone from the forehead of a Hindu idol. The second novel, published first in 1872, is a fantastic mystery which challenges the reader's ingenuity to detect the identity of the heroine.

Conrad, Joseph. *Lord Jim.* New York: Rinehart & Co., Inc., 1957. 369 pp. A triumphant tale of courage involving a young Englishman who lost his honor in a panic and went to settle in a Malayan village. Vivid descriptions of the East in a well-written psychological study.

Cooper, James Fenimore. *The Deerslayer.* New York: Dodd, Mead & Co., Inc., 1952. 573 pp. The beginning novel in Cooper's *Leatherstocking Tales* depicts the adventures of Natty Bumppo, or Hawkeye.

————. *Last of the Mohicans.* Boston: Houghton Mifflin Company, 1938. 372 pp. A swift-moving story of pursuit and capture in the Lake George wilderness during the French and Indian wars.

Costain, Thomas Bertram. *Silver Chalice.* New York: Doubleday & Company, Inc., 1952. 533 pp. A long novel about the cup used by Christ at the Last Supper. A young artisan, purchased from slavery to create a decorative casing for the chalice, braves the perils of persecution of the Christians and completes the task. The detailed setting, interesting background, along with the romance of Basil and Joseph's daughter hold the teenager's interest.

————. *The Three Edwards.* New York: Doubleday & Company, Inc., 1958. 432 pp. Gives England's history from 1272 to 1377 during the Plantagenet reign of Edward I, Edward II, and Edward III. The chronicle details happenings in a highly readable and effective manner.

Crane, Stephen. *Red Badge of Courage.* New York: Appleton-Century-Crofts, Inc., 1953. 267 pp. An imaginative and psychological story describing the fear, confusion, and fatigue of a young Civil War soldier.

Cronin, Archibald Joseph. *The Citadel*. Boston: Little, Brown & Co., 1937. 401 pp. Traces the career of a conscientious young doctor "from his start in a mining town in Wales, to the realization of his ambition for a London practice." After years of struggling against mediocrity and indifference, he decides to capitalize on personal charm and make money. A tragic error brings him to his senses.

Dickens, Charles. *David Copperfield*. New York: E. P. Dutton & Co., Inc., 1953. 837 pp. An autobiographical novel reflecting the life in England, especially London, in the early part of the nineteenth century. The book is regarded as Dickens' masterpiece.

————. *Tale of Two Cities*. New York: E. P. Dutton & Co., Inc., 1955. 371 pp. A historical tale of the French Revolution. It is a powerful melodramatic account of the reign of terror leading up to the self-immolation of Sydney at the guillotine.

Dodson, Kenneth. *Away All Boats*. Boston: Little, Brown & Co., 1954. 508 pp. A fictional account of the U.S. naval operations in the Pacific during World War II. Describes details of the life aboard an attack transport.

Dumas, Alexander. *Count of Monte Cristo*. New York: E. P. Dutton & Co., Inc., 1955. 572 pp. The most famous of the author's books in which a sailor acquires a colossal treasure and becomes Count of Monte Cristo.

Forester, Cecil S. *The Good Shepherd*. Boston: Little, Brown & Co., 1955. 310 pp. The tense story of a convoy-escort's encounter with a submarine pack in the Pacific. Gives detailed naval action.

Galsworthy, John. *Forsythe Saga*. New York: Charles Scribner's Sons, 1946. 921 pp. A trilogy of the Forsythe family. Includes: *The Man of Property* (1906), *To Let* (1921), and the two interludes, "The Indian Summer of a Forsythe" and "Awakening."

Goodwyn, Frank. *The Black Bull*. New York: Doubleday & Company, Inc., 1958. 264 pp. Rare quality and poetic perfection are evident in this story of a black bull which escapes from a Texas loading chute and is fought by Robelin Algeria, a young Mexican cowboy.

Gunther, John. *Inside Russia Today*. New York: Harper & Brothers, 1958. 550 pp. All phases of Russian life, economic and political, are covered as well as some history and a "who's who" of Russian leaders. Interesting and illuminating incidents.

Hardy, Thomas. *Return of the Native*. New York: Dodd, Mead & Co., Inc., 1950. 470 pp. Against the wild and solemn scenery of an imaginary heath, this drama of "passion and nemesis is enacted." Clym

Yeabright and his mother, Eustacia Vye, are fine impersonations of human longing, disillusionment, and endurance.

Hillyer, Robert. *The Relic and Other Poems.* New York: Alfred A. Knopf, Inc., 93 pp. Brilliant light verse by one of the leading contemporary American lyrists.

Hoover, John Edgar. *Masters of Deceit; the Story of Communism in America and How To Fight It.* New York: Henry Holt and Company, Inc., 1958. 374 pp. Shows the organization and operation of the Communist party and describes party tactics, methods of mass agitation, underground infiltration, espionage, and sabotage.

MacLean, Alistair. *Guns of Navarone.* New York: Doubleday & Company, Inc., 1957. 320 pp. A tense, well-plotted adventure story of fine hand-picked British soldiers and saboteurs on the Greek island of Navarone where they were to silence the guns and free 1,200 British men pinned on a neighboring island.

MacLeish, Archibald. *J. B.* Boston: Houghton Mifflin Company, 1958. 153 pp. The dramatic retelling of the story of Job in modern terms. This verse play has been called "a shining landmark in the history of American poetry."

Murray, A. A. *The Blanket.* New York: Vanguard Press, Inc., 1958. 192 pp. Unforgettable characters and scenery, thrilling excitement, and suspense are the primary ingredients of this African adventure which reveals the dramatic conflict between primitive and civilized justice.

Najafi, Najmek. *Reveille for a Persian Village.* New York: Harper & Brothers, 1958. 273 pp. A factual account of social life and conditions in Iran, told through the experiences of a young native's devoted mission to her mountain village. A fine sequel to *Persia Is My Heart.*

Pasternak, Boris Leonidovich. *Doctor Zhivago.* New York: Pantheon Books Inc., 1958. 558 pp. The central figure in this highly proclaimed novel which won the Nobel Prize in Literature is Yuri Zhivago, a typical product of the upper-class, prerevolutionary Russia. It is a terrifying account of "disintegration of the human soul under stress," and will challenge the better readers.

Roberts, Kenneth Lewis. *Northwest Passage.* New York: Doubleday & Company, Inc., 1937. 709 pp. Major Robert Rogers, an American ranger commander during the French and Indian War, leads an expedition against the Indian town of St. Francis in 1759 and dreams of finding an overland route to the Pacific.

Sienkiewicz, Henryk. *Quo Vadis.* Boston: Little, Brown & Co. 1943. 422 pp. A narrative of Nero's time. Gives a vivid picture of Roman life during the first century and contrasts the licentiousness of paganism with the spiritual beauty of Christianity.

White, T. H. *The Mountain Road.* New York: William Sloan Associates Inc., 1958. 347 pp. When Philip Baldwin, a civilian turned soldier, leads his small demolition team through a retreat from a Japanese attack in 1944, he learns much about his men, China, the savage ironies of war, and about himself.

————. *The Once and Future King.* New York: G. P. Putnam's Sons, 1958. 677 pp. An epic narrative which tells of King Arthur and his times in a humorous and exciting manner. From the adventures of the boy Arthur to the tragic last days of the Round Table the story will hold the attention of the reader.

Wouk, Herman. *The Caine Mutiny.* New York: Doubleday & Company, Inc., 1952. 494 pp. A novel about the navy personnel aboard a minesweeper in the South Pacific during World War II. Portrays various kinds of personalities, including a psychopathic case.

Suggested Book Lists for Parents

Arbuthnot, May Hill. *Children and Books,* Rev. ed. Chicago. Scott, Foresman and Company, 1957. 684 pp. $5.50.

Best Books for Children. New York: R. R. Bowker Co., 1959. 190 pp. $2.00.

Booklists from the Child Study Association of America, available by writing to 132 East 74th Street, New York 21:

> *Books About Parents and Their Children.* $.75.
>
> *A Parent's Bookshelf.* Single copies free.
>
> *New Books About Parenthood and Family Life.* $.15.

Books for the Teen-Age, 1958. Annual list of the New York Public Library, Fifth Avenue and 42nd Street, New York 20. $.25.

Books of the Traveling High School Science Library, 3rd ed., 1957. American Association for the Advancement of Science, 1515 Massachusetts Avenue, Washington 5, D.C. 73 pp. $.25.

Children's Books for $1.25 or Less. Association for Childhood Education International, 1200 15th Street N.W., Washington 5, D.C. 36 pp.

Eakin, Mary K. *Good Books for Children.* Chicago: University of Chicago Press, 1959. 273 pp. $5.95.

Eaton, Anne. *Treasure for the Taking,* Rev. ed. New York: The Viking Press, Inc., 1957. 322 pp. $4.00.

Evans, Ben. "Ally of the Gifted," *Saturday Review,* 41-42, November 1, 1958.

Fraiberg, Selma H. *The Magic Years*. New York: Charles Scribner's Sons, 1959. 305 pp. $3.95.

Growing Up with Books. 250 titles classified by age and interest. New York: R. R. Bowker Co. $.10 each.

Hymes, James. *Before the Child Reads*. Evanston, Ill.: Row, Peterson and Company, 1958. 96 pp. $2.00.

Jacobs, Leland. "Hallmarks of Good Informational Books," *The Reading Teacher*, 115-116, December, 1958.

Jefferson, Benjamin. "Some Relationships Between Parents' and Children's Preferences in Juvenile Literature," *Elementary School Journal*, 212-218, January, 1958.

Larrick, Nancy. *A Parent's Guide to Children's Reading; How Parents Can Help*. New York: Doubleday & Company, Inc., 1958. 258 pp. $2.95.

Los Angeles County Public Library. *The Family Read Together*. The Library, 322 South Broadway, Los Angeles 13. Single copies free.

Reference Books for the Home. Enoch Pratt Free Library, Baltimore, Maryland, 1958. 8 pp.

Young, Marion. "A Report on Self-Selection in Reading," *Elementary English*, 176-181, March, 1958.

REFERENCES USED IN COMPILING THE BIBLIOGRAPHY

American Library Association. *A Basic Book Collection for Junior High Schools*. Chicago: American Library Association, 1950. 76 pp.

American Library Association. *Booklist; a Guide to Current Books*. Chicago: American Library Association, 1959 issues.

American Library Association. *The School Library and the Gifted Child*. Chicago: American Library Association, 1958. 108 pp.

Arbuthnot, May Hill, *et al. Children and Books*. Chicago: Scott, Foresman and Company, 1957. 684 pp.

Bulletin of the Children's Book Center. Chicago: University of Chicago, January, 1958, to May, 1959 issues.

Children's Catalog, 9th ed. New York: H. W. Wilson Co., 1956 (also 1958 and 1959 supplements).

Current Books: Junior Booklist of the Secondary Education Board. Milton, Massachusetts: The Board, March, 1959. 58 pp.

Standard Catalog for High School Libraries, 7th ed. New York: H. W. Wilson Co., 1958 (with 1958 and 1959 supplements).

References

Chapter One

[1] Barzun, Jacques. "The Place and the Price of Excellence," *Vogue*, Vol. CXXXIII: p. 139, February 1959.

[2] Morgan, Antonia Bell. "Identification and Guidance of Gifted Children," *Scientific Monthly*, Vol. LXXX: p. 171, March, 1955.

[3] Witty, Paul. "Education Programs for the Gifted," *School and Society*, Vol. LXXXVII: p. 167, April 11, 1959.

[4] Barlow, Fred. *Mental Prodigies*. New York: Philosophical Library, 1952.

[5] Barrat, Robert. "Child Prodigy or Literary Hoax?" *The Commonweal*, Vol. LXIII: pp. 535-537, February 24, 1956.

[6] Wiener, Norbert. *Ex Prodigy*. New York: Simon & Schuster, Inc., 1953.

[7] Hirshberg, Al. "Prodigy at Harvard," *Saturday Evening Post*, Vol. CCXXX: pp. 38–39+, September 14, 1957.

[8] Slenczynska, Ruth and Biancolli, Louis. *Forbidden Childhood*. New York: Doubleday & Company, Inc., 1957.

[9] Cox, Catherine M. "The Early Mental Traits of Three Hundred Geniuses," *Genetic Studies of Genius*, Vol. II, edited by L. M. Terman. Stanford, California: Stanford University Press, 1926.

[10] Miles, Catherine Cox. "Gifted Children," *Manual of Child Psychology*, 2nd Ed., edited by Leonard Carmichael, p. 1002. New York: John Wiley & Sons, Inc., 1954.

[11] Bayley, Nancy. "On the Growth of Intelligence," *American Psychologist*, Vol. X: pp. 805-818, December, 1955.

[12] Conant, James B., Chairman. *The Identification and Education of the Academically Talented Student in the American Secondary School*, p. 16. Washington, D.C.: National Education Association, 1958.

[13] Witty, Paul. "Every Parent and Teacher a Talent Scout," *National Parent-Teacher*, Vol. LI: pp. 4-6, June, 1957.

Chapter Two

1 Miles, Catherine Cox. "Gifted Children," *Manual of Child Psychology,* 2nd Ed. edited by Leonard Carmichael, p. 1008. New York: John Wiley & Sons, Inc., 1954.
2 Barclay, Dorothy. "A Set of Basic Family Values," *New York Times Magazine,* p. 41, July 13, 1958.
3 Terman, Lewis M. "The Discovery and Encouragement of Exceptional Talent," *American Psychologist,* Vol. IX: p. 224, June, 1954.
4 Terman, Lewis M. and Oden, Melita B. "The Gifted Child Grows Up," *Genetic Studies of Genius,* Vol. IV. Stanford, California: Stanford University Press. 1947.
5 Martin, Alexander Reid. "A Study of Parental Attitudes and Their Influence Upon Personality Development," *Education,* Vol. LXIII: pp. 596-608, June, 1943.
6 Harris, Dale B. "What Child Development Has To Say to Guidance Workers," *Journal of the National Association of Women Deans and Counselors,* Vol. XXII: pp. 99-105, March 1959.
7 Travers, Pamela L. *Mary Poppins.* New York: Reynal & Hitchcock, 1939.
8 Dostoevski, Feodor. *The Brothers Karamazov,* Translation revised by Princess Alexandra Kropotkin, International Collectors Library, American Headquarters, p. 482, Garden City, New York, 1949.
9 Harris, Dale B. "The Climate of Achievement," *Child Study,* Vol. XXXIV: pp. 8-14, Summer, 1958.
10 Barzun, Jacques. "The Place and the Price of Excellence," *Vogue,* Vol. CXXXIII: pp. 139-141+., February 1, 1959.
11 Barbe, Walter B. "Case Study of a Gifted Family," *Education,* Vol. LXXIX: pp. 45-48, September, 1958.
12 Strang, Ruth. *An Introduction to Child Study,* 4th Edition. New York: The Macmillan Company, 1959.
13 Schweitzer, Albert. "Schweitzer's Words: Light in the Jungle," *New York Times Magazine,* p. 73, January 9, 1955.

Chapter Three

1 Fletcher, Margaret I. *The Adult and the Nursery School Child.* Canada: University of Toronto Press, Toronto, 1958.
2 Cohen, Dorothy H. and Stern, Virginia. *Observing and Recording the Behavior of Young Children.* New York: Bureau of Publications, Teachers College, Columbia University, 1958.
3 Mearns, Hughes. *Creative Power: The Education of Youth in the Crea-*

tive Arts, Second Revised Edition. pp. 116-118, New York: Dover Publications, Inc., 1958.

[4] Murphy, Lois Barclay. *Social Behavior and Child Personality.* New York: Columbia University Press, 1937.

[5] Valentine, C. W. *The Normal Child and Some of His Abnormalities.* 3300 Clipper Mill Road, Baltimore, Maryland: Penguin Books, 1956.

[6] Gilbreth, Frank B. and Carey, Ernestine. *Cheaper by the Dozen.* New York: Thomas Y. Crowell Company, 1948.

[7] McConkie, Gwendolyn W. and Nixon, Arne J. "The Perceptions of a Selected Group of Kindergarten Children Concerning Reading." Unpublished doctoral project, Columbia University, Teachers College, 1959.

[8] Repplier, Agnes. *Eight Decades.* Boston: Houghton Mifflin Company, 1937.

[9] Barbe, Walter B. "Guiding the Reading of the Gifted," *The Reading Teacher,* Vol. VII: pp. 144-150, February, 1954.

[10] Stott, Leland H. "The Persisting Effects of Early Family Experiences Upon Personality Development," *Merrill-Palmer Quarterly,* Vol. III: pp. 144-159, Spring, 1957.

[11] Myers, Garry Cleveland. "Parents and the Gifted Child," *Education,* Vol. LXXIX: pp. 17-18, September, 1958.

[12] Murphy, Lois Barclay. "Emotional First Aid for the Young Child," *Childhood Education,* Vol. XXXII: pp. 205-207, January, 1956.

[13] Strang, Ruth. "When Should Parents Stop Children's Quarrels?" *Growing,* Vol. XI: pp. 3-5, April-June 1959.

[14] Allen, Frederick H. "The Dilemma of Growth—for Parents and Children," *Child Study,* Vol. XXXV: pp. 4-7, Spring, 1958.

[15] McCarthy, Dorothea A. *Measurement of Cognitive Abilities at the Preschool and Early Childhood Level.* Princeton, New Jersey: Educational Testing Service, 1958.

[16] Strang, Ruth. "Reading Development of Gifted Children," *Elementary English,* Vol. XXXI: 35-40, January, 1954.

[17] Roeper, Annemarie. "Nursery School: A Place To Adjust or a Place To Learn?" *Child Study,* Vol. XXXVI: pp. 3-9, Spring, 1959.
Laycock, Samuel R. "Counseling Parents of Gifted Children," *Exceptional Children,* Vol. XXIII: pp. 108-110, 134, December, 1956.

Chapter Four

[1] Hollingworth, Leta S. *Children Above 180 IQ Stanford-Binet.* New York: World Book Company, Yonkers-on-Hudson, 1942.

[2] Barclay, Dorothy. "Time Out for Hobbies," *New York Times Magazine,* p. 48, June 2, 1957.

[3] Northway, Mary L. "When Friendship Is in Flower," *National Parent-Teacher,* Vol. LI: pp. 17-19, November, 1956.

[4] Harris, Dale B. "The Climate of Achievement," *Child Study,* Vol. XXXIV: pp. 8-14, Summer, 1958.

[5] Oaks, Ruth E. "We Tried to Keep Them Reading Through Our Summer Library Plan," *The Reading Teacher,* Vol. VII: pp. 178-182, February, 1954.

[6] Ojemann, Ralph H. "Basic Approaches to Mental Health: The Human Relations Program of the State University of Iowa," *Personnel and Guidance Journal,* Vol. XXXVII: pp. 198-206, November, 1958.

[7] Crowder, Thora and Gallagher, James J. "The Adjustment of Gifted Children in the Regular Classroom: Case Studies," *Journal of Exceptional Children,* Vol. XXIII: pp. 353-363+, May, 1957.

[8] Brenner, Anton. "Nature and Meaning of Readiness for School," *Merrill-Palmer Quarterly,* Vol. III: pp. 114-135, Spring, 1957.

[9] Eaves, Robert W. "Ready for High Adventure!" *N.E.A. Journal,* Vol. XLVIII: pp. 42-44, April, 1959.

[10] Bissex, Henry. *If You Want Your Child To Read.* Printed for Essie Olive Abeel Private School, Inc., 293 Lookout Avenue, Hackensack, New Jersey.

Chapter Five

[1] Pritchard, Miriam. "Total School Planning for the Gifted Child," *Exceptional Children,* Vol. XVIII: pp. 143-147, February, 1952.

[2] Strang, Ruth. "Manifestations of Maturity in Adolescents," *Mental Hygiene,* Vol. XXXIII: pp. 567-569, October, 1949.

[3] Strang, Ruth. *The Adolescent Views Himself.* pp. 95, 170, New York: McGraw-Hill Book Company, 1957.

[4] Witty, Paul. "Enriching the Reading of the Gifted Child," *Library Journal,* Vol. LXXX: pp. 2619-2623+, November 15, 1955.

[5] Kemp, Charles F. *The Church: The Gifted and the Retarded Child.* St. Louis: The Bethany Press, 1957.

[6] Wilder, Thornton. *Our Town,* p. 80, New York: Coward-McCann, Inc., 1938.

[7] Bland, Phyllis. "Helping Bright Students Who Read Poorly," *The Reading Teacher*, Vol. IX: pp. 209-215, April, 1956.

Chapter Six

[1] Terman, Lewis M. and Oden, Melita H. "The Gifted Child Grows Up," *Genetic Studies of Genius*, Vol. IV: p. 57. Stanford, California, Stanford University Press, 1947.

[2] MacFarlane, Jean W. "Intellectual Functioning in High School Girls and College Women," *Journal of the National Association of Women Deans and Counselors*, Vol. XXI: p. 5, October, 1957.

[3] Cutts, Norma E. and Moseley, Nicholas. *Bright Children*, Chapters XI and XIII. New York: G. P. Putnam's Sons, 1953.

[4] Sargent, Porter. *Handbook of Private Schools*. Published annually by the author, 11 Beacon Street, Boston 8.

[5] Katz, Martin. *You: Today and Tomorrow*. Princeton, New Jersey: Educational Testing Service, 1959.

[6] Barclay, Dorothy. "Child in a New Neighborhood," *New York Times Magazine*, p. 53, October 5, 1958.

[7] LeShan, Eda J. *You and Your Adopted Child*. Public Affairs Committee, 22 East 38th Street, New York 16, 1958.

[8] Terman, Lewis M. "The Discovery and Encouragement of Exceptional Talent," *American Psychologist*, Vol. IX: p. 228, June, 1954.

Chapter Seven

[1] Morris, Glyn. "Helping the Gifted Child in Rural Areas," *The Exceptional Child*, Vol. XXII: pp. 161-162+, January, 1956.

[2] Diederich, Paul, *Journal of the National Association of Women Deans and Counselors*, January, 1960. Washington 6, D.C.

[3] Strang, Ruth. *The Adolescent Views Himself*. New York: McGraw-Hill Book Company, 1957.

[4] Hoppock, Anne *All Children Have Gifts*. Washington, D.C.: Association for Childhood Education International Press.

[5] Havighurst, Robert J. and DeHaan, Robert F. *Educating Gifted Children*. Chicago: The University of Chicago Press, 1957.

[6] Conant, James B. (Chairman of the Conference). *The Identification and Education of the Academically Talented Student in the American Secondary School*, The Conference Report, February, 1958. Washington 6, D.C.: National Education Association, 1958.

[7] Havighurst, Robert J.; Stivers, Eugene; and DeHaan, Robert F. *A Survey of the Education of Gifted Children.* Supplementary Educational Monograph No. 83. Chicago: The University of Chicago Press, 1955.

[8] Passow, A. Harry; Goldberg, Miriam L.; Tannenbaum, Abraham; and French, Will. *Planning for Talented Youth.* New York: Bureau of Publications, Teachers College, Columbia University, 1955.

INDEX

Date Due